THE CIVIL SERVICE RIFLES IN THE GREAT WAR

The CIVIL SERVICE RIFLES in the GREAT WAR

'All Bloody Gentlemen'

JILL KNIGHT

Pen & Sword
MILITARY

First published in Great Britain in 2004 by
Pen & Sword Military
an imprint of
Pen & Sword Books Ltd
47 Church Street
Barnsley
South Yorkshire
S70 2AS

ISBN 1 84415 057 7

A CIP catalogue record for this book is
available from the British Library

Printed and bound in England by
CPI UK

Pen & Sword Books Ltd incorporates the Imprints of Pen & Sword Aviation,
Pen & Sword Maritime, Pen & Sword Military, Wharncliffe Local History,
Pen and Sword Select, Pen and Sword Military Classics and Leo Cooper.

For a complete list of Pen & Sword titles please contact
PEN & SWORD BOOKS LIMITED
47 Church Street, Barnsley, South Yorkshire, S70 2AS, England
E-mail: enquiries@pen-and-sword.co.uk
Website: www.pen-and-sword.co.uk

Contents

I am delighted to contribute a foreword to this book which describes an impressive but forgotten piece of Civil Service history: how a generation of public servants responded to their country's call ninety years ago.

There is, rightly, widespread debate today about the standards to be expected in our public services and about the qualities of the men and women who work in them. But no one would argue that in a modern civil service there is no place for the time-honoured virtues displayed by the Civil Service Rifles: loyalty, courage, devotion to duty.

These men were volunteers and their spirit lives on. At the beginning of the twenty-first century about a third of our Reserve Forces draw their strength from people working in the public sector. And the tradition of voluntary service – of making an extra, unsung contribution – flourishes today in other areas like education, health and social care.

But attractive as these parallels may be, the experiences and achievements of those 'ordinary' civil servants of 1914 must be unique. From Festubert through the Somme to the victorious 'Hundred Days', they rose to the extraordinary challenge laid on them. And in doing so, many lost their lives. Theirs is a powerful and moving story; it is also one with relevance today.

Sir Andrew Turnbull KCB CVO

Introduction

'This mob's all bloody *gentlemen*'[1] complained an old Regular soldier of the 60th Rifles on joining the Civil Service Rifles in France in 1918. This back-handed compliment neatly captures the character of the pre-war territorial regiment which recruited among 'civil servants and their friends'. These were Whitehall clerks and men from City offices, well-educated and articulate, who served as part-time soldiers in a regiment they considered their 'select club'. In the Great War, with their ranks swelled by volunteers of similar character, two battalions served with distinction on the Western Front and in Greece and the Middle East. These clerks, bureaucrats, insurance men and bank staff made efficient, self-disciplined and courageous soldiers. They were bound together by strong bonds of friendship, loyalty and regimental pride – a potent *esprit de corps* which sustained them through the most appalling experiences and losses.

What has intrigued and impressed me as I researched this book is that by the time the 'bloody gentlemen' label was applied in August 1918, hundreds of the original men had gone – killed, wounded or moved on to be officers in other units. The gaps had largely been filled by eighteen year-old conscripts, rushed out from England in the panic following the German offensive in March. Yet the regiment's original character was still recognizable. The more I learned of their war story, the more remarkable this continuity seemed. I discovered that it owed much to a careful recruiting policy at home and to the chance survival in France of influential individuals, who in 1918 trained the young newcomers and taught them the 'Civil Service' ways. The regiment was fortunate, too, in being well led by some inspirational Regular commanding officers who recognized and respected the qualities of these unusual soldiers. But above all, I came to see the survival of the distinctive regimental character as a tribute to the many individuals who served in the Civil Service Rifles – casualties and survivors alike. In writing this book I aimed to place these men back in their social and professional context and to bring their awesome story once more to public attention. They deserve our remembrance.

Jill Knight
August 2004

1. Desmond Young, *Try Anything Twice*, Hamish Hamilton, 1963, p112

Chapter One

Victorian Volunteers and Edwardian Terriers

Walter Humphrys photographed in 1917.

On a balmy summer evening in 2002, the last Civil Service Rifleman returned to Somerset House. A small, frail but alert figure in a wheelchair, Walter Humphrys came, just a few weeks short of his 105th birthday, to honour the men he served with in the Great War. The responsibility of being the last survivor lay heavily upon him but he felt it his duty to make this final pilgrimage. It was a strong sense of duty too which inspired him, as a young clerk in the Post Office Savings Bank, to volunteer for the army. Like so many of his contemporaries, he had enlisted at the headquarters of the Civil Service Rifles in the government offices at Somerset House, beside the River Thames.

That evening in 2002, the Bishop of London rededicated the regimental war memorial. Over twelve hundred of the fallen were remembered once more in the place where their regiment was mobilized in those innocent days of August 1914. As the Last Post sounded, ex-Private Humphrys' thoughts went back to the horribly wounded men he had tended as a stretcher-bearer at the Battle of Messines; to the pals in his Lewis gun team knocked out one by one during the withdrawal from Bourlon Wood; and to the critical day in March 1918 when the rest of his company was surrounded and cut down in the massive German advance and Private Humphrys himself was taken prisoner.

Such experiences could hardly be imagined by the crowd which gathered round him on the river terrace that July evening, anxious to shake the hand of a man who fought on the Western Front. Patiently he posed for photographs and reached deep into his memory to answer the many questions from relatives of his old comrades. Soon he slipped away, leaving the party to enjoy the stirring spectacle and music as his regiment's successors sounded the retreat in the square. As he left Somerset House for the last time, Walter was pensive. 'You never forget them, you know', he muttered as his chair was lifted into the taxi. 'You never forget'.

Walter Humphrys was a remarkable survivor of a remarkable period in our history. He stands as a representative of the men whom he outlived but never forgot. He enlisted because he thought the cause was right; it was a matter of being able to face himself in the mirror. He was wounded and suffered extreme privations as a soldier and as a prisoner of war. On getting home he declared 'despite the experience, I believe England to be worth it all'. In later years he talked of the special comradeship in the Civil Service Rifles, a regiment he remembered for the number of educated men in the ranks and for the way 'the officers treated us like they treated themselves'. Walter's service on the Western Front lasted two years in a lifetime of over a century. But it exposed him to intense experiences and pushed him to the limits of his endurance. The sensations remained with him, quite literally, until the day he died in 2003. This is the remarkable story of men, like Walter Humphrys, whose early lives and experiences as civil servants contrasted so starkly with the challenges they faced in the mud of France and Flanders, the mountains of Macedonia and the deserts of the Middle East.

The regiment to which government clerks flocked in 1914 was a leading territorial battalion of the London Regiment. Its members were clerical staff from central and local government and financial houses in the City. It had a venerable history and was proud to trace its origins to the Napoleonic wars, when volunteers were organized to protect the country from invasion and to keep order while the army was overseas. In this period, gentlemen of the Stamp Office at Somerset House stepped forward, as did officers at the Custom House and Excise Office and staff at the Bank of England. The volunteer units were disbanded following the peace treaty of 1815. Four peaceful decades were to pass before bugles echoed in the stairwells of Somerset House and the martial spirit once more stirred in the bosoms of government clerks.

Civil Service Rifle Volunteers (CSRV)

The modern history of the regiment begins in 1859 with the birth of the Volunteer movement, which so caught the imagination of the Victorian middle classes that by the following summer there were well over a hundred thousand volunteers throughout the country. The stimulus for this patriotic effusion was once again a fear of invasion from France. When formation of Volunteer units was authorized, civil servants were quick to respond. Their enthusiasm is evident in a declaration signed by all the clerks in the Patent Office:

> As loyal subjects and servants of the Crown, we, the Clerks in the Great Seal Patent Office, offer our services as a body to join a rifle corps, for the preservation of the peace of these realms. We are prepared to provide our own weapons and dress, and the duties of those who are absent on drill or otherwise will be cheerfully performed in lengthened hours of service by those remaining in the Office.[1]

The Audit Office organized an inter-departmental meeting and sent a petition to the Prime Minister seeking arms and accoutrements, which it was felt that junior civil servants could ill afford. The government's

The earliest picture of the Civil Service Rifle Volunteers, drawn by Captain Angell to commemorate the first 'march-out' at Wimbledon, April 1860, in 'torrents of rain'. Expenses of the outing were defrayed by a collection of ten shillings per man.

response was not encouraging: it did not intend to supply arms to any Volunteers and would make no exception for civil servants. The Treasury sounded a warning note which prefigured the government's attitude in 1914:

> *However desirous my Lords may be of forwarding the Volunteer movement, they do not feel that they can properly allow of any interference with the time devoted to the duties of the Civil Service which are indispensable of themselves and would be equally so in the event of War.*[2]

In response to public agitation, the government soon relented on the question of arming the Volunteer units and towards the end of 1859 the civil servants began to organize. The Audit and Post Offices were first to raise a corps, closely followed by Customs, Inland Revenue, Whitehall departments and the Admiralty. Inter-departmental discussions opened on the question of forming a brigade, choice of uniform apparently proving so contentious that Customs decided to go its own way.

From the beginning these corps attracted enthusiastic recruits, from senior officials down to the lowliest messengers and office boys. Junior staff who could not afford a uniform or a subscription of ten shillings or more were assisted by a fund, raised through voluntary donations in the wider Civil Service. Those who were too elderly to fulfil all the drill requirements became honorary members and were allowed to parade in uniform wearing an identifying red sash. Thus at the first drill in Westminster Hall on 25 November 1859, all grades were represented:

> *Very many of the leading Government officials shouldered arms in the ranks side by side with their less fortunate colleagues.*[3]

In 1860 the War Office approved a combined corps, to be known as

21st Middlesex (Civil Service) Rifle Volunteers (later renumbered 12th Middlesex). From its first days this Service-wide corps had influential friends and supporters. The Prince of Wales agreed to be Honorary Colonel and later granted the title *The Prince of Wales' Own*. The commanding officer was Lord Bury, pioneer of the Volunteer movement and subsequently a minister at the War Office. Charles Kingsley was the first chaplain. The early nominal rolls resemble a 'who's who' of the Victorian Civil Service, indeed of literary and scientific society. Several permanent secretaries and other distinguished figures enrolled, including the great Civil Service reformer, Sir Charles Trevelyan; the inventor of the Penny Post, Sir Rowland Hill; Sir Ralph Lingen of the Education Office; Sir Robert Hamilton, then at the Board of Trade; and Professors Huxley and Tyndall. The corps also attracted talented men of literature and the theatre: novelists Anthony Trollope and Edmund Yates, both employed by the Post Office; dramatist and librettist W S Gilbert, who doubled as a clerk in the Privy Council office; and prolific dramatist Tom Taylor, best known as a later editor of *Punch* but whose day job was Secretary of the Sanitary Department.

On 15 June 1864, 400 Civil Service Rifle Volunteers were inspected by the Prince of Wales at Somerset House. They went through all their movements 'with creditable steadiness...faced to the front, formed fours, and prepared to receive cavalry...the two front ranks kneeling, the two rear ranks ready for file firing'. Illustrated London News, 25 June 1864

This august if somewhat colourful membership seem to have enjoyed dressing up for balls, amateur dramatics and concerts as much as they loved appearing in uniform for marching, drilling and shooting. Even in their 'very elementary stage of military knowledge and discipline', they were opinionated and argumentative and required tactful handling by Lord Bury. They were typical 'gentleman volunteers' – members of a Victorian movement which the historian Hugh Cunningham cautions against taking too seriously and whose history before 1914 'belongs to comedy not tragedy'. The members of the later, more sedate regiment regarded their eccentric and colourful predecessors with amused pride. This is evident in the tone of Lieutenant Merrick's historical account published in 1891 and also in the fact that tales of W S Gilbert stage-managing the corps' amateur dramatics were still being quoted affectionately in recruiting literature as late as 1913.

In its first thirty years, the CSRV's activities settled into an annual routine of instruction and drills, marches, camps and competitions, with a corresponding increase in standards. A grey uniform was adopted, to which later was added

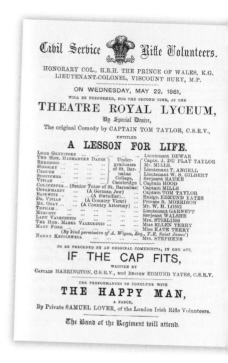

The early regiment attracted an enthusiastic, somewhat colourful membership, with strong literary and theatrical connections. The Editor of Punch, *Tom Taylor, wrote this play for the amateur dramatic society. Other famous names appear among the cast.*

royal blue facings and silver lace. The badge and the blue flag bore the 'Plume of the Prince of Wales' and his motto *Ich Dien*. Eight companies recruited from particular offices: A Company from the Audit Office (later called Exchequer & Audit Department), General Register Office, National Debt Office and British Museum; B and C Companies from the Post Office; D and E Companies from Inland Revenue and Royal Courts of Justice; F and G Companies from Whitehall and the War Office; and H Company exclusively from the Admiralty. These arrangements remained substantially the same until 1914, except for a few adjustments, the most significant of which was the addition in 1866 of a strong company of clerical staff from the Bank of England.

Somewhat surprisingly, given the stratified Service from which its members came, the corps was democratic in spirit. Apart from the major and adjutant, officers were generally promoted from within. New recruits would begin as privates, regardless of Civil Service rank. The officers were not a class apart; indeed they often commanded their social and professional equals. Relations between the ranks were respectful but friendly – a tradition which endured right down to the Great War era and was then a significant factor in morale.

A VETERAN!

Civil Service Captain. "WILL—HE—AH—STAND POW-DAR?"
Dealer. "'POWDER!' WHY HE WAS ALL THROUGH THE BATTLE O' WATERLOO THAT CHARGER WAS!!"

Victorian Volunteers made a rich target for humour. A volunteer unit composed of civil servants had even more comic possibilities, as this cartoon of 1866 suggests.

Department heads would urge new staff to join the corps, as a way of performing a patriotic public service in an agreeable manner. Like other employers, the Service stood to gain from encouraging volunteers, since it was generally claimed that these made fit, disciplined and respectful employees. It does not appear, however, that this was the only or even the main reason for the official patronage the regiment enjoyed. It was a Service-wide institution which brought men from different departments into social contact, thus oiling the wheels of official business. By the 1890s about 3,000 civil servants had passed through the ranks and many of these had subsequently attained high official posts. The CSRV was 'their' regiment and they could commend it to their juniors with pride.

An outstanding example of the regard in which the CSRV was held is the apparent ease with which £3,000 was obtained in 1892 for a headquarters building within Somerset House: every penny was raised in advance through an appeal, chiefly among the upper reaches of the Service. A school of arms established in the new

Regimental march 'God Bless the Prince of Wales'

REGIMENTAL MARCH PAST.

"GOD BLESS THE PRINCE OF WALES."
[*By permission of the Publisher,* J. H. LARWAY, 20, Newman Street, W.]

Among our ancient mountains,
And from our lovely vales,
Oh! let the prayer re-echo,
"God bless the Prince of Wales!"
With heart and voice awaken
Those minstrel strains of yore,
Till Britain's name and glory
Resound from shore to shore!

CHORUS—Among our ancient mountains,
And from our lovely vales,
Oh! let the prayer re-echo,
"God bless the Prince of Wales!"

Should hostile bands or danger
E'er threaten our fair isle,
May God's strong arm protect us,
May Heaven still on us smile;
Above the throne of England
May fortune's star long shine!
And around its sacred bulwarks,
The olive branches twine.

REGIMENTAL CALL.

The following Bugle Call has been adopted as the "Regimental" Call. The Regimental Call precedes every bugle call when in Camp or Quarters with other Regiments, and is thus used to denote that the Call which immediately follows it applies only to our Regiment. An "aide memoire" in the shape of simple words is printed below the music which will assist every Member to recognize and remember it, Sounded unexpectedly and followed by the "Assemble" or "Fire Alarm," this Call will be obeyed by every Officer and Man within hearing doubling at once *in silence* to the Parade Ground or Alarm Post.

(Ci - vil Ser - vice Vol - un - teers.)

(Ci - vil Ser - vice Vol - un - teers.)

Regimental bugle call

13

building attracted new recruits and improved the CSRV's performance at tournaments and competitions. W 'Fuzzy' Marsh, who won medals in sabres, bayonet-and-sword and foils at the Royal Military Tournament in 1903 and 1906, recalled:

> On 'open' nights...there was quite a jam. On the 'off' evenings the premises were used for social purposes and for a few drills and lectures. There was a very efficient Signalling Section which sparked and flagged around at all hours. Competition and a keen spirit of rivalry kept men on their toes. Ropes, wrestling mats, bars, bells and weapons were always available, and the indescribable smell of mixed sweat and dust became known and loved by all. It was a fine life. There was a never-ending stream of keen and skilled men ready to devote themselves to bringing on the youngsters, as well as top-class professional instructors.[4]

In the 1890s the corps flourished and membership rose to a peak of 956 in 1901. Though nominally a rifle regiment, it carried out line drill under a succession of regimental sergeant majors from the Guards. It had a good reputation as one of the élite London units known as the 'Grey Brigade', after the colour of the full dress uniform. The regimental rule book for 1899 claimed that the corps offered the 'advantages of what is practically a select and popular social club'. Membership was limited:

> The privilege of admission is...reserved to gentlemen in the clerical establishments of HM Government Offices and of the Bank of England, but in certain special cases relations and friends of Civil Servants are allowed to join, if approved of...

And on the subject of discipline:

> Anything in the nature of brawling, swearing, coarse conversation or songs should never be permitted, but should be immediately stopped by the senior soldier present. Recruits usually join the Regiment at the most impressionable period of their lives, and association with the Corps should always be for good, never for evil.

The South African War

Volunteers could not legally serve overseas unless enlisted into the Regular army. When the deteriorating situation in South Africa prompted Volunteer units to offer their services, the government was reluctant to accept. It changed its mind after the 'black week' of defeats at Magersfontein, Stormberg and Colenso in December 1899. It accepted various offers, including one from the Lord Mayor of London to raise and fund the City Imperial Volunteers. There was a huge rush of existing London volunteers to join and those who were unsuccessful applied to other units, notably the Imperial Yeomanry. In all, 136

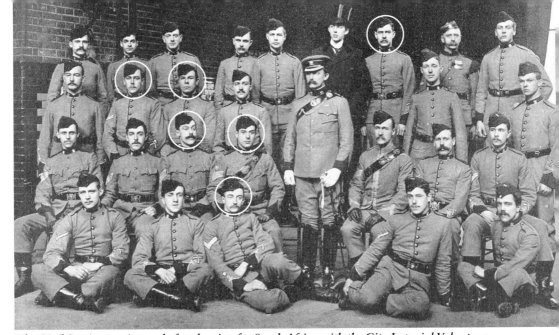

The Civil Service contingent before leaving for South Africa with the City Imperial Volunteers in 1900. The six circled men later served overseas in the Great War.
First row (at back): Pte Stephens, Pte Boot, Pte Ross, Pte Henderson, Pte Hildred, Lord Bury, **Pte Grimsdale**, Pte W Reed, Pte Page. Second row (standing): Pte H Fisher, **Cpl Hart**, **Pte Haylett**, Cpl Mears, Col the Earl of Albemarle, Pte McKenzie, Pte Buckland. Third row (sitting): Sgt Worsfold, Sgt Harris, **Sgt Brett**, Col-Sgt Oliver, Sgt Ager, Cpl Cripps, Cpl Harper. On ground: L/Cpl Reading, Pte Wheeler, **Cpl Newson**, L/Cpl Tebbutt, Pte Crick.

members of the CSRV served in South Africa with these units, of whom five died.

The Territorial Force

The experience of the South African war, combined with growing anxieties about Europe, prompted a fundamental reform of the armed forces. From 1903, defence policy was based on an assessment that there was no risk of invasion, only of raids, and that the army's major role would be overseas, either in India to combat a Russian threat or, as now seemed more likely, in Europe facing a German threat. In his reforms the Secretary of State for War, R B Haldane, sought to turn the auxiliary forces into a better organized and more efficient second-line army. It would repel raids at home and provide reserves which, after six months' training in wartime, could reinforce the first-line army in the field.

Haldane encountered political difficulties which led him to compromise and dilute his reforms. Anticipating opposition from the well-connected Volunteer lobby, he drew back from imposing an overseas service obligation, relying instead on individuals and units to volunteer in an emergency. Moreover, he began to emphasize the home defence role of the proposed new 'territorial army'. Thus when the loosely organized

A clear message. Recruiting postcard for the Territorial Force, formed in 1908.

Volunteer Force was replaced in 1908 by the more strictly regulated Territorial Force, there was uncertainty over its role in any future war. This was a factor in the difficulties faced by the regiment after mobilization in 1914.

Under the new arrangements the CSRV became the 15th (County of London) Battalion the London Regiment (Prince of Wales' Own Civil Service Rifles). Together with other units of the old Grey Brigade, now clothed predominantly in khaki, it formed 4 London Brigade in 2nd London Division. Members were enrolled for four years and could re-enrol or leave as 'time-expired'. Terms were more onerous, with compulsory attendance at camp and fines for non-compliance. After some initial anxieties about the effect of the new statutory liabilities, the

Officers of the Civil Service Rifles in mourning for their Honorary Colonel, Edward VII, in 1910. Five years later those circled went to France as '17th March Men'. Middle row: William Clark (Patent Office), James Kinsman (Treasury Solicitors), William Newson (Westminster Fire Office), Allan Trembath (Prudential Assurance, killed at Festubert), George Grimsdale (Inland Revenue), Robert Branthwaite (Home Office). Bottom row: Richard Chew (London County Council)

One of two CSR detachments at Edward VII's funeral – one marched with arms reversed, the other was in a Grey Brigade party lining the route. The Daily Telegraph *was impressed by the smartness and physique of these 'cream of London's Territorials'.*

reconstituted battalion settled into a routine of drills, camps, competitions and instructional tours, much of it now organized at brigade and divisional level. A large number transferred from the old corps, so that regimental character and *esprit* continued unchanged. The

recruiting base had widened to include clerical staff of the London County Council, Metropolitan Water Board, insurance companies and banks as well as all the London government offices. There was also a company of cyclists. Recruits often graduated from the Civil Service Cadet Corps, formed in 1903, or from school or university cadet units. Schools with traditional links to the Civil Service Rifles included City of London School, Christ's Hospital and several grammar schools in and around London.

The pre-war Civil Service

In 1914, the regiment had been in existence for fifty-five years – a period which coincided almost exactly with the evolution of the modern Civil Service. The earliest Volunteers of 1859 belonged to a very small Service, less than 18,000 strong. Radical reforms had already been proposed by the eminent civil servants Sir Stafford Northcote and Sir Charles Trevelyan, but had yet to be fully implemented. The system of appointment by political patronage was still largely in place and early members of the regiment would still have recognized elements of the Civil Service satirized by Charles Dickens in *Little Dorrit* or by Anthony Trollope in *The Three Clerks*.

By 1914 the Service had grown to 270,000 non-industrial staff. Apart from the greatly expanded Post Office (which accounted for 209,000 and which had its own regiment, the Post Office Rifles), the increase was due to the mass of social legislation introduced from 1906. Government activity now extended into old age pensions, national health insurance and labour exchanges. These substantial new areas required complex administration by armies of numerate clerks. Appointment through

Clerks at their desks in the Post Office Savings Bank in West Kensington. The Bank had a strong contingent in the regiment before and during the war. National Archives (NSC 27/2(12))

Charles Quinton about 1912. From his state secondary school in Portsmouth, Quinton passed the highly competitive exam for entry into Exchequer & Audit Department. He served in 2nd Battalion throughout the war and was severely injured, losing a leg, in October 1918.

Family of C J Quinton

patronage had been abolished and replaced by the principle of open competition, formally adopted in 1870. Promotion was by merit rather than seniority. Competitive examination in literary and scientific subjects was now the accepted method of appointment - from the loftiest Indian Civil Service clerk down to girl sorters and messenger boys in the Post Office.

In the immediate pre-war years, an estimated eighty per cent of the population was employed in manual labour. Opportunities for 'white collar' jobs were eagerly sought after. Clerical posts in the Civil Service were attractive, not so much for the salaries, which at clerical level were meagre, but for the security of employment offered. Other inducements were the prospect of steady promotion with increments, paid holidays and sick leave and retirement pensions. The 'white-collar' nature of their work gave even the lowest paid civil servants a certain social status. For bright boys from lower middle- and working-class homes it was one of the few ways open for advancement. The social standing of civil servants was reflected in a rigid dress code: white shirt with starched collar, tie and three-piece suit, the ensemble completed in winter by bowler hat and umbrella and in summer by a boater. The hat, it appears, was a potent status symbol: 'I shall have to get a hard hat' wrote the working-class boy Douglas Houghton on joining the General Post Office, 'There is no-one here who wears a cap; even little chaps of twelve and thirteen years have hard hats'.[5]

Douglas Houghton, 'hard-up and homesick' as a temporary boy clerk. The Civil Service was an attractive opportunity for bright, ambitious working-class boys like Houghton, son of a Derbyshire lace-maker.

Lady Houghton

Entry into the élite administrative class (or first division) was extremely limited and achieved by few, chiefly graduates from Oxford and Cambridge. A more realistic aim for the majority was one of the large clerical classes which carried out the bulk of Civil Service business and were broadly equivalent to what until recently were called the executive and clerical grades. Principal entry levels were at fifteen or sixteen for temporary boy clerks and between seventeen and twenty for second division clerks. In 1913, 1,354 candidates competed for 495 boy clerk vacancies. Competition for the more coveted second division clerkships was much keener, with 2,140 competing for 100 places. Examination papers ranged across the school curriculum, with at least six compulsory subjects including a foreign language. A small number of departments had no first division men and instead employed an intermediate grade above the second division. Examinations for intermediate posts were even harder and designed to attract boys between eighteen and nineteen and a half from 'good public schools' who were not going to university.

The Civil Service offered a progressive career, within certain defined limits. Prospects for boy clerks were poor, given their temporary status and low starting wage of fifteen shillings a week, which would equate today to approximately £35. In a system which was criticized by a Royal Commission report in 1914 and which would soon be phased out, boy clerks were automatically discharged at eighteen unless they passed another examination. They could compete for a limited number of permanent posts in the next layer up (assistant clerks) or aim higher, for the second division, in competition with external candidates. In spite of being allowed extra marks for each year of service, success was not assured and many boys spent two years 'cramming' in their free time in an effort to avoid being thrown out at eighteen.

It was barely possible for a boy to survive comfortably in London lodgings and maintain a respectable appearance on fifteen shillings a week. 'Moonlighting' was common. In 1913 Douglas Houghton left a 'fairly comfortable' home in Derbyshire for a boy clerkship at the Post Office. His letters home reveal the typical preoccupations of his grade: how to eke out his wages to cover meals and keep his clothes washed and mended and how to achieve promotion. Even if a boy clerk managed to progress to assistant clerk, the salary was still modest (£45 to £150 a year or, in today's terms, approximately £2,146 to £7,156). At a salary below £100 (about £4,770) it was difficult to maintain an independent household. It was common for clerks to postpone marriage for several years until they earned enough to graduate from Spartan digs to a rented suburban house.

Examination timetable for boy clerks, 1913. Candidates had to take 8 subjects. Competition among 15 and 16 year olds for these temporary positions was fierce. If appointed, they were paid fifteen shillings a week. Most members of the CSR in the war were 'second division' civil servants but some of them would have begun as boy clerks.
Kathryn E W Blunt.

Entry to the second division brought security of tenure and better prospects. The salary scale was £70 to £300 (equivalent to about £3,340 to £14,313). A clerk might expect to approach the top end in his late thirties or early forties, by which time he would be comparatively well off, possibly socially above his parents, and able to afford a reasonably sized house and a live-in servant. He could compete for a small number of staff clerkships or an intermediate appointment at salaries of up to £400 (£19,084). In theory he was also eligible after eight years for promotion to the first division but in practice the huge gulf between the two divisions was rarely crossed. Leslie Pearce of the Board of Trade would have achieved it had he not been killed in the war. This reminiscence by his sister reveals the dramatic change in circumstances which would have ensued:

'Ba'...spent all his free time studying for his First Class level exam. Once passed this threw all sorts of careers open to him. He was in the middle of the exam when called up as a Territorial in 1914 and had done so well his Chief told Father that 'Ba' would not have been asked to take it again, but would go straight into the First Class (£500 a year – riches!) But till the war he got one pound ten shillings a week, lodged with a now married ex-parlour maid of Granny's for one pound a week, which included washing, mending and general mothering. An occasional weekend train trip to Axminster cost three shillings and sixpence.[6]

Compared with manual workers, even junior civil servants enjoyed enviable conditions. They worked a seven-hour day with half an hour for lunch and usually a half-day holiday on Saturday. The regime varied between departments. The Post Office Savings Bank was known for hard work and strict discipline. According to Houghton, boy clerks there had 'no leisure whatever while at work and are taken no more notice of than messenger boys and receive no more consideration and courtesy'. Staff at the Board of Education complained of a 'caste system', in which inspectors appointed straight from university constituted 'a privileged class separated by an almost impassable gulf from the mass of clerks below'.[7] The Post Office, on the other hand, was described as 'easy-going'. Houghton 'rubbed shoulders with the mighty and shared their prestige and leisurely official life'. Three boy clerks who passed examinations to become tax clerks in 1915 also reported favourably:

Assistant clerks do their tasks mechanically, but a Tax Clerk must use his brains all the time...the Surveyor treats us as equals ...All confirm the fact that the Tax Office is the heaven of the Civil Service.[8]

Saturday afternoon soldiers

In the immediate pre-war years the Civil Service still gave the regiment official support. Recruiting posters were displayed in government buildings and membership was encouraged by senior officials, sometimes in terms implying an element of duty:

The well-known head of a large Government Office made a habit of enquiring of all newcomers to his Department as to what, if any, was their hobby. Failure to give a satisfactory reply elicited the advice that the youngster should join the Civil Service Rifles, and the advice from such a source was – well, bound to be good.[9]

The Civil Service Rifles (CSR) was not the only unit which civil servants joined. There was competition for recruits among the leading London territorials, which charged subscriptions and were known as 'class' corps. Excepting Scotsmen who, it was understood, might prefer to join the London Scottish, civil servants were expected to join the CSR. *Red*

Tape, the magazine of the Assistant Clerks' Association, declared 'The duty of civil servants...[is]...to join the Service regiment', pointing out that drills were arranged to suit office hours and it was an advantage to associate with one's own colleagues.[10]

For individuals, duty was perhaps mixed with other motives, as this recollection by a member of the London Rifle Brigade suggests:

> Among foremost London clubs before the war could be numbered the headquarters of half a dozen of the leading Territorial battalions. Such regiments as the Artists Rifles, the Civil Service Rifles, the Honourable Artillery Company, the London Rifle Brigade, the London Scottish, and the Kensingtons. ...In those days the offices in the City worked longer hours than they do now, and Saturday mornings off were by no means so prevalent. At the same time the amusements offered were less, and sport was not so well organised...Accordingly the young men in the banks, insurance offices, the Civil Service and the City generally joined the famous Territorial battalions as much for their social activities and for the facilities for exercise and sport provided as for any other reason. Friends would join the same battalion almost on leaving school...Amongst the senior non-commissioned officers...were... gentlemen wearing the ribbons of the Boer War...by now respectably married men with families, and certainly the last thing on their minds was that they would shortly be fighting for their country in a great European war.[11]

Notwithstanding the CSR's special place in the affections of departmental officials, misgivings were stirring in the Treasury. As early as 1899, 'special objections' had been raised to the idea of a regiment of civil servants leaving their duties to serve overseas. Only a small number had served in the Boer War. Now, with a greater conflict in prospect, the Treasury questioned whether civil servants should be territorials at all:

> It is very expensive to train up as a territorial at a cost of over

Sergeants at territorial summer camp, Abergavenny 1913. They are wearing the light grey full dress uniform with royal blue facings and flat caps for 'walking out'.

> *£12 per annum a man who in time of actual mobilisation would almost certainly be required in his Department, and so not available for military purposes...It is doubtful whether it is really in the public interest that civil servants should be territorials at all. The work of most civil departments would be greatly increased in the event of war and the double call on the civil servant would tend to the inefficiency of the Department if he went out and the disorganisation of the Territorial Force if he stayed. For sentimental reasons however it is no doubt important that Departments should give their officers all reasonable encouragement to join the force. The existing arrangements seem ...quite sufficiently liberal – if not over liberal – for this purpose.[12]*

The so-called liberal arrangements for attendance at the fifteen-day annual camps were resented, especially by married men. If a civil servant attended the whole camp, he was allowed a week's special leave with full pay in addition to army pay, rations and allowances. Civil pay for the second week was paid only if a man gave up a week of his annual leave entitlement; alternatively he could take a week's special leave without pay. Several parliamentary questions called on the government to set a good example to employers by paying civil servants for the second week. The Treasury did not budge, citing the need to pay substitutes in addition to salaries of absent men.

Despite these discouraging official signals, pre-war camps were well attended by civil servants, most of them forgoing a week's leave. For the lowest paid, it substituted for a holiday; and for many it was the high point of the year:

> *Camp! What splendid memories are revived by the mere mention of the word camp. The life in the open air, the spirit of comradeship which prevails, the feeling of fitness, to say nothing of the glorious thirst generally associated with life under canvas, appeals strongly to the average man.[13]*

Another affectionate recollection, by Eric Phillips, encapsulates the appeal of the pre-war CSR:

> *The years when Civil Service Riflemen kept their rifles and bayonets with their kits at home and went at times to the office in uniform before attending parades...the annual Easter trainings among the indulgent Guards at their Depot at Caterham; the summer-time excursions for musketry to Bisley, and Runnymede, and Rainham; the winter Saturday route marches round the outskirts of London, with their mighty high teas; the occasional 'night ops' in Richmond Park; the annual church parade in the grey, blue-faced dress uniform at Westminster Abbey; and the great review by King George V of the two London Divisions in Hyde Park in the summer of 1913.[14]*

E Company with Lt E A Coles about 1913. Seated extreme left is a youthful Paul Davenport (GPO), later Captain and Adjutant of 1st Battalion. Seated fourth, fifth and sixth from left are Sgts Brightman (Patent Office) and Jolliffe (Board of Trade) and 2/Lt H T Lewis - all '17th March men'. The third officer is 2Lt Davies, killed at High Wood. Seated second from right is Sgt 'Bulldog' Harris (Stationery Office), killed at Jerusalem. In second row, above and to right of Jolliffe, is George Eager (Inland Revenue) who featured in CSR recruiting literature in 1915 'looking very much at home in a trench'. Eager was killed at Messines in 1917.

In 1911, camp at Dover was overshadowed by the deteriorating political situation. It seemed that the regiment 'might be called on for more serious work'.[15] The call did not come for another three years. Camp in 1914 was to be on Salisbury Plain. Harry Old, of the Board of Agriculture, recalled the battalion assembling at Somerset House on the

evening of Saturday, 1 August:

> *Rumours were current that the portending event would almost certainly cause some alteration in the training plans, and many anticipated that our destination would be to some place of defence on the East or South coast.*

In fact the battalion did get as far as Salisbury Plain, arriving in the early hours of Sunday morning. But it returned within twenty-four hours. Eric Phillips recalled:

> *'That Sunday night...Reveille sounded barely an hour after Last Post, and that eerie call heralded the greatest phase in our regimental history'.*[16]

1914 Daily Telegraph Cup team marches into Pirbright camp for the tough annual shooting competition. The regiment won four times in a row 1902-05. The team shown here includes Paul Davenport, Tommy Dodge (killed at Loos) and 'Doodle' Lovelock (killed in Flanders 1918).

The order came to pack up immediately and return to London. This was thrilling, if confusing, as Ralph Thompson described:

> *I shall never forget the excitement of that moment. 'War has been declared', said one. 'They are sending us out to France right away', wailed another. 'They can't do that without an Act of Parliament' snorted a third. 'What they'll do will be to mobilise us and keep us under arms until Parliament has passed a law enabling it to send us abroad' said a fourth.*

On arriving in London early on Monday, the battalion marched to Somerset House, passing newspaper placards declaring 'ENGLAND PREPARES FOR WAR'. Mobilization instructions were issued and the men dismissed. They paraded again on Tuesday and Wednesday, by which time war had been declared. Thus began 'the greatest phase' in the regimental history.

1. Quoted in *Patent Office Centenary*, HMSO, 1952, p 40
2. *Civil Service Corps of Rifles: Proceedings of Inland Revenue Sub-Committee 1859-1888* (Royal Green Jackets Museum)
3. *The Volunteer Service Gazette*, Vol 1, No.8, December 15, 1892
4. QW & CSR RMA *Newsletter* Vol 2, No.2, May 1951, p 95
5. Rt Hon Lord Houghton of Sowerby: *a memorial tribute to his life and work*, published by Lady Houghton CBE, 1998, pp 6-10
6. K H Pearce, *Decades: a life story*, privately published, 1998
7. *Royal Commission on the Civil Service*, Fourth Report 1914 [Cd.7338], Appendix 6
8. Rt Hon Lord Houghton of Sowerby, *op cit*
9. CSR *Gazette*, Vol 1, No.4, December 1923, p 6
10. *Red Tape*, No.13, October 1912
11. Bryan Latham, *A Territorial Soldier's War*, Aldershot, 1967
12 Memorandum of March 1914, National Archives (T1/11617)
13 *Red Tape*, No.12, September 1912 p 12
14 E E Phillips (No.1181) article in *The Times*, 18 May 1938, p 10
15 Quoted in *The History of the CSR*, 1921, p 45
16 E E Phillips, *op cit*

Chapter Two

'The 17th March Men'

In the first week of the war there was unprecedented activity and excitement at Somerset House. Over eight hundred Civil Service Riflemen had returned from their interrupted camp on Salisbury Plain, turning the government offices into a temporary barracks. Soldiers camped in the corridors of the Inland Revenue and ate their meals lying in the square. There was much to do before the battalion could report that it was fully mobilized. These early preparations for war were not without their comic touches. After medical inspection, the men lined up in the quadrangle:

> *We parade; our kit is inspected; we are served out with identity discs giving our rank, name and religion; we are lined up (one is always lined up to do any thing in the Army) to have our bayonets sharpened – which is only done on mobilisation – something like real war, this! We feel as if we are going to die in the field of battle next day! At first, one of our men is detailed to turn the grindstone, and each man brings his bayonet singly, till some bright spark amongst the officers concludes that from the present rate of progress, we shall be ready by about the end of the war, so the whole lot are packed off to the cutler's in a taxi.*[1]

On the first day of the war, men of B Coy ride through Hyde Park on a bus pressed into service by Captain F Woodbine Parish. Sgt Teddy Green recalled 'When we saw our beloved 'Gasper' draw his sword and commandeer the bus, we all felt we were really in the war as real soldiers'. On the top deck are R G Bools and N B Skertchley of the Savings Bank, also H W Hartill a civil servant killed at Loos. Daily Mirror/Deborah Lake

As the Hackney carriage with its warlike cargo lumbered out of Somerset House, the men paraded before the Adjutant, Captain Parish, who announced that they were now under military law. In a theatrical demonstration of his new powers, Parish – an immaculate, six-foot, Regular officer of the 60th Rifles – led a small party into the

roadway. Drawing his sword, he waved down a bus crowded with office workers bound for the City. The startled driver lurched to a halt and Parish, having turned off the passengers, ordered him to turn round and drive to the magazine in Hyde Park. Here the men loaded 250,000 rounds of ammunition, pressing into service a second bus for the return to Somerset House. Emboldened by the Adjutant's dashing example, Sergeant Brett stepped out and commandeered another bus, this time to collect rifles from the Tower of London. Brett, who had then over twenty years in the regiment and wore South Africa and long service ribbons, recalled:

> *I was quite amused at the way* [the passengers] *took their misfortune; nobody grumbled, but all accepted it with good humour. Having told the driver to proceed to the Tower, we were soon back at Headquarters with the rifles.*[2]

Outside the Strand entrance sentries stood guard with bayonets fixed, facing a throng of curious onlookers and would-be soldiers. Even before Lord Kitchener's preliminary call to arms on 7 August, the country had been swept by a wave of patriotism. Hundreds of young men were stepping forward. One of these, eighteen-year old Kenneth Wills, was on his way to the recruiting office at Great Scotland Yard. Noticing the 'military stir' at Somerset House, he decided to go in and apply for a commission in the Civil Service Rifles (CSR), proffering the certificate from his school officer training corps. Far from being welcomed, he was told with undisguised amusement that in *this* regiment all commissions were given from the ranks; if he wanted to join the ranks he had better come back later and join the queue![3]

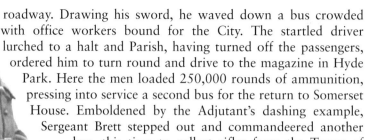

The Adjutant Captain Parish, nicknamed 'Gasper' after his middle name Woodbine. On outbreak of war he announced 'You're under military law now, I've got power over you - and, by gad, I mean to use it!' But his bark was worse than his bite and the men were willingly turned by him into efficient soldiers for active service. In 1917 Parish commanded the 1st Battalion for a brief but memorable period in the Salient. His early death in 1921 was partly attributed to a head wound sustained on the Somme. Sheila Parish

Underlying the excitement and activity was much uncertainty. Nobody was clear what the regiment's role in the forthcoming conflict might be. Despite the intention of the Haldane reforms of 1908, the job of the Territorial Force in wartime was still seen as home defence. Territorials understood they would be embodied in a national emergency, but most in the CSR had never expected to go abroad and had not signed the optional commitment to serve overseas.

Kitchener, when appointed Secretary

Crowds outside CSR headquarters in the Strand, early in the war. One private recalled the excitement: 'We rush to the gates of Somerset House every morning at seven to learn the news, till an officer or a sergeant comes along and shouts, 'That'll do! No crowding at the gates there! Get back, all of you!' Neil Bright

of State for War on 5 August, had immediately foreseen a long war and the need to raise a 'new army' to fight and win it. But he chose to start from scratch, rather than base the expansion on the Territorial Force, which he is said to have disparaged privately as a 'town clerks' army'. However, Kitchener did make clear on 10 August that he would accept for foreign service any territorial units which volunteered en bloc (later defined as units in which at least sixty per cent had volunteered). These developments raised the hopes of those CSR men who were keen to get to France before the fighting was over.

For a regiment of civil servants there remained crucial unanswered questions. Would the government allow them to go? Would it continue to pay them and keep their jobs open? As early as 4 August the Metropolitan Water Board, which had a strong contingent in the regiment, announced it would guarantee the position, salaries and wages of staff who joined the colours. The Board of the Prudential Assurance Company passed a similar resolution on 6 August, aiming to protect enlisted employees from 'pecuniary loss and anxiety'; other London authorities followed suit.

But the government's position on pay for enlisted civil servants remained unclear until 11 August. The previous day the Prime Minister announced to Parliament that posts would be kept open for civil servants; that their military service would count for pension and increments; that married men would receive *half* their civil pay; but that

29

single men would receive *no civil pay* (emphasis added).[4] This caused dismay in the regiment. Clearly, it would be a disincentive for civil servants to go overseas. Since they were the largest professional group, there now seemed little chance of getting the sixty per cent required for the whole regiment to go to France. Urgent intervention was needed at the highest level.

The CSR was doubly fortunate in its Adjutant, F W Parish. He was an experienced professional soldier and administrator with the ability to turn the battalion into a credible fighting unit. He was also a man of initiative and dash, with good personal connections to the Liberal government which he could turn to the regiment's advantage and did. As soon as the announcement about Civil Service pay was known, Parish sought and obtained a meeting with the Prime Minister, Herbert Asquith (before, it was said, the latter had had his breakfast) to put the civil servants' case. Parish was persuasive. In an unusual about-turn, the Treasury cancelled the arrangements announced by the Prime Minister and agreed that all ranks would continue to receive full civil pay, from which army pay and allowances would be deducted. There would be no distinction between married and unmarried men.[5]

Thus a major stumbling block to foreign service was removed. But uncertainty remained as to whether individual civil servants would be allowed to go. Heads of department were willing to give permission where work could be absorbed or dispensed with. At Customs & Excise about seventy assistant clerks, whose statistical work had diminished on outbreak of war, were allowed to enlist. Exchequer & Audit Department released thirty-seven examiners, on the basis that those left behind would work longer hours and audit certain accounts 'with a somewhat light hand'. Most departments made an effort to reorganize in order to allow some men to go. But soon the war began to impose additional responsibilities on the Civil Service and departments were reluctant to release staff at all, let alone in the numbers that applied.[6] These were precisely the problems the Treasury had foreseen from the regiment's earliest days.

Initially, the War Office concurred with the Treasury. The Army Council declared on 8 August that, the establishment of the Territorial Force being practically complete, 'members of the public service can most usefully display their patriotism in the present emergency by furthering the smooth work of the Departments in which they may be serving'.[7] This, combined with Treasury reluctance to authorize the employment of substitutes, meant that some civil servants were prevented from joining or rejoining the CSR. One member, Eric Phillips, recalled:

> *Some of the best trained were forbidden to accept the foreign service obligation; some were prevented from attending at headquarters to be embodied at all, and others who had been*

embodied were recalled by their Departments. There were men in the last category who flatly declined to return to civilian duty and for long afterwards flourished letters and telegrams threatening them with dismissal; but in the end they 'got away with it'.[8]

Not everyone got away with it. At least two civil servants were dismissed from the Board of Trade for enlisting without permission. One of these was Michael Joffe, a boy clerk at the Patent Office, who was killed at Messines in 1917.

Training at Somerset House

While the arguments reverberated around Whitehall, the CSR remained at Somerset House. A daily routine developed of parades and route marches, usually to Regents Park or Battersea Park for drill, musketry instruction, physical training and practice attacks. It was arduous carrying equipment weighing sixty pounds:

To the civil-servant-soldier, just from his particular department, this weight was a decided burden to cart about over five or six miles or more of London's hot, hard and dusty streets. The first two or three of these marches were productive of a good many blisters and rubbings on the feet.[9]

In the patriotic atmosphere, soldiers travelled free on buses and trains and were generally made a fuss of. This sudden popularity was bemusing. John March recalled going with his colour sergeant, Bernard Jolliffe, to a public house in the Strand. Jolliffe was a clerk in the Board of Trade though he looked every inch the old soldier, with his luxuriant moustache and medal ribbons. March was astonished to be offered a drink by a total stranger. 'Take it, laddie', whispered Jolliffe: 'he thinks you are a hero now the war is on'. March observed:

We territorials were looked down upon by 'the man in the street' as poor fools who seemed to have nothing better to do with our spare time. But on declaration of war everything changed as if by magic and we became overnight public heroes.

The number mobilized on 5 August had been 869. The full establishment of 1,000 was soon made up and a waiting list formed in the expectation that a second battalion would be authorized. Old members flocked back: men in middle age like R H 'Dump' Haylett, W B 'Bill' Hart, and 'Darli' Darlison – all veterans of the South African War. These experienced territorials were made NCOs and set to work training the battalion for war. Before leaving Somerset House, the commanding officer Lieutenant Colonel Hayes, an assistant principal at the Admiralty with many years in the regiment, made several appeals for foreign service volunteers. Even after worries about pay and job security had been resolved, the response was not generous. Less than half the officers and men stepped forward. It did not help that the Colonel himself did not volunteer, for personal reasons, and some afterwards attributed the poor response to his lack of leadership. This criticism may be unfair, since there was also hesitation in the ranks of other London territorial units.[10] There was a feeling, voiced in the newspapers, that asking territorials to go abroad was not quite 'playing the game'. Kitchener was moved to issue a statement acknowledging that many territorials might have good reasons for wishing to remain at home and allowing that some units could be designated for home defence.[11]

'Kicking our heels in Hertfordshire'

When the battalion left London on 16 August for training with the rest of 2nd London Division in Hertfordshire, the foreign service question remained unresolved. Along with other battalions of the Grey Brigade, the CSR set off in scorching heat from Marble Arch. The march took two days, with an overnight camp at Edgware, to billets in and around Bedmond, between Watford and St Albans. The officers were accommodated in houses but most of the men slept on floors in public buildings and even on straw in barns, a new experience which foreshadowed the discomforts in France. Training began:

> The first two or three days...were spent in company drill, visual training and 'belly flopping'...that very important part of our training consisting of doubling over all sorts and conditions of ground in full marching order and in flopping down on the ground on the instant that the sergeant blows his whistle. The enemy ...has then to be fired at. This flopping goes on for an hour or two and when the enemy are sufficiently close, the charge is ordered. This is done amidst cheering.[12]

In Hertfordshire some of the men were billeted in farms. 'We slung our equipments off and laid down on the straw to contemplate our new "homes". Most of us had attended annual territorial camps, but never had we been put into a barn to work out our salvation'.

H Coy return after church parade to their billet at St Andrew's School, Watford in October 1914. Note the crowd of small children around the band in the rear. Dr E Old

Lt Col R G Hayes, who commanded in turn the 1st, 2nd and 3rd Battalions in England. He was seriously wounded in an accident while supervising trials of the Madsen gun in 1918. A sergeant, Charles Hill, was killed in the same accident.

Harry Old from the Board of Agriculture was among those anxious to get overseas. He recalled the 'foreign service' question was raised again:

> *Men had now had time to think the matter over and discuss it with others. Colonel Hayes, however, showed no enthusiasm, but carefully explained that enlistment for imperial service was purely voluntary, and in this way the response was much smaller than it might otherwise have been. Captain Newson, the only foreign service Captain, appealed so strongly to H Company that the large majority undertook the additional obligation.*

Soon afterwards, separate 'home service' and 'foreign service' sections were formed. Colonel Hayes left to command the new 2nd Battalion at Somerset House. Within a few days this too was full and had its own waiting list. Hayes was succeeded by the Earl of Arran, a cavalry officer who had commanded the CSR in Volunteer days. He remained only two months with what was now called the 1st Battalion, but injected a new sense of pride and direction. The Earl issued a strong, enthusiastic appeal for volunteers, urgently needed to reinforce the British Expeditionary Force. The response was much more positive but still insufficient. To make up the shortfall, men were drafted from the new 2nd Battalion. Llewelyn Edwards, just released from the Board of Trade, was thrilled to be chosen despite having no previous military experience:

> *The Earl of Arran has...bucked things up a lot. ...Attended by some of the 'army men' and the doctor, [he] came up to Somerset House to pick out men. ...The 2nd Battalion paraded; about 180 of us are trained men, old Territorials, OTCs etc; these were drawn up separately. The Earl and his 'staff' inspected these and, with the exception of a few considered to be of inadequate physique, the lot were accepted for transfer...They did it pretty carefully, as they only had to select one man in every four. They examined each man's physique very carefully; height went for something, but I believe they looked for a good chest, good legs and healthy appearance more particularly. Some questions were asked too. I was very much*

relieved when the Earl curtly ordered me to 'fall out' to join the ranks of the lucky chosen ones.

The resulting draft joined the 1st Battalion on 5 November. Meanwhile there had been so much lobbying by civil servants wishing to enlist that the matter was raised in Parliament. On 9 September Lord Redesdale proposed a scheme whereby 'old civil servants, old bank managers, solicitors, men of letters, men of business' should be drafted in to free up more civil servants to join the colours. He argued:

Civil Servants are burning to do something for their country in this hour of need. And you can hardly imagine a better class of men from whom to draw recruits...They are many of them University men, some have gained high honours, and all of them have had the highest possible education; they are just the men who would be able to supply what we are told is in these days the greatest necessity in the case of every soldier – the brains behind the rifle.[13]

Drawing by J. Etherington-Bartholomew.

THEY ALSO SERVE WHO ONLY——STAY AND WORK.

"Civil Servants would probably do better work for their country by adhering to their departmental duties than by asking to be enrolled as raw recruits."
—*The Marquis of Lansdowne in the House of Lords.*

This cartoon from the Civil Service magazine 'Red Tape' **in October 1914 suggests a romanticized view of the soldier's life.**

The government stuck to its policy, maintaining that the brains would be better deployed in departments at home. But the high educational qualifications of those civil servants who did manage to enlist soon brought them to notice as potential officer material. Over the next few months as many as three hundred left from both battalions for officer training, most of them destined for other units. This exodus would continue throughout the war. The 2nd Battalion's waiting list was quickly used up and by February Colonel Hayes was leading recruiting marches through London. The regiment was officially open to 'all men of good character between nineteen and forty' but it still wanted men from 'the same walk of life' as those who had joined in peacetime.[14]

Eventually the 1st Battalion was brought up to strength for overseas service. But because of its hesitant start and the time needed to train the late arrivals, it was not among the first London territorials sent to France. Of the old Grey Brigade, the London Scottish was first to go in September, followed by the Queen's Westminsters and Kensingtons in early November. The CSR men felt keenly that theirs was the only Grey Brigade

Members of Lt Col Hayes' recruiting party in the Strand, aiming to persuade more civil servants to enlist. The man, who is wearing a CSR lapel badge, looks like a civil servant.

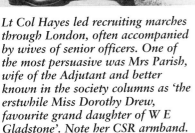

Lt Col Hayes led recruiting marches through London, often accompanied by wives of senior officers. One of the most persuasive was Mrs Parish, wife of the Adjutant and better known in the society columns as 'the erstwhile Miss Dorothy Drew, favourite grand daughter of W E Gladstone'. Note her CSR armband.

Sheila Parish

Battalion left behind. As a City clerk, Norman Blackaby, recalled:

> We were afraid we shouldn't be in the fighting at all. Everyone was saying the war would be over by Christmas. Well, Christmas was approaching and here we were kicking our heels in Hertfordshire.

Inevitably the delay was blamed on the men who had not volunteered. Bad feeling grew. Kenneth Wills, after being gazetted to the 2nd Battalion, spent a short spell with the home service detachment in Hertfordshire. He was there when Lord Kitchener visited:

> Kitchener inspected the whole division, foreign and home service detachments all parading, though formed up separately.... he made a little speech in his blunt gruff style and wound up by saying that the home service detachments were quite as precious too as the foreign service detachments. After this, of course, we were always being referred to as the 'quite as precious too's'

The antagonism was not always expressed so light-heartedly. Harry Old recalled it spilling over into 'an unfair and destructive raid on a home service company, for which the offending party receive severe

'Kicking our heels in Hertfordshire'. Men of 7 Platoon at Bedmond. All but one went overseas on 17 March 1915. Four were later commissioned and two were killed while still in the CSR: G S Scarr, T Dwane, Mather, F F Cork, P J Tickle, Archibald 'Long' Andrews, A J Pack, L J Price, A L Brinn.

punishment'. Eventually the two detachments were parted permanently, the home service men being transferred to the White City in London.

Why volunteer?

There is much in the letters and memoirs to suggest that young men were attracted by the idea of adventure and excitement not present in their desk-bound existence as civil servants. There are also references to patriotism and suggestions of peer pressure to 'do the right thing'. Albert Robins of the Board of Trade afterwards claimed to speak for his fellow civil servants:

> Why did people volunteer? Patriotism? King and country? I doubt whether this was the reason. Fundamentally, though not clearly or fully expressed, there was a feeling that there was a conflict between might and right. Certain things had happened and were continuing to happen that were wrong and could not be allowed to continue. The Germans had violated Belgium...and... France; the danger of domination of one nation by another was a reality...It was...not a claim that war put things right but that it left open the possibility of the right and stood up to the bully. So, voluntarily, off to the recruiting station.

Reorganization

The battalion was restructured along Regular army lines. Companies were reduced from eight to four (A, B, C, D), each consisting of 250 men commanded by a captain (or a major in the case of one company), with another captain as second in command. Each company had four platoons commanded by subalterns. The company commander was responsible for tactics, discipline and conduct of his company as a whole, with the second in command looking after pay, rations and equipment. Following a decree that all company commanders would be mounted, a number of officers took riding lessons. The old rank of

RSM A Toomey a Regular soldier of the Scots Guards. Had been RSM since 1907 and, with Captain Parish, trained the battalion for active service. Toomey was proud of the 17th March men. He left in 1915 to take a commission, but always remained in touch and attended reunions after the war.

36

The senior NCOs with Col Renny, Capt Parish, Lt Carlisle and Capt/QM Clark. All of the 52 senior NCOs were pre-war men. 19 were later commissioned and of those remaining in the CSR, 11 were killed.

colour sergeant gave way to two key posts per company: company sergeant major (CSM) and company quartermaster sergeant (CQMS). These important posts were all occupied by pre-war men. Specialist sections were set up, including transport (drivers, saddlers, farriers and grooms), machine gunners and signallers. Individuals were earmarked for additional duties such as clerk, storeman, batman, officer's servant or scout.

The foreign service detachment eventually got its chance to go to war, along with the other battalions of 2nd London Division, which was selected as one of the first complete territorial divisions to go to France. This was decided in late October but rumours continued to circulate about whether and when it would happen. Training was progressively intensified during winter and it was not until mid-March that the moment finally came. On Monday, 15 March Captain Parish announced to loud cheering that the battalion would embark for France on Wednesday, St Patrick's Day. This date, 17 March 1915, later came to assume historic significance for all Civil Service Riflemen.

The transport section at Watford. It was the proud boast of these men that they never lost an animal through sickness, only enemy action.

The 1st Battalion of March 1915

The 1st Battalion which sailed to France in March 1915 was around 1,080 strong, including thirty-three officers and fifty-two senior NCOs. Despite its new structure and personnel and its advanced state of training, the battalion was readily recognizable as the pre-war unit it had been. Of the three professional soldiers who exercised the greatest influence over its training, two had been on the permanent staff before the war: Captain Parish as Adjutant since 1913 and Sergeant Major A C Toomey of the Scots Guards as Regimental Sergeant Major (RSM) since Volunteer days. The third was Colonel A M Renny, the elderly commanding officer who had succeeded the Earl of Arran in November 1914. Renny was the son of a Victoria Cross winner, from a prominent Indian Army family. With his diminutive stature, white walrus moustache and impressive seat on a horse, he had an uncanny likeness to Field Marshal Lord Roberts, or 'Bobs' to the troops. All this, plus remarkable energy for a man of his age, won him immediate popularity.

Since mobilization, the senior staff had been supported by men steeped in the old regimental ways. There was a substantial pool of common background and experience – professional, military and social. The great majority in the ranks had pre-war experience, as had all the senior NCOs and nearly ninety per cent of the officers – most of these with the CSR. There was a strong contingent which had served before 1908, including at least nine with service in South Africa. Tradition is highly valued in military units. While the CSR had but one battle honour, it was nevertheless proud of its Volunteer past and of its achievements in sports and shooting. It had been customary to pass something of the ethos on to new recruits:

> As an old CSR man, I can vouch for the fact that in pre-war days the young soldier was undoubtedly well grounded in the history and traditions of the regiment, not so much by means of lectures, but by association with older members of the Regiment, who were constantly reminding the youngsters of what the Regiment had done in the past, and what they, the youngsters, were expected to do.[15]

By the time the 1st Battalion left for France, every member had received some exposure to the ways of the old regiment, either directly or through contact with older members.

Who were the 17th March men?

The majority of 17th March officers and men came from the Civil Service, Bank of England, London County Council and City offices. Since mobilization the number of civil servants had reduced: some were not allowed or chose not to go overseas; some were transferred as NCOs to the 2nd Battalion; and a good number had left for officer training.

Jean Lindley

The CSR was very much a 'family' regiment, as is demonstrated by these inter-related Isleworth families. Above: Mr Henry Trembath (organist and composer) with wife and 7 children, of whom 6 served in the war. Standing from left: Francis, Allan and Charles, all in C Coy, CSR. Allan and Charles had served in South Africa; Allan was killed May 1915. Arthur (extreme right) was killed later serving in East Surreys. Below: the 4 sons of Mr W B Newson (a businessman). William (first left) and Reginald (second right) joined the CSR and served in South Africa. Both returned to the regiment in August 1914. William commanded the 1st Battalion early 1916 and was seriously wounded when his horse stepped on a mine. Reginald, later commissioned in the Royal Fusiliers, was married to Hilda Trembath (above, seated right).

A Newson

But they were still by far the largest group, accounting for at least a third and probably a much higher proportion of the battalion. The 350 civil servants who can be identified on the 17th March nominal roll came from thirty departments and were predominantly from the second division and intermediate class. The largest contingents came from GPO (clerical rather than postal staff), Savings Bank, Inland Revenue, Customs and Board of Trade.

Very few first division men were released for military service and only three can be identified among the 17th March officers; any who had managed to leave their departments and join the ranks were likely by 1915 to have been creamed off for commissions. The second division was a large class which performed a wide range of duties calling for different levels of skill. It encompassed men of varied educational backgrounds including graduates and those who had left school at sixteen, but it was filled predominantly by those with a grammar school education. Second division men came from a surprisingly wide range of social backgrounds. As well as providing an avenue of advancement for working-class

Arthur and Geoffrey Gaze as prefects at Oundle School. Both became civil servants and by the outbreak of war held commissions in the CSR. Geoffrey was killed at High Wood in 1916. Arthur served as Adjutant and later CO of the 2nd Battalion. Jennifer Gaze

boys, the clerical grades still attracted those from middle-class homes who needed 'to earn a modest bread and cheese' as Arthur Roberts, from a public school in Liverpool, described his reason for becoming a government auditor. As a class, the second division had a history of discontent about pay and promotion prospects. They considered that their competitive selection and work experience qualified them as professionals able to fill posts reserved in most departments for the first division. They resented the barrier to their entry on merit into that élite body of university men who, with reasonable competence, could expect to rise to earn at least £1,000 (around £47,710 today).

The wartime CSR thus contained a large body of officers and men sharing the characteristics of the second division of the Civil Service. They were well-educated, self-disciplined and used to operating in a rule-bound, hierarchical environment. They displayed a self-confidence derived from having achieved their positions on merit and they enjoyed the dignity and status this gave them. They tended to be rank-conscious and prepared to work hard for further advancement. Few would probably have claimed to be gentlemen in the traditional sense of wealth or breeding. But in education, manners and dress they were distinctive. This description by Llewelyn Edwards is revealing about the attitudes of a group of second division clerks from the Board of Trade:

> *I sent in a special application at once for permission to go and enlist. This was not granted at once, but on August 28th I and two other fellows in the Department were told that we could go. At that time the Public Schools lot had not been started. The only thing for people of our sort was what was called the 'City Battalion' of the Royal Fusiliers. We went up to their headquarters but found that they were just full up. I had seen something of the sort of people enlisting in the ordinary Kitchener's Army and I wasn't going in that lot! The City Battalion people said that the best thing we could do was to get into a good Territorial regiment.*

After the war Albert Robins, who had been a boy clerk in 1914, commented:

> *There was a saying that in the army you 'met all kinds'...but...the men in our battalion were mostly good comrades and of the same background, that is city white collar workers, civil servants, bank clerks or office workers. Most of these had passed some examinations to obtain their job. They were used to mental work..... Far from comprising 'all kinds' they were mostly of one kind socially and culturally. As far as other kinds were concerned, I never met any artists, farmers or squires, college or university lecturers, miners or railway men. I never came across any titled people, in fact any in a social class above my own.*

There is some personal information available for most of the thirty-three 17th March officers. There were thirteen civil servants from nine departments, eight from the London County Council and offices in the City, three recent university graduates or students and one wealthy 'man about town'. Most had some pre-war connection to the CSR and only three or four had Regular army backgrounds. The second in command was Major Richard Chew from the architects department of the London County Council. Their average age in 1915 was thirty-four overall and twenty-nine for captains and subalterns. The three oldest were Colonel Renny (sixty), Surgeon Captain Branthwaite from the Home Office (fifty-six) and the Quartermaster W H D Clark from the Patent Office (fifty-five). Nine had been to university; sixteen had attended public or private schools and two had been to grammar schools. Where occupations of fathers are known, the majority were in professions or other middle-class occupations: medicine, law, Civil Service, army, navy, academic world and business. Many 17th March men were work colleagues and friends; a lot had attended the same schools; and a number were related, either directly or by marriage. These relationships

The 17th March officers in 1915. Front row: 2Lts G C D Stevens, HRE Clark*, B Scott*, Lts A C H Benké, G C Grimsdale, T H Sharratt, F R Radice, Capt G E Stokes; Middle row: [?], Capt/QM W H D Clark, Capt F W Parish, Sgn Capt R W Branthwaite, Major R Chew, Col A M Renny, Major H V Warrender, Capts W F K Newson, A E Trembath*, H H Kemble*; Back row: Capt G A Gaze*, [?], Lts L Davies*, R Chalmers*, JCP Kinsman, JCD Carlisle, H T Lewis, F C Olliff, G G Bates, [?], [?], Lts B Barnes, A Roberts*, H M Crofts. * Killed

Sheila Parish

A historic day. 1st Battalion leaving Watford station on Wednesday 17 March, 1915. The surviving '17th March men' commemorated this day until the 1980s.

crossed all ranks and there was no deep divide between officers and men.

This, then, was the unit which left Watford by train in the grey early morning of 17 March 1915. Lieutenant Arthur Roberts described the departure:

> The people of Watford turned out en masse to see us off and I am afraid there are many broken hearts left behind. The people have been awfully good and took to our fellows wonderfully. They could do nothing too much for us and as I was going to the parade ground on the last morning I met a girl coming away weeping bitterly and unrestrainedly. The same old story!

The battalion embarked at Southampton that evening on four ships (*Balmoral, City of Chester, Jupiter* and *Munich*) and after a calm crossing arrived at Le Havre the following morning. Fully laden, they toiled up the hill to spend the first night in France under canvas in biting

CSR on board for France. At Le Havre they complained there were no signs of the war and no welcoming crowds of pretty French girls. J R Rickard

cold. Despite their impatience to get to the front, some must have wondered what the future would hold. None could surely have realized that the war would last nearly four more years, still less that the regiment would lose more men killed than had filled those four ships from which they had just disembarked.

1. *CSR Gazette*, Vol 7, No.2, July 1929
2. Brett, *Memories of a CSM*, privately published, p 10
3. After this first rebuff, Wills was successful in getting a commission through London University OTC. He served in the 2nd Battalion throughout the war.
4. *Oral Answers, House of Commons*, 10 August 1914, Col 2243; Treasury Circular 15814/14 of 10 August 1914
5. Treasury Circular 16490/14 of 11 August 1914
6. CUST 49/369 (National Archives); letter from Sir H Gibson of 31 March 1915, T1/11844 (National Archives)
7. War Office letter of 8 August 1914, CUST 49/369 (National Archives)
8. E E Phillips (No.1181) article in *The Times*, 28 May 1938, p 10
9. 'FW', *St Martin's-le-Grand*, Vol XXV, 1915, p 32
10. See, for example, article on The Rangers by Arthur Potton in *Firestep*, Vol 3, No.1, May 2002
11. *The Times*, 14 August 1914, quoted in Peter Simkins, *Kitchener's Army*, Imperial War Museum, 1988
12. 'FW', *op cit*, p 34
13. Parliamentary Debates, 9 September 1914, Col 582
14. *The Times*, 25 February 1915, p5; contemporary CSR recruiting leaflet
15. *CSR Gazette*, Vol XI, No.1, April 1933

Symbolic painting by Henry Sayer (cartoonist of 'Red Tape' and CSR member) for regimental Christmas card 1914. Note the menacing German eagle in the clouds. This bird appears again – vanquished – in Sayer's Christmas card for 1918 on page 218.

Chapter Three

France 1915: 'Many Little Items of Dirty Work'

The battalion's first year in France coincided with twelve months of disillusion and disappointment for the Allies on the Western Front, as their offensives failed to achieve the desired breakthrough. In autumn 1914 the Germans had been pushed back, but still occupied large areas of France and practically all of Belgium. As spring 1915 approached, the French commanders were determined to find a way to eject them. At that stage, the British were ill prepared for a large-scale offensive. Kitchener's New Armies had still to be trained and the munitions industry had to be expanded and properly organized. Some politicians were looking elsewhere than Western Europe to achieve a victory. Nevertheless Britain – then the junior partner in the alliance – acquiesced in the French proposal for a combined offensive campaign in 1915 involving attacks in Champagne, Artois and around Verdun.

The CSR, as part of 140 Brigade, 47th (London) Division, arrived on the Western Front on 18 March.[1] This was just after the first British action of the 1915 campaign which began at Neuve Chapelle on 10 March. That offensive started well but halted after two days. There were few gains in exchange for huge casualties. In the reorganization which followed, 47th Division was diverted from its original destination of Ypres to the area around Béthune, where it would be based for a year. The division was allocated a stretch of front extending 6,000 yards northwards from Cuinchy and the men spent their first year in a flat, undistinguished coal-mining district where the landscape was dotted with mining towers and slag heaps. When not in the line, they were billeted in villages like La Beuvrière, Sailly Labourse and Les Brebis, which they came to know well.

1915 was described in the CSR *History* as fairly quiet and uneventful though punctuated by 'incidents' in which the battalion became 'acquainted with the realities of war'. The chief incidents came on the fringes of two battles – at Festubert in May, and at Loos in the autumn – and finally in a 'hot corner' known as Hairpin Trench in December. In retrospect the battalion's historian gave these events less prominence than the greater horrors and privations which followed. But it is clear from contemporary accounts that these 'incidents' then appeared to the participants as some of the worst experiences that could be endured.

First taste of the trenches

The first three weeks were spent in training at Cauchy à la Tour. This was a sleepy village about eighteen miles from the front line, reached after a train journey of twenty-four hours and a gruelling fifteen-mile march. On 22 March, Field Marshal Sir John French, accompanied by Generals Haig and Munro, inspected the battalion. The Commander in Chief's cheering if laconic remark, 'The men are splendid', was subsequently used on recruiting posters at home. At Cauchy, Harry Old began a journal which provides valuable glimpses of day-to-day life and of Old's personal reactions to it. On 4 April, he wrote:

> By putting some paper next to my skin, in my trousers, taking some quinine and wrapping myself up warmly, I have avoided a cold ...A service of Holy Communion was held early this morning... about 100 ...paraded at 6.30 am for this voluntary celebration ..... It seemed peculiar, and somewhat bloodthirsty, to kneel before a peaceful altar loaded with a haversack, water bottle, entrenching tool, bayonet and 120 rounds of ammunition and with a rifle just behind. The Chaplain read the sixth commandment in a firm voice, and not a man winced at the thought of the arms which he had deliberately brought into that hallowed area, to be consecrated in the cause of blood.

The first, eagerly-awaited experience of the front line came on 8 April when the battalion was attached to 4th Guards Brigade for instruction

A card game in sleepy Cauchy à la Tour, the village near Béthune where the battalion spent its first weeks in France in spring 1915.

At Cauchy the battalion trained 'somewhat impatiently, for three whole weeks'. Here the Machine Gun section are holding a field day.

in trenches astride the La Bassée Canal. Unknown to the troops, this sector was to be the pivot for the forthcoming Battle of Festubert. During pre-war training the battalion had formed a high regard for the Guards. Norman Blackaby of B Company recalled with amusement:

We were fortunate in being allowed to go into the trench where the Guards were holding a section of the line. To our great surprise we saw all these burly fellows with black beards – we thought they were Russians. But as soon as they opened their mouths, 'effing and blinding', we realised of course they were Guards from Caterham!

'The Keep', an old farm building close to the front line at Givenchy where the battalion did its first trench duty. In the yard were flowerbeds, laid out by the 4th Guards Brigade and nicknamed St James's Park. Not to be outdone, the CSR planted their crest in privet hedging. The scroll of the Prince of Wales feathers is just visible behind the sandbags.

The Guards were by now old hands in trench warfare and taught the newcomers survival techniques as well as the local geography. The CSR *History* records this first front line experience as disappointing. War was not as exciting as anticipated, but 'a thing of drab monotony, of dull routine, of the avoidance of being killed, of an invisible enemy'. Givenchy was swampy, bleak and desolate. The trenches were shallow and afforded little protection. Nevertheless the battalion's first solo trench duty on 13 April was greeted with renewed excitement. John

47

March of C Company recalled:

> For one short spell, perhaps five minutes, my section of the trench was shelled by whiz-bangs, the German 3 inch field gun, and I have never been so frightened before or since. The 'whiz' of the shell seemed to have a venom specially directed against poor me! But I got used to it later, and learned that if one stuck tighter than a postage stamp to the front of the trench there was not too much danger from them as long as the first one missed, and prompt evasive action was taken.

Three tours in quick succession were generally peaceful and uneventful despite some casualties from snipers. The first two men to be killed were Privates Pulman of the Local Government Board and Albert Snellgrove of the Post Office Savings Bank. Of the four pals who carried Pulman's body at a moving service in Béthune Town Cemetery, two would themselves be dead within six months.

In 1915 artillery ammunition was in short supply and there was much improvisation. Lieutenant Radice recalled:

> Unless there was something on, very few shells were sent over from either side. Our trench mortars were very primitive, drainpipes dug out of the streets of Givenchy to which a flange had been soldered at one end. The projectiles were jam tins filled with explosives, like the hand grenades of the period, only larger.

The battalion then had nearly a fortnight's break from the trenches. This was spent at La Beuvrière, where football and swimming were interspersed with hard training for the forthcoming offensive. Harry Old and his pals in 15 Platoon had found the front line exciting. During the march back they had sung all the way. Old, who celebrated his twenty-first birthday at La Beuvrière, was developing a personal philosophy which would sustain him through 1915 - his darkest year. On 27 April, he wrote:

> We all enjoyed our experiences in the trenches and for my part I should like to be in the excitement surrounding them instead of in this village. A soldier's first duty is generally considered the care of his rifle, but I think on this game his first duty is to know how to look after himself. This is especially the case in cooking meals in the trenches. The tea – without milk unless we had had the foresight to bring some condensed milk – we made at breakfast was more appreciated than any other drink at any other time. We cooked our meals on braziers, made by riddling with holes old tins, buckets or mess tins. Extra dainties, such as toasted cheese, Oxo, and fried eggs made our meals more tasty. Dirt could not be avoided, so we treated it as non-existent.

On 22 April the Germans launched an attack about twenty-three miles

Burial services were well attended. The early death of Albert Snellgrove from a sniper's bullet caused great shock. He was 39, one of many older men from Volunteer days who re-enlisted in 1914.

48

further north, beginning what became known as the Second Battle of Ypres. The Germans used gas for the first time, in contravention of the Hague Convention. Soon afterwards the first, rather primitive gas masks were issued. Called 'smoke helmets', these were flannel hoods with goggle eyepieces.

By the end of April, after six weeks in France, the battalion had spent barely seven days in front line trenches, but already the attrition of original men had begun. The casualties were two killed, one died of sickness and five wounded. Greater losses came from other causes: eighteen to officer training (of whom all but six were destined for other units) and a number evacuated due to sickness, including an outbreak of German measles. Two subalterns, Radice (Post Office) and Benké (Home Office) were embarrassed to be sent home with what they considered a child's ailment, the more so when their ship was packed with seriously wounded and gassed casualties from Ypres. Both soon recovered and were posted to the 2nd Battalion.

The Battles of Aubers Ridge and Festubert

Festubert, like Neuve Chapelle, was part of the British effort to assist the French to break through the German defences. The French army concentrated on Vimy ridge, while the British objective was further north – Aubers ridge, which rose no more than forty feet above the plain but was sufficiently commanding to be strategically important. The battalion's role at Festubert was alternately to hold the line and provide working parties, particularly for repairing the sandbagged breastworks which passed for trenches in the low-lying, swampy ground. They were also called upon to provide bombing parties and make almost nightly patrols in no man's land. Festubert was afterwards regarded as the CSR's baptism of fire. Though they were not sent 'over the top', it was here that they first suffered significant casualties.

The British attack began on 9 May and was renewed on 15-18 May. It failed to break through. The battalion was in the line when the intense artillery bombardment began early on 9 May. Later they held the line to the south of the heavy fighting around Festubert. In this period there were over forty casualties, including seven killed. Harry Old recorded:

> We had experience of war with full force in all its aspects, its excitement, its thrillingness and its gruesomeness. We know what shelling is now. All day long, and at times in the night as well, the whole district around was alive with shells.

Lieutenant Roberts described supporting an attack by another battalion:

> We supported them with rapid fire till our rifles were too hot to hold. They reached the trench and then dropped in one by one. It was a thrilling sight. Then they bombed their way along and the explosion of bombs was punctuated by the most horrible silences.

I can't explain how horrible those silences were. It was a ghastly night. The rain came on and transformed the place into a sea of mud, so thick that walking was a matter of utmost difficulty. You simply stuck.

An unfortunate series of incidents beginning on 23 May (Whit Sunday) compounded the CSR's losses. This was during the final phase of the battle, when 47th Division was holding the line Festubert-La Plantin-Givenchy. Part of the German trench system opposite La Plantin had been captured and repeated efforts were now made to clear and consolidate it, principally by Canadian troops and 8th Londons (Post Office Rifles). The enemy resisted stubbornly over two days and many lives were lost on both sides. The CSR supplied patrols to collect intelligence in no man's land. They also lugged boxes of bombs and empty sandbags to the captured trench and worked at night on a new communication trench, trying to dig quietly with picks and shovels behind a flimsy hessian screen.

On Whit Sunday night a carrying party was shelled, killing three and wounding five including Second Lieutenant Clark, who died later. Clark, who had been commissioned from Cambridge University in August 1914, was the son of the battalion's Quartermaster, W H D Clark, an official of the Patent Office and prominent CSR man from Volunteer days. This was the first of many family tragedies played out in the regiment, in which so many men were related. Another popular subaltern was killed in an unplanned operation in no man's land, as he rallied a party of Post Office Rifles bombers, directing them from the parapet. 'Cissie' Chalmers was also a Cambridge man who had enlisted in May 1914. He was admired for his valour and had been mentioned in dispatches for daring reconnaissance work. His death made a big impression. The same night, eight volunteers went to help the Post Office Rifles in their desperate extended struggle to clear the captured German trench opposite. The operation was successful, all the enemy occupants being killed, but the return was made under fierce fire. Of the eight bombers, only four got back alive, and two of these were wounded. Arthur Roberts wrote home:

1181 Pte E E Phillips, pre-war territorial and 17th March man. At Festubert he was so badly wounded that on leaving hospital he became an instructor in England. Originally a civil servant, he was for many years military reporter of The Times, *often signing his articles '1181'.* Pat Phillips

Our bombers, boys all of them, were heroes and mostly died for it. They ran along the parapet chasing the Germans back with their bombs and when their bombs were done they took to their bayonets. When they were wounded they still went on.

This incident led to the CSR's first gallantry awards, the four surviving bombers being awarded the Distinguished Conduct Medal.

The final blow at Festubert, mentioned in all the memoirs, was the death of Captain Trembath, a senior and respected member from Volunteer days. One eye-witness recorded the incident which occurred while digging a communication trench:

1940 Pte A J F Tracey of the Board of Education – one of four bombers killed on Whit Monday in a successful operation to clear a German trench.
Croydon Local Studies Library

We were shelled very heavily all the way up and had several casualties. We...commenced digging for all we were worth...we were making splendid headway when the Germans...opened rapid fire on us...The two killed were...Captain Trembath...and my friend Private Smith. ...They were next and next but one to me in the trench and both lost their lives while an attempt was being made to bring under cover two wounded lieutenants who were directly in front of us.[2]

Allan Trembath, from Prudential Assurance, had won the Distinguished Conduct Medal and been commissioned in the field in South Africa. Ralph Thompson recalled his skipper as 'thoroughly efficient, a strict disciplinarian but very just – in one word a *soldier*'. Trembath's two brothers served in the battalion and, as with the Quartermaster's son, many felt they shared in a family bereavement.

On 25 May the CSR gave covering fire to 142 Brigade as it attacked at Givenchy, on the right. Again, the attack was initially successful but the gains could not be consolidated or extended because of fierce enfilading fire. This was effectively the end of the Battle of Festubert. That night the Germans could be heard digging themselves into a new position and at dawn on 26 May the remaining post opposite, which had caused such trouble to the Canadians and Post Office Rifles, surrendered. The battle had pushed forward the British line several hundred yards but the coveted Aubers ridge remained in German hands.

The battalion spent 27 May cleaning the captured trench, evacuating prisoners and casualties and burying the dead. Harry Old recalled a German officer refusing food from a private and instead requesting the attentions of a British officer. The newly commissioned Lieutenant Ind, from the Local Government Board, proved 'scrupulous in matters of army etiquette' and complied with the request. They were still under constant shell fire. Lieutenant Roberts described the appalling scene:

Everywhere the most awful collection of debris of all sorts, dead men, dying men, equipment, clothing, rifles twisted and bent in the most fantastic shapes. Literally piles of dead men one on top of another in pools of blood. A veritable shambles and a place of utter desolation as the result of the fearful artillery fire it had undergone followed by the bombing and bayonet charges.

The battalion buried an estimated 350 in three days – most of them London territorials. For long afterwards the name Festubert conjured up gruesome memories.

IN MEMORIAM
'THEIR NAME LIVETH FOR EVERMORE'

SHANKS – In memory of my friend DOUGLAS BROWN SHANKS, aged 19, Civil Service Rifles, killed in action by my side at Festubert. May 27, 1915

York Rickard was deeply affected by the death of his chum Douglas Shanks, killed by a sniper. They had enlisted together from the Metropolitan Water Board in August 1914. Rickard placed this notice in the Daily Telegraph *in 1969, 54 years after the event.* J R Rickard

On 31 May the battalion marched to Béthune for rest and recovery. During May they had lost nearly ninety men as casualties, of whom twenty-eight were killed. Forty-seven had been evacuated sick and seventeen left for officer training. Most of the battalion's dead lie in Brown's Road Cemetery, Festubert. The short committal services were well attended; Private Flook of A Company was buried by two of his school fellows from Christ's Hospital.

Summer 1915 – recovery and reorganization

The early summer months provided a pleasant respite. The weather was fine and on the whole the billets were good. In some parts the trenches were almost hidden by long grass and corn and everywhere no man's land was ablaze with cornflowers and poppies. Best of all, the war in this particular sector was temporarily quiescent. True, there were inspections, working parties, listening patrols, and long tours in the line, but these were uneventful and interspersed with 'much cricket and feasting and very little drill'. This was, according to the CSR *History*, 'a bon war'. In early June the French handed over a section of line south of the La Bassée Canal. Norman Blackaby recalled trenches:

> ...left in an indescribably disgusting manner...alive with mice. We had to burn most of the stuff we came across...our people were pretty adamant about cleanliness, etc. But we couldn't avoid getting loused up. Our occupation was getting rid of these lice.

Both Captain Parish and Brigadier General Cuthbert had reputations as sticklers for cleanliness. The men complied cheerfully when they could see it was necessary for reasons of hygiene or discipline. But they resented and ridiculed 'spit and polish' for its own sake, such as buffing the metal part of entrenching tool handles. Private Edward Loxdale recorded in a spoof *War Gazette* in July:

> A favourite pastime with the NCOs is for them to come to us

'After sleepy Cauchy, Béthune was voted top hole'. The Place du Beffroi, crowded with British troops waiting to board London buses to take them up the line. In 1915 Béthune was relatively undamaged. When the CSR returned in 1918, this square had been devastated.

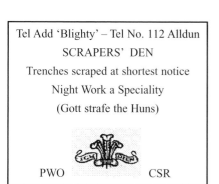
*Notice on the door of an elaborate
dugout in trenches near Grenay, June
1915.* Liddle Collection/Dr E Old

*when we are at meals or asleep and inform us that
IT WILL NOT BE NECESSARY TO DUST THE
TRENCHES.*[3]

Despite the divergence in standards of trench
hygiene, relations with neighbouring French troops
remained good. Joint celebrations marked the
hundredth anniversary of the Battle of Waterloo.
Paddy Brett recalled:

*On June 18th...100 years after the Battle of
Waterloo, Sergeant Hilton and myself entertained
the French Corporal and his senior soldiers...We
felt we were making history, having a few drinks
together at the estaminet – as comrades-in-arms.*[4]

In the front line at Vermelles the regime seemed to
Norman Blackaby like 'live and let live':

*We had working parties going out to repair broken wire. You
could hear only a few hundred yards away German soldiers doing
the same thing and the low murmurs as they got on with it. ...They
didn't poop off at you, so you didn't poop off at them.*

John March recalled how, from an advanced sap, it was possible to walk
about fairly freely at night and on one occasion he bumped into the
Adjutant and Captain Gold 'strolling around' in no man's land. During
the summer the first home leave was granted and there were changes in
personnel. Some of the older officers, including Major Chew, were
withdrawn and replaced by younger
men. Colonel Renny went on leave
and did not return, on health
grounds. The men were sorry to lose
their 'little Indian colonel' who,
despite his age, had proved an
energetic and inspiring leader.
Command passed to Major
Warrender on promotion. Initially
seen as a rather aloof Guards officer,
Warrender later grew in the men's
esteem as he led them through a
succession of harrowing actions in
1916. They found him somewhat
intriguing. A wealthy, middle-aged
bachelor and man-about-town,
Warrender was known to move in
exalted social circles. He was
rumoured to have been a confidant

*Washing day at C Coy's billet, Haillicourt, July 1915.
Getting in and out of such billets usually involved
negotiating a dung heap in the centre of the yard.*

'Then and now' views of Noeux-les-Mines cemetery, 1915 and 2004. The graves in the foreground are of victims of an accidental explosion at the nearby bomb school in July 1915: Sgt W K Evans, Pte J H Bunce and Pte C H Taylor. The plot where the man is walking in summer 1915 would shortly be filled with casualties from Loos, several to a grave. Their headstones are visible in the modern photograph, crammed in staggered rows. Hedley Malloch

of the late King and his name had been romantically linked with that of Lady Randolph Churchill.

The campaigns of 1915 were dogged by shortages of artillery ammunition. At home, the munitions industry was now being organized on a grand scale by Lloyd George. This led to the recall of civil servants, including the quartermaster, W H D Clark, to set up the new ministry. Meanwhile in France there was a call for volunteers to replace bombers who had been lost. The new men, including Harry Old, were trained at the bomb school at Noeux-les-Mines. Lieutenant Roberts was made battalion bombing officer or, as he put it, 'president of the suicide club'. Roberts' first home leave had been a mixed blessing:

> Leave...has left me absolutely unsettled...All those things of home have attained new values for us since the war...England, home and beauty.

Several pre-war territorials became time-expired after four years' service. To those contemplating re-engaging for the duration of the war, a reward of a month's leave was offered. Norman Blackaby signed on and took the leave, while his sergeant 'put down his rifle and went straight back to his office, because his time was up'.

At home, the debate about releasing civil servants to enlist rumbled on, with letters in *The Times* and questions in Parliament. The War Office had begun to relax its policy of encouraging civil servants to remain in their jobs. In April, Lord Kitchener said he 'looked with confidence to the heads of departments to arrange...for the necessary permission to be freely given'. The Board of Trade responded by announcing that all men in the labour exchanges and unemployment insurance department could go, their places being filled by temporary women officers. Similar blanket releases were made from the land valuation department. For those still denied permission, there was the unpleasant experience of being handed white feathers in the street. To try to counter this, special 'HM Civil Service' badges were issued.[5]

In France, drafts were arriving only spasmodically and the battalion was already under strength. Fighting strength reduced every month until dipping below 700 in January 1916, after which it would pick up steadily in the run-up to the Somme battles. The 3rd (later Reserve) Battalion had been formed in England in May 1915 under Colonel Hayes and was the main provider of reinforcements. Recruiting leaflets made no bones about the reason for needing 500 more men in France immediately: 'to repair the wastage of war'. Another 500 would be needed in six months, and a further 500 after that. Despite opening the ranks to 'all men of good character', the CSR still aimed at 'civil servants and their friends'. Regimental publicity emphasised the contrast between the former desk-bound existence of the men and the challenges they faced in the front line, as soldiers and as manual labourers. News of the first medals, won on Whit Monday at Festubert, appeared in the *Daily Express* in July under the headline 'HOW FOUR DCMs WERE WON BY LONDON CLERKS'. The article included an interview with an insouciant Private Brantom and a quote from a proud RSM Toomey:

> *It is almost impossible to realise that, less than a year ago, they were just ordinary civilians, with no greater excitement in life than pushing a pen in a Government office.*

The four were all pre-war territorials: H Harris of the Estate Duty Office (subsequently commissioned), W H Brantom of the Board of Agriculture (soon to be commissioned, then killed in 1916), Sidney Lawrence of the National Health Insurance Commission (killed in 1916) and S W Mills of the Metropolitan Water Board. The three civil servants were all assistant clerks, a class whose terms and conditions had long been contentious. *Red Tape* noted with heavy irony that the public found the act of bravery splendid because:

> *everything in a Civil Servant's conditions and training is unheroic. The successful Civil Servant is all too often the timid, careful vindictive* [sic] *man. And the people knowing this, never sympathise with Civil Servants, however badly they may be treated. Yet these men were Civil Servants.*[6]

In France, Llewelyn Edwards' keenness and leadership potential had been noticed and he was encouraged to apply for a commission. He was hesitating, as were junior civil servants in other units, in case he ended up with less pay. In some circumstances a civil servant, especially if married with children, could be financially better off by remaining a private or NCO. This financial disincentive to junior civil servants taking commissions was a source of complaint throughout the war. By the time Edwards faced it, two parliamentary questions had already been put, asking the government to change the rules, which it declined to do.

While Edwards pondered the pros and cons, the battalion went into the front line at Mazingarbe. Now fully experienced in trench discipline, their turn came to instruct new arrivals from the 15th (Scottish) Division. Captain Parish recorded in the war diary on 20 July: 'They seemed disappointed as they did not jump over the parapet and they thought an attack ought to take place every day'. These keen Scots would not have long to wait: they were among the first of Kitchener's New Army troops to be blooded, in the culminating offensive of the 1915 campaign – the Battle of Loos.

The Battle of Loos

When the battalion went into trenches at Maroc on 1 September, preparations for the offensive were well advanced. The men joined nightly working parties, straightening out the front line at a point opposite and slightly to the north of two long parallel embankments of mining spoil. This was the Double Crassier, just behind the German line south-west of Loos. On 17 September the men were taken by London buses to Les Brebis and were briefed the following morning by Colonel Warrender on their role in the forthcoming battle. Private Portch of 16 Platoon recalled 'we were very keen and excited'. Warrender announced that while the battalion would be in reserve for the actual attack, it had been picked for a special, highly secret job – carrying gas cylinders up to the trenches in 47th Division's sector.

The British were to use poison gas for the first time at Loos, in retaliation for gas used by the Germans at Ypres. This was before the days of organized transport and light railways, so along the whole length of the battle front thousands of cylinders had to be manhandled

Slag heaps at Loos known as 'Double Crassier'. A whole CSR platoon was practically wiped out here, running across with boxes of bombs under heavy fire, 25 September 1915

up to the line before being hoisted into position in special bays. The men recalled these fatigues as the worst ever for sheer physical exertion. Each cylinder weighed nearly 200 pounds and took two men to carry. They were slung on poles and manoeuvred with the greatest difficulty along miles of narrow, winding trenches. The battalion emerged from completing this awkward and exhausting task on the early morning of 19 September and returned to Haillicourt, again by bus.

Before the battle opened on 25 September, instructions were issued to destroy letters and diaries. Judging by the number of surviving accounts, many CSR scribblers disobeyed. The job of 47th Division was to secure a defensive flank at the southern end of the whole attack. Of the four battalions of 140 Brigade, the 6th and 7th Londons were to attack from opposite the Double Crassier, where the Germans had dug a second line behind their front line. The 8th Londons (Post Office Rifles) were in close support, with the CSR further back in brigade reserve. From these reserve trenches the whole battalion witnessed the unfolding battle. At 0550 gas and smoke operations started. Forty minutes later the infantry, wearing smoke helmets, advanced towards the Double Crassier.

Both the 6th and 7th Londons reached the first German line without many casualties, but encountered resistance at the heavily defended second line. The Germans did not appear incapacitated by the gas and were able to counter-attack. The Post Office Rifles were sent to reinforce the 7th Londons who were in danger of losing their foothold on the Crassier. When they, too, got into difficulty, men from two platoons of CSR's B Company, twenty-six strong, were sent over carrying bombs. Twelve were killed and only four returned unhurt. Private Lloyd of the Post Office Savings Bank was one of the few to get across and through the German wire:

> At the signal, we all got out of the trench and pulled our smoke helmets down so that we couldn't tell t'other from which. At another signal, forward we all went, each man carrying bombs weighing about 60lbs in all, but before going many yards they felt as many tons. The distance was only about 300 yards, but it took me at least eight minutes to get across. The helmet was stifling, so I hadn't much opportunity of observing things, but I saw the impenetrable wall of smoke and the number of shells bursting on my left. I kept falling down under the weight of the bombs, getting up and stumbling a few more yards. Presently I came to the barbed wire which, thank goodness, was blown to atoms. Having reached the trench, I threw my bombs in, then doubled up and collapsed in a heap at the bottom. Our sergeant, who arrived a few seconds before me, was shot through the mouth by a Hun, who immediately put his hands up after doing it. Somebody else dealt with him.[7]

Most of the party had been hit by machine-gun fire before reaching the German trench. Only six got onto the Crassier itself. Of these but one survived: Corporal Chinn, also of the Post Office Savings Bank. As his five companions became casualties, Chinn made three journeys up the side of the Crassier, carrying each time as many bombs as he could collect. Meanwhile Lloyd was oblivious to the struggle raging around him:

> I lay for at least an hour before coming round and never have I been in such a state before, covered from head to foot in slimy mud. ...I tried to find some of my pals and at last discovered 4 of them, and we remained together all day in a German officer's dugout. At dusk we made our way back to our old line, and found we were the only ones left of the 26 who started, and one of these was wounded. It was a veritable hell...I felt very sick at losing all my chums. Some of the best they were. Of the four left, three were NCOs, so I am the only private to return.[8]

The 47th Division secured its objectives on the first day and for the remainder of the battle was required to defend and consolidate its gains. For the CSR this involved two nights' hard labour, digging a new communication trench between

Three of the few survivors of 6 Platoon after the Battle of Loos. Sgt Tyler, Cpl Seys (India Office) and Cpl Chinn (Post Office Savings Bank)

what were now the former British and German front lines. Men lying out in the open as covering parties were frozen to the marrow. Meanwhile to the north and east an incredibly complex and bloody battle raged on. On the first day the village of Loos had been captured but further north the attack had failed. There was a desperate need for reinforcements, which arrived too late. On 27 September the men witnessed the unforgettable sight of the 3rd Guards Brigade advancing under fire to attack Hill 70. They moved across open ground, as Norman Blackaby described, 'as though they were on Salisbury Plain...steady as a rock'.

Overall the battle was a failure. The early gains could not be exploited because the reserves were too far back. This led ultimately to the removal of Sir John French and his replacement as commander in chief by Sir Douglas Haig.

When the battalion left the line on 29 September the men were in a state of extreme exhaustion. Harry Old recorded that this period had been 'almost unbearable in its severity'. Llewelyn Edwards described the aftermath of battle:

> We were finally relieved...and, in pitch darkness and pouring rain, made our way across the open...stumbling along in the greasy

mud and great pools of water, picking our way amidst the indescribable debris of a battlefield – if you hadn't seen what this debris is like you couldn't possibly imagine what an extraordinary mess a battle makes! My god we were in a state too – covered from head to foot in slimy mud, bearded like the – and very worn out. After a few hours halt in the village (unable to sleep owing to being pretty nearly frozen to death!) ...[we] had to march 13 miles.

The CSR men killed at Loos were buried at the northern end of the Double Crassier, but their graves did not survive and they are commemorated on the Loos Memorial. While the battle raged, the French army had considerable initial success in Champagne; further north they captured Souchez and made advances on Vimy ridge. But they too failed to achieve the desired breakthrough and a general halt was ordered. In fact the offensive was to rumble on for another three weeks and, after a short rest, reorganization and training at Verquin and Noeux-les-Mines, the battalion was involved in an attack north-east of Loos on the village of Hulluch.

Hulluch

The CSR, temporarily attached to the 1st Division, moved to reserve trenches at Vermelles on the evening of 12 October ready to support the attack, which opened the following day with a discharge of gas and smoke. This was intended to provide cover as the infantry cut thick wire entanglements which long-range artillery had proved unable to destroy. In fact the gas served to warn the Germans that the attack was imminent. When the smoke cleared, men of the Black Watch came under intense fire as they struggled with wire-cutters. After heavy losses, the Scots were left holding the line from which they had started. The CSR narrowly missed being sent over the top when a second attempt on the barbed wire was called off at the last minute.

Llewelyn Edwards reported somewhat laconically: 'We had a great view of the fight (in so far as the gas and smoke screen permitted!) as we lay in support trenches, though we were rather heavily shelled and lost a lot of men, as is always the case with the supports in an attack'. In the misty dawn of 14 October, Private Hurst of B Company was shot by a sniper:

His case was so desperate that three stretcher bearers tried to take him to the rear over the open at the back of the trench - the mist having closed down a little. Unhappily, as soon as they had started the mist lifted and the Germans shot two of the bearers before anybody realised what was happening - I watched all this myself.

The stretcher-bearers managed to crawl back but Hurst had to be left out all day. Later, Captain Farquhar and Private Probyn crawled out with morphine and water for the desperately wounded man. He was finally rescued after dark but died at the dressing station. The CSR stayed in the line burying the dead until late on 17 October. John March commented: 'One only has to bury a very few real dead men under fire to realise there is no glory or romance in war'. Harry Old recorded this time as 'no doubt the roughest of our experiences up to date'. Worse was to come.

Before returning to the trenches at the end of October, Harry Old became a reserve bomber. This meant he had to drag four bombs in a sack wherever he went, 'like a rag and bone merchant'. One man lugged his sack all the way to his billet, only to discover that he had brought the trench rubbish sack. On 31 October the CSR began fourteen days in 'some of the most wretched trenches it is possible to conceive'. Llewelyn Edwards described the gruelling five-mile march over a 'sludgy squidgy plain', passing through the captured village of Loos to some poorly-dug and very exposed trenches. Harry Old recorded:

> It rained practically every hour of this period...the Germans poured onto our position such a dose of shells as we had never before experienced over such a prolonged time...huddled against the side of the trench, with our groundsheet over us, and with one corner of it hooked onto our bayonet to keep the rifle dry, and so spent the time smoking, muttering, shivering, even blubbering... simply enveloped in mud.

Private Deubert of the Metropolitan Water Board lost his entire kit, buried under a mud slide. All digging had to be done by night, so there was no rest. The discomfort was shared by officers and men alike. Lieutenant Roberts wrote:

> My mind carried a vague recollection of trenches and then more trenches, and then more and mud up to your eyes, incessant shelling, unceasing rain, and through it all a great 'unwashedness'. In fact we had a hell of a time...Just think of keeping your clothes and boots on, probably wet through for 16 days, imagine rubbing your teeth round with your handkerchief when they get too thick with all the food sodden; in fact every d—- thing sodden.

Casualties from the shelling were high and Edwards' little coterie experienced some 'rather narrow shaves'. The appalling conditions produced a steep rise in sickness figures: three officers and 102 men reported sick during November, the second highest monthly total of the entire war.

Morale

Under the trying conditions in autumn 1915, when attacked by the weather almost as ferociously as by the enemy, the battalion managed somehow to sustain its morale. Some writers are surprisingly frank about being on the point of breakdown. It seems, however, that they were capable of very quick recovery. Llewelyn Edwards, for example, at the end of the thirteen-mile march from the Loos battlefield, reported that after a good night's sleep he was 'right as rain again and already the beastly sights ...are beginning to fade in the memory'.

Harry Old admitted more than once to breaking down in tears. On 10 November, after a particularly gruelling fatigue, he collapsed: 'Halfway through my [sentry] duty I could stand the agony no longer. I sank down completely exhausted'. But he too recovered quickly after being carried to an improvised dugout and put to bed wrapped in a blanket. Next day he was able to return to duty feeling refreshed. Tours in the trenches always alternated with periods behind the line when, between fatigues and training, it was possible to get baths and clean underwear, receive letters and parcels, and perhaps watch some kind of entertainment. There was sympathy and support, too, from the transport, cooks and storemen who at this stage of the war had at least some respite from these front-line conditions. Private R York Rickard of D Company recorded on 18 October:

> Have made 'duff' on two occasions this week...very much appreciated by the boys. They are having a rougher time than we cooks are and am willing to do anything for their comfort. Thank God I am a cook and more often than not have some sort of a roof over my head at night even if only a barn with rats for company. Shall try and stay on this job all the winter. It is a snip job.

Perhaps one of the most important factors in sustaining morale were personal friendships and bonds fostered by communal living and shared dangers. These could inspire men to 'soldier on' rather than let down their pals. Harry Old explained it thus:

> Without any mental strain, one forgets the conventions of civilised life and reverts more and more to the more primitive stage of living. The artificial barriers of reticence imposed by the conditions of cultured life cease to exist; soldiers share one another's joys and sorrows, their pleasures and their pains, and become as intimate with one another's feelings and secrets as little children, all unmindful of the larger things of life.

These feelings could become intense when a man was separated from the battalion and cause him to hasten back, even when this meant returning to discomfort and danger. Corporal Cornwell of A Company was one of several to describe a sort of *nostalgie du régiment*. After recovering from a slight injury in June, he had kept enquiring at the base camp when he could rejoin the battalion, prompting the exasperated officer in charge to remark that he couldn't understand why a corporal in the CSR should 'kick up stink about getting back'!

The men also developed psychological ploys, like 'grousing', a universally accepted outlet for feelings of anger and frustration. Harry Old referred to grousing as 'the very life and soul of our existence in this hog-like life'. Edward Loxdale, one of the battalion's most prolific scribes of 1915, wrote in an essay entitled *The Terrier at the Front*, published after his death:

> *He used to be clamorous about his rights; now, his one privilege is to grouse. He was ease-loving and pleasure-seeking; now he submits to the most rigorous discipline. His time is divided between soul-saddening drill and detestable trenches. His amusements are 'slating the Army' and 'strafing the enemy'. He anathematises the Army wholeheartedly, root and branch, from top to bottom, lock, stock and barrel. He criticises its organisation, methods, and all its works. He is irreverent about 'Red Hats'. He says the 'Army is an ass', and if he had his time over again – well, he would join it again. He is starved, sweated, insulted, 'fed up', and far from home. BUT HE IS HAVING THE SPORT OF HIS LIFE; WITH ALL ITS FAULTS HE SAYS 'IT'S THE FINEST WAR WE'VE EVER HAD'.*[9]

Temporary relief

On 15 November the battalion was at last withdrawn and went with the whole division to Lillers, an undamaged town fifteen miles back. Here the men had an extremely enjoyable month's rest, with only some mild training and one route march to spoil it. The contrast with the trenches was almost unbelievable. All the recollections seem to involve food. Norman Blackaby recalled the excitment: 'There was a shop open and we could buy *patisserie*! Just imagine! We felt on top of the world'. York Rickard and his pals found a private billet for one franc a week each and

'Our territorials at the front...muddy but cheerful' ran the title of an early official film shown in British cinemas. The battalion was filmed marching out of the line to Noeux-les-Mines on 15 November 1915. This frame shows the cookers apparently brewing up on the move, the slag heaps of the Loos battlefield just visible in the distance. IWM (FLM3676)

'We all fell in love with Lillers and soon forgot our troubles'. The battalion thoroughly enjoyed two rest periods in Lillers in winter 1915/16.

enjoyed a 'splendid dinner...best since been in France: soup, rabbit, roast pork, potatoes, salad, apples, coffee, cigs, all for one franc fifty'.

Llewelyn Edwards became a lance corporal and finally decided to apply for a commission. On 12 December he asked his mother to approach any senior officers of her acquaintance to ask for him to be commissioned into their regiment: 'If not, you see, I should have to be gazetted into any old crowd the army liked to shove me into!' He had had a marvellous time at Lillers, playing the piano for the battalion concert, and would be sorry to leave. This was Edwards' last letter: he was killed on 21 December in the CSR's last 'incident' of 1915 – at Hairpin trench.

12 Platoon posing at Lillers, 4 December 1915. A typical group of 17th March men: only two were not later killed or commissioned or both. Back: L S Martin, H E Jacobs, H S Hundleby, F A Coward, E Loxdale (the poet), R J Thompson. Front: E W Kettle, A G Rose, R R Nicol, G F Ives. IWM (Dept of Docs, Capt R J Thompson, 78/58/1).

Hairpin trench

In the second week of December, 47th Division went into the north sector of the Loos salient, which included the Quarries and the Hohenzollern Redoubt – a particularly unsavoury part, with many half-buried bodies lying around from recent fighting. The Hairpin was an infamous fifty yards of captured enemy trench which was fiercely contested. The Germans still occupied sections to the right and left, and were blocked off from the captured section by double barricades of sandbags, just sufficient to keep them out of bombing range. The captured section was linked to the British front line by two long parallel saps, so completing the 'hairpin'. As if the Hairpin were not unpleasant enough, subterranean noises could be heard, indicating that the Germans were tunnelling to lay a mine. It was justly described as a hot corner.

Just before daylight on 20 December, Harry Old was awakened by the sound of bombs as the Germans rushed a sandbagged barricade in the Hairpin. There was an urgent call for reserve bombers. Feeling 'that thrill which is produced by the expectation of danger', Old and his chum Frank Matthews rushed with the other reserve bombers towards the Hairpin. Neither of them reached it. As they ran, bent double, along the shallow communication trench, a rifle grenade burst among them, killing Matthews and severely wounding Old. Norman Blackaby recalled this incident:

> You were more or less enfiladed on either side and they were firing both artillery and rifle grenades. Everything was bursting all around, casualties were happening. It was all we could do to get stretcher bearers up to get them away.

The Germans retained control of the barricade and a counter-attack was organized for the same evening, to be carried out jointly by the CSR and 7th Londons. Second Lieutenant Thompson of the Royal Fusiliers led the CSR's remaining bombers and some bayonet men from B Company, including Llewelyn Edwards, over the top on the right of the Hairpin. The plan was to jump into the German trench and bomb along it, while a party of 7th Londons restored the disputed barricade. According to the CSR *History*:

> From the outset there was not the slightest chance of success. However, 2nd Lieutenant Thompson and the NCOs and men with him went to their end unflinchingly, and though the enemy put down an impenetrable barrier of bombs, rifle grenades and machine-gun bullets, the tragic scheme went on until all officers and NCOs taking part had been put out of action.

A rare view inside Hairpin trench, a notorious 'hot corner' near Loos where the CSR lost many men on 20/21 December 1915.

1813 Pte Harry Old from the Board of Agriculture. Severely wounded in the chest by shrapnel at Hairpin trench. After a long convalescence he was able to return to work in Whitehall.

Liddle Collection/Dr E Old

3007 Pte P C Lennard from the National Health Insurance Commission. Seriously wounded at Hairpin trench and died nine days later at St Omer. Croydon Local Studies Library

This incident described in Lloyd's Weekly News, 20 February 1916, *took place during the emergency in Hairpin trench in December. Leonard Druett was a civil servant at the Ecclesiastical Commission.*

There were many valuable lives lost on that night unfortunately, as it turned out, to no purpose, for the Germans a few days later blew up the whole trench and a number of the 23rd Londons, who were holding it, went with it.

So ended the life and short military career of Llewelyn Edwards, almost sixteen months to the day since leaving his desk in the unemployment insurance branch of the Board of Trade. Meanwhile Harry Old lay on a stretcher at the advanced dressing station. Seriously wounded in the chest but still conscious, he watched and waited all day and throughout the following night as the wounded arrived – 'the fruits of the Hairpin stunt'. He was anxious for news of his pal of nine months, Frank Matthews. Eventually he learned from Lieutenant Grimsdale, who arrived with a gunshot wound in the shoulder, that Matthews had died from head wounds. The Hairpin 'stunt' resulted in about 120 casualties among the Londoners. Twenty-three of the dead were CSR men; many more, like Old, received wounds which would keep them in England for the rest of the war. All but four of the battalion's dead have no known grave and are commemorated on the Loos Memorial.

Christmas 1915

As Christmas approached, the Divisional Staff issued orders to pre-empt a truce of the kind which had erupted spontaneously in some places at Christmas 1914. But those still mourning the losses at the Hairpin were in no mood for fraternizing with the enemy, or even for their own festivities. Their first Christmas in France was spent in trenches and cellars at Vermelles and by New Year the battalion was back in the unhealthy area of the Hohenzollern Redoubt. Early on New Year's Day an enemy mine exploded and a party went to attempt consolidation of the crater. In this action Private Chambers, badly wounded, was rescued under fire by Drummer Hogwood and Corporal Tickle, both of whom were later awarded the Military Medal. At the Hohenzollern Redoubt Edward Loxdale scribbled his last, for he, too, was killed on New Year's Day. Three days earlier, his musings on the stoicism of the soldier in wartime had ended prophetically:

> All that interests him is that the cause he is fighting for is a good one. So he suffers the indignities of army life, grouses a little, and carries on. HE REALISES THAT HE IS IN THE VALLEY OF THE SHADOW.[10]

Loxdale lies today in Quarry Cemetery, a sunken chalk pit near Auchy-les-Mines, hard by the Hohenzollern Redoubt where he was killed.

End of the first year in France

In mid-January the battalion returned to the Loos area, where they found that both Allied and enemy trenches now ran across the Double Crassier. Trenches and communications had been improved but Loos itself was completely ruined and no accommodation remained above ground. The battalion spent the time constructing defences. One last period in reserve at Lillers heralded the move of 47th Division to a new area further south, which included the edges of Vimy ridge. While the battalion in France reflected on its first year, a historic regimental event took place in Winchester: a dinner on the first anniversary of the departure for France. It was resolved that such reunions would be held annually so long as any 17th March men should live to attend them. Thus began a tradition which lasted over seventy years. Present in 1916 were over a hundred who were temporarily in England following wounds or sickness. The rather riotous event was presided over by Captain Grimsdale, now recovered from his wounding at Hairpin trench.

In the first year the 'wastage of war' had accounted for 130 dead and over 200 wounded. In addition, 170 had left for officer training. The CSR had not yet been sent 'over the top' as a battalion. In assessing the first year the *History* declares that the battalion had, as a unit, undergone little real alteration. 1916 would change all that.

1. 4 Bde of 2nd (London) Division until names changed in May 1915.
2. Letter from staff member of Beckenham Council, published in a local newspaper.
3. Private Edward Loxdale, *A souvenir of a soldier*, 1916.
4. T P Brett, *Memories of a CSM*, privately published.
5. *The Times*, 22 March 1915, 14 April 1915 (p5); *Red Tape* No.44, May 1915 (pp 129-131); *Territorial Service Gazette*,18 September 1915 (p 186).
6. *Red Tape*, No. 47, Vol IV, August 1915.
7. *Territorial Service Gazette*, 11 December 1915, p 380.
8. Private Lloyd was killed in action in the Ypres Salient on 14 July 1917.
9. Loxdale, *op cit*.
10. *ibid*

Chapter Four

France 1916: 'Damned Silly Orders'

After a year of frustrated efforts and heavy losses on the Western Front, a new Allied strategy was agreed in December 1915. It was now accepted that the enemy could only be decisively defeated by fully coordinated efforts in the main theatres. Three simultaneous offensives were planned on the Western, Russian, and Italian Fronts. The British and French were to mount a combined offensive in the area known as the Somme. But the German attack on Verdun in February distorted this scheme. It put the French army under so much pressure that the British were called upon to play a greater role than they were ready for.

While plans were laid for this great Anglo-French offensive, in which the battalion would play its part, life continued with the familiar alternation of short periods in the front line, support, reserve and on working parties. Even in a relatively quiet period, there was a steady trickle of casualties. Over a hundred were recorded between February and May, including twenty fatalities. These losses would eventually be made up by reinforcements from England, where the rules on enlistment were now being radically altered.

Recruitment in England

During 1915, in the face of mounting casualties and a fierce public debate about conscription, the government reluctantly accepted that it could no longer rely on voluntary enlistment. Lord Derby's scheme, under which men could attest voluntarily then wait to be called up, was introduced in 1915. This was quickly followed by full conscription under a series of Military Service Acts from January 1916. The procedures for releasing civil servants were now the same in all departments. Men of military age were divided into three categories. Those who could be spared at once were automatically released when their turn came under the Derby Scheme or when conscripted. Those who could not be spared for the time being were to be released 'at the earliest opportunity'. A small number of men were exempted due to the 'indispensability' of their work. This last category was very small but included practically all the remaining decision-making, or first division, clerks. No fit men of military age were taken on for 'ordinary administrative or clerical work' and many vacancies were filled by women.[1]

In contrast to the early volunteers, Derby men and conscripts had much less choice of regiment, as reinforcements were sent wherever the need was greatest. Hundreds of civil servants released under these new arrangements ended up in a variety of units. However, for those who still wanted to join the Service's own regiment, whose exploits were followed with interest in government offices, there was still a way to do so. Under a special dispensation allowed by the War Office to a handful of London 'class' corps, the CSR was able to continue enlisting men directly until late 1917. It seems likely that the reason for this concession was the ability of these units to attract potential officers into their ranks.[2] Civil servants would specify on attestation that they wished to serve in the CSR and, if accepted, would be told to report to Somerset House when they were eventually called up. Thus even during conscription reinforcements were, as the CSR *History* put it, 'much the same class of man as joined...in pre-war days'.

Recruits were trained at Hazeley Down near Winchester, where the Reserve Battalion had moved from South-West London in January 1916. The men lived in camp but mixed freely in local villages, where they found a warm welcome. Their basic training lasted thirteen weeks and then they were liable to be drafted overseas. Groups of thirty to forty men, known as 'the draft', were segregated during final training. Alec Reader was on a draft in February 1916: 'Am working very hard at present, trench digging, bomb throwing, bayonet fighting, etc, and we do all our work in full war kit'. Albert Robins recalled the final preparations:

> *There was some attempt at toughening* [the Draft] *...up. There was inoculation and draft leave. A certain amount of one's kit was*

'The sites around Winchester... hallowed for all time with memories of brave men who were in our midst for awhile and then passed away to the great adventure'. The Hazeley Down cross still stands among the fields where so many young recruits were trained in 1916 and 1917 to replace men already lost in France, Greece, Egypt and Palestine.

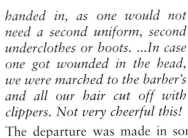

Two portraits of 532005 Pte A L Robins, Board of Trade: the more serious pose on enlistment and the informal one when on the draft for France, after having his head shaved and with the wire removed from his cap. The pipe in his hand prompted family and friends to send Robins tobacco. Pals in France thought he would have done better to be photographed eating tinned fruit.

Brotherton Library, University of Leeds

handed in, as one would not need a second uniform, second underclothes or boots. ...In case one got wounded in the head, we were marched to the barber's and all our hair cut off with clippers. Not very cheerful this!

The departure was made in some style. Colonel Hayes would hold a farewell parade at which he wished them luck and exhorted them to live up to the fine tradition already established by the 1st Battalion. The draft would then be cheered off as they marched to the station, led by a band. Small crowds of local people would gather to watch. Arthur Armfield recalled 'marching on air with excitement'. Anthony French described the men of his platoon:

They were of course heterogeneous but all were fired with a will to acquit themselves as first-rate soldiers. Which they did, every one. When the day came for our heads to be shorn and for the regimental buglers to lead us down the hill as a draft to Twyford station the platoon marched as one man.[3]

In France the draft did final training at the divisional base depot before going up the line. Senior regimental officers were distant figures to the average private, but they made special efforts to greet new arrivals personally. Anthony French recalled a welcome interview with Colonel Warrender, who enquired solicitously after French's family (whom he had never met) and posted him to B Company so he could be among friends. Most of these young men were at least nineteen, the minimum age for overseas service. Some drafts, however, included boys who had exaggerated their age in order to get overseas quickly. Sometimes a boy's physique gave him away. Edgar Powell and Vic Blunt both attempted to enlist at seventeen, but the medical officer was not taken in and rejected them for foreign service. Others managed to sustain the deception. In early 1916, Anthony French, an apprentice accountant, Alec Reader from the Post Office Telephone Service and Arthur Armfield, a banking apprentice, were all still under nineteen when put on the draft for France.

The Vimy ridge sector

In April the battalion moved to the west slope of the northern spur of Vimy ridge. Canadian troops won an epic victory here in 1917 but a year earlier it was relatively quiet with little firing on either side. The Germans occupied a dominant position on the ridge and the British hold on the western side was somewhat precarious. The front line was not continuous, but consisted of detached posts about a hundred yards apart. Getting to these outposts involved crossing the exposed Zouave valley. This ran west of the ridge and the Germans would regularly send a rain of shells along it.

On the surface an atmosphere approaching 'live and let live' prevailed. Below ground the war was pursued more aggressively. Both sides were digging mines under no man's land. When finished, these tunnels would be packed with explosives and blown up. Without waiting for the dust to settle, infantry from both sides would rush forward to 'occupy' the resulting crater and 'consolidate' the lip. The aim was to advance the line by the distance of the crater, or at least as far as the lip nearest one's own line. The men had to be permanently alert, ready to exploit any explosion. The constant strain of listening and the expectation of being blown sky-high at any moment were wearing on the nerves. Colonel Warrender summed it up as 'a loathsome

A glimpse inside a CSR billet. Relations were generally good, though one Madame was reported to claim, unjustly, 'English soldat do no work and eat too much'.

form of warfare'.[4] On 29 April there were three explosions. One of these destroyed part of the line on the battalion's right, causing heavy casualties among the 6th Londons. During a fierce bombardment, two sections of bombers and two Lewis gun teams were sent to occupy the resulting crater. Despite twelve casualties, the operation was successful and resulted in immediate gallantry awards to Sergeant Knapp and Corporals Nottingham and Smedley.

Arthur Roberts had experienced four months of 'England, home and beauty' following a fall from his horse the previous November. On return he found D Company much changed. All the subalterns were new and many original men had gone – casualties, commissioned or promoted to NCOs in other companies. The new men, however, were 'very good indeed'. Roberts enjoyed the new responsibility of commanding the company. He thought this 'a better job than office work' and wondered what chance he might have of an army career after the war. He would not survive to find out.

The loathsome warfare continued, with the blowing of five mines under the German line on 15 May – a spectacle observed by the battalion from comparative safety on the Lorette Spur. The Germans then reverted to more traditional warfare, shelling systematically over several days. This culminated in a massive bombardment and infantry attack on 21 May.

Disaster on Vimy Ridge

On that gloriously hot Sunday the battalion was in reserve at Camblain l'Abbé. The men were having tea when suddenly the bombardment began. It could clearly be heard, even from six or seven miles away. Barely an hour later they were on the road in full kit. When they halted at Villers-au-Bois, small groups stood around speculating on what was up, while others played cards. It was clear from the officers' faces that something serious was afoot. A superstition had developed that it was unlucky to win money before going into the line. As they finished their card game, 'Driver' Andrews confided to Francis Martin that he was certain to 'go under' that night. Andrews' pessimism was well placed: he and many others in B Company did not survive the disaster that was to overtake them on Vimy ridge.

As they pulled up the hill from the village, some engineers on the road shouted 'This way for the orchestra stalls!' A clear view opened up towards the ridge, about four miles ahead. Years later, Lance Sergeant Frank Watts recalled:

> It was as awful a sight as could be imagined. From end to end [the Ridge] was covered with a thick cloud of grey smoke, lit here and there by the twinkling flashes of shell bursts. Seen across that peaceful looking countryside it seemed unreal, fantastic, but there was no-one so new to warfare that he did not know what it meant.[5]

The *Official History* states that such a bombardment had never before been experienced. Though of unprecedented intensity, the barrage was confined to about a square mile and was the first 'box barrage' of the war. It almost obliterated the front and support lines and severed all communications. The pounding continued for four hours, whereupon the enemy easily overran the front line and switched the bombardment onto the Zouave valley, to catch British reinforcements coming up.

Meanwhile the battalion stumbled along a narrow communication trench in fading daylight, through a barrage of tear gas. At Cabaret Rouge they were issued with extra ammunition and bombs. They were to attempt a counter-attack in the dark over unfamiliar ground and with no guide. B Company under Captain Farquhar was leading. Weighed down by their extra load, the men struggled through the barrage in the Zouave valley and arrived exhausted at a small hut of sandbags which passed for headquarters of the 8th Londons (Post Office Rifles). A counter-attack was being hastily organized with a mixed force consisting of B Company, details of Post Office Rifles, and a company of 18th Londons. The 6th and 7th Londons were to cooperate on the right.

There was no time for reconnaissance or liaison or for briefing the men. B Company moved off at 0210, Captain Farquhar having arranged the men in two waves for their hopeless task. Afterwards the editor of the CSR *History* had difficulty producing an authoritative account. It appears that in the darkness and confusion B Company never made contact with the other units. There was no artillery or other support. Francis Martin, in the first wave, recalled:

> *Moonlight on bayonets. Captain Farquhar and Mr Scott in front with walking sticks and revolvers. Machine gun fire hellish – chaps going down in dozens 20 yards from Boche. Reggie Watson and I only left standing. Decide to wait for second wave in shell hole. The second wave came over – none reach us – Boche standing on parapet throwing bombs into wire. Reggie & I fire 50 rounds apiece. Rifles choked with earth.*

Most were killed or wounded before reaching the objective. The few who could continue, like Martin and Watson, found the German wire impassable and took cover in shell holes. They lay out all day, sweating in the heat and expecting to be blown to bits by trench mortar fire. Eventually they managed to crawl back under cover of darkness. They discovered a number of men from the second wave had advanced little further than the trench marking the recent British line. Among these had been Frank Watts:

> *I saw by the light of a flare, our platoon sergeant cursing some men who wanted to stop in...[the trench]. He was threatening them with his bayonet and shouting 'Get out, you b——ds!' In front.... the attacking party seemed to melt away and I soon began to feel*

Capt H B Farquhar who, with another popular officer Lt Scott, led B Coy up Vimy ridge on 21 May and was never seen again. He was from the National Insurance Audit Department and had served in the Matabele and Boer wars.

James B Farquhar

rather lost and strongly disinclined to go any further. I dropped into a shell hole with a half-hearted suggestion to myself that I only wanted to take stock of things for a minute.[6]

The other companies had fared better. A Company stayed behind to bring up rations while C and D followed B through the valley. C Company under Captain Gaze was ordered to assist the 18th Londons. Two platoons of C under Second Lieutenant Osborne went forward but, unable to establish contact, secured a trench as a defensive flank and sent out parties looking for wounded. D Company, led by Captain Roberts and CSM Brett, was ordered up the slope to support B Company but found only small, scattered parties. D Company then got into and consolidated the support line trench. Apart from two intense bombardments in the afternoon and evening, 22 May was relatively quiet, allowing the divisional staff to establish where the front line now lay. Another counter-attack, also unsuccessful, took place that evening but by then the CSR had been relieved.

The battalion's losses exceeded one hundred. B Company had been badly mauled in 1915; now the remnants were all but wiped out. Casualties were reported as nine killed, ninety-eight wounded, and fifteen missing, including Captain Farquhar and Lieutenant Scott. A few bodies were recovered immediately and buried on the ridge but these graves did not survive the later fighting. Of the twenty-seven who died between 21 and 23 May, all but three are now commemorated on the Arras Memorial. The fate of the missing men long remained in doubt. When the battalion returned to Vimy ridge in mid-July, it was quiet enough to send out search parties to recover bodies from the German wire, where Captain Farquhar was last seen. But definite identification was not possible and Mrs Farquhar received well-meaning but conflicting accounts of her husband's fate. During the summer she and other relatives anxiously sought news from survivors and through the Red Cross. Requests for information were still appearing in the *Territorial Service Gazette* three months later. Some relatives nursed hopes, not fully dashed for over two years, that the missing men were prisoners. Original men comprised almost forty per cent of the dead and missing. These were prominent pre-war members like CSM F Howett of the India Office, Lance Sergeant A J Andrews of the Board of Agriculture and Sergeant Chick from London County Council.

Recovery

On 25 May, the survivors marched in deep gloom to Calonne Ricouart and began reorganizing. Drafts of around 200 arrived. Alec Reader, having experienced his first real action, wrote to reassure his mother he was safe. He had lost all his kit and was making do with stuff inherited from a casualty who had, Alec complained, been 'very careless with his

The Lord Mayor of London (in overcoat) inspects D Company's cooker at Camblain-Chatelain on 11 June 1916. General Barter and Major Newson look on. 2500 Pte R Y Rickard, visible behind the cooker, remained a cook throughout the war and became used to such inspections. In 1917 he complained 'Posh, Posh, Posh all the time. D Company cooker only one reported clean'. IWM (Q623)

socks'. Seven decorations were awarded and twelve men were mentioned in dispatches. One of the most popular awards was to 'Bulldog' Harris, CSM of C Company, who worked at the Stationery Office. In a rare distinction for an NCO, he was awarded the Military Cross:

> *For conspicuous gallantry. After a counter-attack he went out and bandaged wounded men in broad daylight. He moved about under constant machine gun and rifle fire.*

One of those Harris had been searching for, but never found, was his old friend 'Kaffir' Howett, CSM of B Company. These two civil servants had served together since 1908 and had been inseparable. Frank Watts recalled how the survivors eagerly scanned newspapers for reports of their adventure but were disappointed. The situation on Vimy ridge, said the communiqué, remained 'unchanged'. The 47th Division overall lost heavily and the divisional history questions whether the higher command was justified in incurring this scale of losses for the maintenance of such a risky position.

Despite the depressing effects of the losses, the battalion resumed social life while reorganizing at Calonne Ricouart. The weather was warm and the men patronized estaminets and enjoyed sports days. A battalion revue was a howling success. The Adjutant censored the script

but the cast still managed to get away with a merciless lampoon of Regular army 'spit and polish'. The climax was an audacious impersonation by Private Teasdale of General Cuthbert alias 'General Brasso'. The revue even merited a mention by Major Newson in the war diary: 'very topical and very well played'.

'A forbidden topic of conversation'

On 13 June the battalion moved further north to the Angres sector. Here they were to mount a raid, one of several such ploys along the line which were designed to confuse the enemy in the run-up to the Somme offensive. Morale had evidently been quickly restored after the Vimy ridge operations, for there was no shortage of volunteers. According to Anthony French:

2488 Sgt Bugler S H Moxon and friends at Bruay, June 1916. These little girls took immediately to a Tommy who spoke fluent French. Before enlisting, Moxon was leading trumpet in the London Symphony Orchestra. He had a chest expansion of 6" and his party trick was to 'breathe in', sending his tunic buttons flying. He was killed while carrying a wounded man to safety near Ypres on 25 October 1916.
IWM (Q640)

Had all volunteers been accepted, each raid would have been a major offensive. Married men with families, then those who had most recently been in bayonet reach of the Boche, were automatically ruled out. Company and platoon commanders sorted out the rest.[7]

About a hundred men and five officers were chosen and began rehearsing behind the lines. Arthur Armfield, selected as Lieutenant Fallon's runner, recalled the disappointment among those left out. Two parties were to cross no man's land, enter the enemy trench at different points, then bomb their way along it towards each other. The CSR *History* is reticent about the raid on the night of 3 July: 'a dismal failure... a forbidden of topic of conversation in CSR circles'. The Germans apparently suspected an attack and, as the raid was about to begin, put down a box barrage. The north party managed to get close enough to discharge bombs into the enemy trench but the south party was held up by wire and had to withdraw. Armfield recalled

The raiding party...equipped with Mills hand grenades, rifles and fixed bayonets, coshes, wire-cutters, etc, each man's faced blackened with charcoal, moved forward as silently as possible to the front line trench and took up position...The night was particularly dark, still and silent, accentuating the all-round tension. At zero hour our guns opened up with a heavy barrage...

75

Immediately the German artillery replied with an equally heavy barrage on their own front line, across no man's land and around us...a terrifying inferno...We were all pinned down on the firestep or flattened against the wall of the trench.

So disabling was the barrage, Armfield did not even set off across no man's land. Francis Martin did cross and afterwards recorded tersely:

Black faces – wet night. Crawl across no man's land. Hell. Got back half an hour later...Killed my first Boche certain – got his bayonet [in my] left hand.

Second Lieutenant Brantom of the Board of Agriculture, a 17th March ranker subsequently commissioned, was killed. Thirteen were wounded, including Lieutenant C W A Millar, another original. Millar had seven operations for his injuries, eventually having to resign his commission in 1918.

The battalion had one short and fairly quiet tour on Vimy ridge before heading south. Around this time some cross-posting of drafts began, as casualties mounted on the Somme and other units were short of men. By the end of July significant numbers of CSR men were attached to other units, particularly the 13th and 19th Londons. This poignant account from Private P D Mundy demonstrates how a disappointed draft reacted to being sent to another regiment. Mundy was a 'Derby man' who had joined the CSR by preference, before being called up.

4090 Cpl Francis A Martin, local government official from Reading. He served in B Coy from December 1915 until injured at High Wood. After recovering was commissioned in the 20th Londons, whose uniform he is wearing here.

Donald Martin

Before we left Havre we were told we were going to be attached to the Kensingtons [13th Londons] instead of the CSR, much to our disappointment...100 dog-tired men starting off each with three-quarters of a hundred weight on his back...It was a scorching hot evening and now and then a man would drop out but at last with footsore feet and...perspiring faces we staggered into a village about 3 or 4 miles behind the line. It was crowded with soldiers who looked at our badge with curiosity. But then curiosity turned into amazement when one of our fellows started singing our regimental march and in a moment it had rippled down the column and we marched into the market place singing 'God Bless the Prince of Wales'. I heard one soldier say to another 'These poor buggers can't know what they're in for'.

Mundy and others on this draft were killed with the Kensingtons during the heavy Somme fighting in September.

Trek to the Somme

At the end of July the battalion began its long trek to the Somme. The great offensive had opened, after a week's bombardment, on 1 July – the bloodiest single day's fighting in the history of the British army. The casualties were staggering: nearly 60,000 in one day of which a third were killed. It was a dreadfully high price for only very modest gains at the southern end of the fourteen-mile British section of the Somme front. Elsewhere the British attack failed to secure its objectives and the planned 'breakthrough' did not materialize. The Somme turned into a grim, protracted struggle which would last until November.

Very little of this bigger picture was known in the battalion at the time. As the heavily-laden column set off from Camblain l'Abbé on 26 July, there was no official word as to where it was bound. The ultimate destination, however, was never in doubt. Since the offensive began it had been difficult to ignore as the distant rumble of guns could be heard even from Vimy ridge. Such news as filtered through was not good and it seemed only a matter of time before the CSR would be thrown in. Letters home spoke of 'the advance' as though one were expected any day. The Colonel himself wrote on 28 July, 'what our movements in the near future are to be is unknown, but one can make a guess'. Sixteen months at the front and a year in command had not inured Colonel Warrender, educated in a more gentlemanly school of soldiering, to the rigours of trench warfare or to the responsibility of taking young volunteers into the line. As he led the battalion towards its biggest challenge yet, the colonel reflected that his divisional commander, General Barter, had been rash to bet him five pounds on hostilities being over before the end of the year. Though he must surely be onto a winner, Hugh Warrender fervently hoped he might lose the bet.[8]

The route was roundabout and took seven weeks. Warrender led on horseback but the men marched with full packs. It was arduous in the scorching heat:

> It was a point of honour never to fall out except to drop in one's tracks...Mechanically you moved on, impelled by some involuntary force to put one leg before the other, every ounce of energy reserved for this effort. A horse-fly would land on the back of your hand as you clung to the sling of your rifle...The last vestige of sweat would evaporate and leave face and hands dry and the skin taut. All blood seemed to drain from the head. The tramp of feet sounded far away. A misty light, subdued yet strangely bright, enveloped your comrades as you stared at the weather-beaten neck of the man ahead and thought of rest and sleep.[9]

Outbursts of singing relieved the monotony. The men harmonized sentimental ballads or belted out ironic, complaining choruses or paraphrased hymns. Black humour and frank vulgarity, like grousing, played its part in maintaining morale. They also sang popular songs such as *There's a long, long trail a winding; An old mill by the stream; Take me back to dear old Blighty; I want to go home*; and, later in the year, *Roses of Picardy*. In the seven weeks before going into action on the

Somme, the battalion spent twelve days on the march, thirty-one in training, and only five at rest. They journeyed in a great arc, north as far as Divion before turning south-west towards Abbeville and finally towards the valley of the Ancre. It was arduous and at times intensely hot. The result was the battalion's highest incidence of sickness in the war: a record 300 reported sick in July and August with a variety of complaints like trench fever, influenza, bronchitis, heat stroke and septic feet.

Under-age soldiers

The CSR *History* records that memories of August 1916 are 'among the happiest of the war'. But there were underlying tensions as each man considered his chances of surviving the next action. Under-age men had particular cause for reflection. They knew that under a new ruling their parents could apply for them to be sent home while still under eighteen, provided they were willing to go. Similarly, boys between eighteen and nineteen could be sent to a training or other unit behind the firing line.[10] However, as Arthur Armfield recalled, the idea of 'quitting' was generally not entertained: 'I had taken on the job and nothing on my part could absolve me from it. That was the prevailing spirit'. Alec Reader was of similar mind. After five months, he had had enough of the 'rotten game' of war: the dirt and squalor, the crippling fatigues, the horror of seeing men wounded and killed, and the apparent futility. He had been in hospital twice, suffering from the effects of gas and from septic feet. Yet he could not bring himself to take advantage of the new ruling:

> It would look rather like running away from the advance...I have decided to stick out here until I get knocked out as that is, in my opinion, the only thing to do.

Later Alec's father arrived in France, having joined an army balloon unit, and suggested organizing a transfer for his son. Honour satisfied, Alec agreed: 'I could never have applied myself, but am only too pleased to shelve the responsibility'. As the battalion drew closer to the battlefield, and the news got out that they were to attack the notorious High Wood, the bureaucratic wheels for Alec's transfer ground agonizingly slowly. The papers had still not come through by early September, when they were at Franvillers, not far from Albert, performing dress rehearsals for the attack.

Arrival on the Somme

In the two months since 1 July, the Somme offensive had ground on, with a number of minor but costly actions and one significant advance. On 14 July a large tract of ground was captured along Bazentin ridge, on which stood the village of Longueval. This was a bigger gain than on 1 July, but the advantage was not exploited and an opportunity was lost for cavalry to take High Wood, north-west of Longueval. The ridge was low but strategically important since it overlooked the plain of Bapaume, one of the ultimate objectives of the offensive. Repeated attempts were made after 14 July to consolidate the gains but these had little success until the end of August, when the Germans were finally ejected from Delville Wood directly east of Longueval. By the time the CSR arrived, High Wood was the last vantage point on the ridge still in enemy hands. It was well known that the Germans had grimly resisted all attempts to dislodge them. The task was now given to 47th Division.

Small wonder then that Alec, realizing that his transfer would not come in time, was pessimistic. There was a valedictory purpose underlying many of the activities at Franvillers. Wills were drawn up and witnessed, 'last' letters were written, and photographs were taken and sent home. Men played cards for money, the more superstitious quickly disposing of winnings. Anthony French summed up the atmosphere:

> [We] *had unappeasable appetites and in me the others claimed to have discovered propensities for coaxing omelettes and coffee from the most forbidding patronne...There was a gay abandon about such entertainment. First there was the wholesome change from interminable greasy tinned hashes...Fresh rolls and butter went far toward restoring self-respect, though the thought that such a meal might well be the last of its kind, or last of any kind, was never far from mind. This was why, at the last village on route, it was customary to spend every centime of one's ready cash, so to ensure against enriching the German treasury in the final reckoning. Then came the plunge into music of every kind and quality...Conversation would range from the latest latrine rumour to the theories of Darwin and Huxley and back.*[11]

On 8 September, Second Lieutenant Eric Townsend, who had been commissioned from his school officer training corps in 1915, began a letter 'Dearest Mother and Father, You are reading this letter because I have gone under...'. He enclosed it with his will. In an attempt to provide some comfort – which in the event proved necessary – he told his parents that:

> *But for this war I and all others would have passed into oblivion ...but...we shall live as those who by their sacrifice won the Great War. Our spirits and our memories shall endure in the proud position Britain shall hold in the future. ...I did not make much use of my life before the war, but I think I have done so now.*

After his death, Townsend's letter would reach a wider readership than he had intended when it was published in the *Daily Mail* and later as a small booklet entitled *The Happy Hero*. By early September Alec Reader had become resigned to the fact that his transfer would not come in time. His letters became increasingly fatalistic in tone, making him sound far from a happy hero:

1 September: Peculiar as it may seem, everybody hopes for a 'Blighty one', more or less. It is one of the few things we have to hope for.

3 September: The reason I don't want parcels...is that I stand [CENSORED] and my benevolence to the rest of the platoon does not exceed letter pads and socks. To give you an idea of how firm my conviction is, I may tell you that I shall [CENSORED] within a fortnight. So why waste good stuff.

Sunday 10 September: We have been told for the last month or so that we are going into the 'real thing' at last and other news calculated to produce 'wind up'. While on church parade we have hymns such as 'Nearer my God to thee', 'For ever with the Lord' etc. They are trying to make us 'resigned to our fate'. Of course the beauty of the game is that although they are always trying to kill us they can only succeed once. It would be painful if we had as many lives as a cat. This is absolutely my last appearance – on paper – for some time to come, as in the place we are bound we shan't get time to sleep let alone write.

This was indeed Alec's final appearance: he was killed five days later.

'We never saw anything quite like High Wood'

Company commanders went forward to reconnoitre the ground and a small party was given a preview of the 'hush-hush' weapon about to be used in battle for the first time. Anthony French recalled:

Covered entirely with tarpaulins and guarded by sentries was a huddle of enormous angular objects perhaps eight or more feet high and tapering away at the tail like prehistoric monsters... We were told to memorise their outline as we should shortly see them in action as a new and formidable weapon.[12]

These were the first tanks. At Sir Douglas Haig's request, sixty had arrived in France by early September and forty-eight were to take part in the attack. The military planners set much store, too much, as it turned out, by these untried weapons. At the time, however, the men were greatly encouraged. York Rickard confided in his diary, 'The 'caterpillars' are going over with the infantry. These are truly marvellous inventions and a great surprise to us'. As a senior D Company cook, Rickard would not be in the attack. Instead he was to prepare hot meals for the men on their return. 'I don't like being left out of it', he wrote, 'yet I am lucky and ought to know it'.

On 12 September the battalion marched through Albert, passing the ruined cathedral with the famous hanging golden virgin and child.

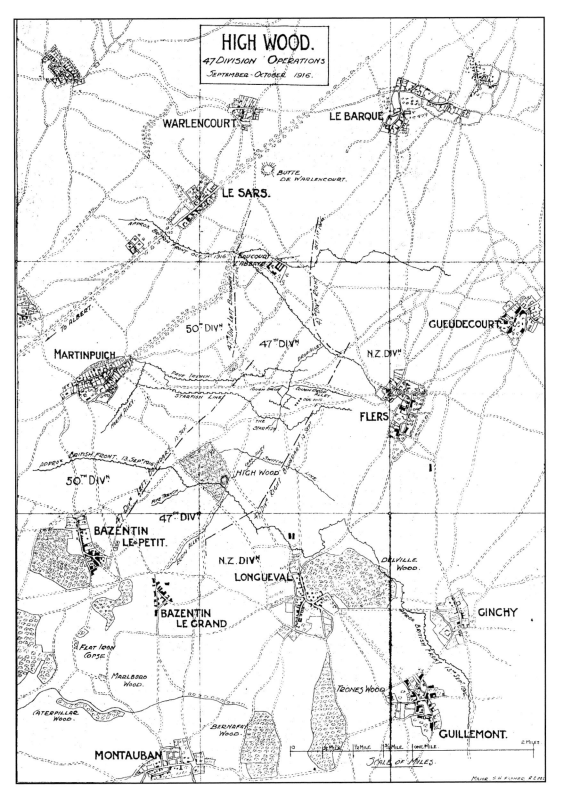

HIGH WOOD.

47 DIVISION OPERATIONS
SEPTEMBER - OCTOBER 1916.

WARLENCOURT

LE BARQUE

BUTTE DE WARLENCOURT.

LE SARS.

APPROX BRITISH FRONT OCT. 1ST 1916

EAUCOURT L'ABBAYE

TO ALBERT

50TH DIVN

47TH DIVN

400N LEFT BOUNDARY

47 DIVN RIGHT OCT 1ST

GUEUDECOURT

MARTINPUICH

PRUE TRENCH

STARFISH LINE

MARTIN ALLEY

TOUGH TRENCH

DROP ALLEY

COUGH DROP

COUGH DROP ALLEY

OUR MINE

N.Z. DIVN

FLERS

THE STARFISH

400N RIGHT BOUNDARY 13 SEPT

SWITCH LINE

APPROX BRITISH FRONT, 13 SEPT 1916.

47 DIVN LEFT BOUNDARY 13 SEPT

DROP ALLEY

50TH DIVN

PIPE TRENCH

HIGH WOOD

47TH DIVN

400N RIGHT BOUNDARY 15 SEPT

BAZENTIN LE-PETIT.

FLERS ALLEY

N.Z. DIVN

DELVILLE WOOD.

BAZENTIN LE GRAND

LONGUEVAL

GINCHY

FLAT IRON COPSE

MARLBORO WOOD.

APPROX BRITISH FRONT 3 SEPT 1916

TRONES WOOD

CATERPILLAR WOOD.

BERNAFAY WOOD.

GUILLEMONT.

MONTAUBAN

0   ½ MILE   ½ MILE   ¾ MILE   ONE MILE   2 MILES

SCALE OF MILES

MAJOR S.H. FISHER R.E DEL

81

Leaving the town, they marched straight into...

> *...a new world of war...we could see freshly-devastated country without being in the battle. All round the slopes were covered with transport of all kinds, and whole divisions of cavalry waiting for their opportunity... heavy howitzers stood in the open, lobbing their shells over at a target miles away...the ground was alive with field-guns. ...All these things, later the commonplace of a successful 'push', were new.*[13]

To the men, this sight was truly impressive. 'Wonderful sights' wrote York Rickard in his diary. The same adjective 'wonderful' is applied to these scenes in the CSR *History*. The night of 13 September was spent under the muzzles of long-range guns in Bécourt Wood. These made 'a devil of a row' so sleep was difficult. In the morning each attacker was issued with two bandoliers of cartridges, two Mills bombs, extra rations and a pick or shovel. As they marched, spread out by platoons, in the direction of Longueval, they began to realize the scale of the imminent battle. Heavy artillery was already in action and aeroplanes buzzed overhead. The battalion was part of a vast movement of men, machines and horses slowly converging on the front. The bulky outline of a tank on the road caused a frisson of interest. Then, passing under a wayside crucifix, they entered a long communication trench. This was Elgin Alley, the final approach to High Wood.

The CSR relieved the 21st Londons along the south-western edge of the wood at 1800 hours on 14 September. After months of fighting, it was in a vile state:

> *We never saw anything quite like High Wood. ...It was a wood only in name – ragged stumps sticking out of churned-up earth, poisoned with fumes of high explosives, the whole a mass of corruption.*[14]

Anthony French characterized the good-humoured exchanges between arriving and departing Londoners:

> *Low-pitched voices continually called 'ware wire! 'ware wire! We slithered down a slope, and under cover of darkness entered a maze of communication trenches where we squeezed unceremoniously past the men we were relieving. Their cold wet garments brushed against our hands. There were whispered greetings: Cheerio chum....Cheerio feller. Hot water laid on?...Yes, too hot. Goodnight old man...Goodnight. Watch the roots further up...Thanks; goodnight. How's things round here?...Quiet; nothing doing for two days...Don't like the sound of that. Cheerio...Cheerio; see you in Berlin...Cheerio.*[15]

The Battle of Flers-Courcelette which began on 15 September

Christ in agony on the cross. The battalion passed this image on the way up to High Wood late on 14 September 1916. It stood at the entrance to Elgin Alley, the long communication trench leading up to the wood.

Thoroton Pocklington Brett CSM, D Company Military Cross

For conspicuous gallantry in action. He took command of his company when the officers had become casualties, and displayed great courage and determination in organising his men, and consolidating the position under heavy fire.

The MC was rarely awarded to NCOs. This one, to Paddy Brett after High Wood, was the battalion's second. The first was won by 'Bulldog' Harris for Vimy ridge.

was planned as a big push by eleven divisions on a broad front. The 47th Division had orders to press home its part of the attack 'with the utmost vigour all along the line till the most distant objectives have been reached'.[16] 140 and 141 Brigades were to advance inside High Wood to take the German front trenches, then press on to capture three successive objectives: the Switch Line (which cut through the wood's north end), the Starfish Line (700 yards beyond the wood), and finally the Flers Line. The aim was to force the Germans out of the wood and well north of it. On 140 Brigade's front, the CSR on the left and 7th Londons on the right were to go over first and capture the German front line and Switch Line. Then the 8th (Post Office Rifles) and 6th Londons were to pass through and take the second and third objectives. On the CSR's left, the battalions of 141 Brigade had similar dispositions and orders. Inside the wood no man's land was very narrow – in places no more than forty or fifty yards. British artillery could not therefore fire directly on the enemy front line without risking its own infantry. Instead of withdrawing the infantry while a bombardment took place (a tactic adopted on the previous two days), the plan for 15 September relied on the new tanks doing some of the artillery's work.

The artillery bombardment at zero would open 150 yards beyond the British line, and thus behind, rather than on, the enemy's front line, then creep further into the German lines. The artillery would also leave hundred-yard 'lanes' free from shells so as not to churn up the ground for the tanks. To compensate for the absence of preliminary bombardment, four tanks were to *precede* the infantry across no man's land, arriving at the German front line at one minute before zero. Tanks would then fire directly on the German line as the British infantry left their trenches. This plan was drawn up against the strong advice of the tank commanders and General Barter, who urged that the tanks go round the edges of the wood and support the infantry from the flanks and behind. They feared that the tanks could not negotiate shell holes and tree stumps. Barter was overruled by the corps commander but in the event he was proved right.[17]

The battalion shared the front line inside the wood with the 17th Londons on the left. A Company was on the edge and to the east of the wood, with B, C and D Companies disposed from east to west inside it. The men knew they faced a daunting task. The Germans had concealed machine-gun nests and sniping posts in the wood and since July many units had tried and failed to dislodge them. 140 Brigade's orders anticipated some difficulty:

> *Arrangements will be made by 7th Battalion to assist 15th Battalion* [Civil Service Rifles] *by attacking from the flank if the latter experience difficulty in occupying German trenches in High Wood.*[18]

As the men waited, packed like sardines in Black Watch Trench, the

This wooden divisional cross stood in the devastated High Wood until replaced in 1925 by a handsome stone memorial. It stands today at the headquarters of the London Irish Rifles in Camberwell.

Roger Goodman

Postcard with romanticized image of a tank 'battle-scarred but victorious'. Inside High Wood, victory was achieved with little contribution from tanks.

tension mounted. Anthony French found it difficult to sleep despite the 'unhealthily quiet' night:

> *Fellows felt for their grenades and tried the pins with a delicate touch. They crammed their magazines with cartridges one over the other and gently drove the top one home in the breech. They crunched a scrap of biscuit for something else to do. I felt the point of my sharpened bayonet and said to myself I'll pull the trigger when it gets as close as that and use it afterwards if necessary and imagine it's a dummy.[19]*

Just before midnight, Lieutenant Middleton took the officers' watches to brigade headquarters to be synchronized. Colonel Warrender visited his company commanders. NCOs went along the trench, checking on sentries and issuing rum. Paddy Brett found Corporal Beazley had joined the sentry in a listening post near the German line, lest he be 'lonely by himself'. Brett asked Beazley to keep close to Captain Roberts when going over the top, as 'he was sure to be well in front of everyone else'.[20] According to the CSR *History*, the first waves of B, C and D Companies began to 'creep up' soon after 0530 and the men in these first waves 'at once' came under German rifle and machine-gun fire from the undamaged enemy front line: 'the fight, therefore, can be said to have started well before zero'. The day had started badly. Worse was to come.

The expected difficulty of this attack, coupled with scepticism about the adequacy of tanks as a substitute for artillery, may perhaps explain why the battalion's officers apparently observed a zero hour thirty minutes earlier than the official zero for the first waves of 140 and 141 Brigades. Faced with the deadly prospect of advancing towards an unsubdued enemy, the CSR may have preferred to start moving under cover of a dark sky at 0550 rather than the near-sunrise of 0620. Another factor which argued for an early start was getting the three companies inside the wood into a straight line with A Company on the right.[21]

84

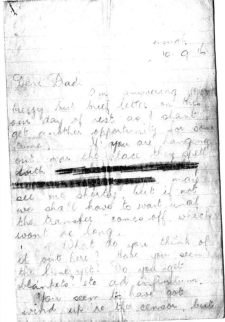

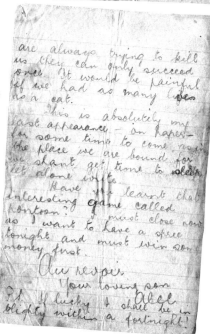

'I have undergone the various emotions caused by war, have seen most things that happen in war and don't think much of it ... War is a rotten game', so wrote Alec Reader after 9 weeks in France. He was under age and could have left the front line, but declined. Alec was killed at High Wood on 15 September, aged 18. Roger Goodman

Alec Reader's last letter to his father: 'Although they are always trying to kill us they can only succeed once. It would be painful if we had as many lives as a cat'. He was killed five days later. Roger Goodman

While the three companies were pinned down in no man's land, news arrived that the tanks were running late. The CSR *History* records that one crashed into the trench containing battalion headquarters, whereupon its commander alighted and asked the way to High Wood. Colonel Warrender's reply was said to be unprintable.[22] The tanks had been due to set off at appointed times between 0540 and 0555. They had difficulty finding the route and, as predicted, were held up by the terrain. Three became stuck early on. Private G V S Mitchell observed the fourth (D13) crawling through survivors of D Company in no man's land. Tank D13 eventually reached the German second line and burst into flames.[23]

The infantry were thus gravely handicapped, with artillery suppressed and tanks starting *behind* rather than ahead of them. The Germans were determined to defend their stronghold and subjected the three CSR companies and the 17th Londons to continuous, murderous fire. The advance was held up for three hours as a desperate fight developed for possession of the wood. Casualties in the three companies amounted to four-fifths of their strength that day. Captain Davies, leading B Company, was killed early on. Captain Roberts, D Company, crawled to within twenty yards of the enemy front trench. He stood up to lead the charge and was shot instantly. When Paddy Brett found him afterwards, Corporal Beazley was lying dead a few yards from him. Captain Gaze, C Company, was wounded but refused to leave his men.

'The Boy Who Died'. 2/Lt E L Townsend, whose last letter to his parents was published after his death in September 1916 from wounds received at High Wood. R Flory

To the right of the wood, A Company, led by Captain Bates, had fared better, capturing two German trenches and pressing on to the Switch Line. They engaged in hand-to-hand fighting and took prisoners before bombing their way down the Switch Line into the wood, where they discovered that B Company had not yet reached the first objective. Men of A Company were killed, including Alec Reader, but casualties were less than inside the wood, where the situation had become confused and desperate. Wave after wave of infantry moved forward steadily, as rehearsed. Finding they could not pass through, they joined in the fight. At one point during the morning no fewer than five battalions of Londoners were embroiled. In the mêlée Brett recalled an officer of the Post Office Rifles crawling up behind and asking 'why we did not get on'. Brett explained the position and the officer crawled away, bent on calling up support from 140 Brigade Trench Mortar Battery.

The implications for the overall advance were grave, for the hold-up allowed a gap to open in the British front which it was imperative to fill. Despite what the *Official History* termed 'reckless bravery of officers and men', it was only after two additional bombardments (one by the artillery and the other a record-breaking trench mortar attack) that German resistance showed signs of breaking. This provided a breathing space. Captain Gaze with Paddy Brett and 'Bulldog' Harris rallied remnants of the three companies and reorganized them for another attempt. This time they were able to carry their objectives. More men were cut down including Captain Gaze, killed while leading the ultimately successful charge. At 1225, Colonel Warrender reported that the Switch Line had been taken. High Wood was at last in British possession.

Decades later, survivors retained vivid and disturbing impressions of the carnage. Paddy Guiton of C Company, who lost a leg, recalled:

> *I saw men torn to fragments by the near explosion of bombs and - worse than any sight – I heard the agonised cries and shrieks of men in mortal pain...*

Practically every survivor could describe witnessing a friend go down beside him. A common reaction was immediate anger, accompanied by a wish for revenge, sometimes fulfilled, followed in tranquillity by intense regret and sorrow:

'It was a wood only in name'. *High Wood after being captured by the 47th Division in September 1916. The churned up ground and fallen trees made it impossible for the tanks to advance as planned.* IWM (50750)

> *In getting up from the trench Sergeant Greenfield directly in front was shot dead, and fell into my arms. It was remarkable seeing all the colour go out of his face, and curiously I felt nothing but great anger at the time; but afterwards I remembered what an exceedingly brave sergeant he was.* (Paddy Brett)
>
> *Trees laced up with barbed wire – machine guns very active. Oscar Jacobs shot dead at my side. Shot the Bosche who killed him.* (Francis Martin)

View of High Wood from Caterpillar Valley Cemetery. It looks so peaceful today but in 1916 it resembled 'Hampstead heath made of cocoa-powder...the natural surface folds further complicated by countless shell-holes...'

> *I heard through the roar of artillery the vicious twang of a rifle bullet and saw Bert [Bradley] pause queerly in his stride and fall stiffly on his side...Desolation of spirit gave way to a rising, fuming, blazing anger fed by primitive, overwhelming emotions, an unspeakable hatred of all mankind,...I nursed my hate and thought only of revenge. (Anthony French)*[24]

Later, when presented with the opportunity to take that revenge, French hesitated:

> *His mouth was open, his face was all dirt, his eyes stared up with a frightening expression of idiocy. My bayonet was lowered, my fingers were on the trigger ...I left him there to the mercy of others and plodded on, filled with rage and determined to destroy something worthy of hate.*[25]

Phase two of High Wood

The exhausted remnants spent the rest of the day consolidating a new position beyond the captured Switch Line, which had been only the first of the division's three objectives for the day. This was dangerous work, as Brett recalled:

> *Just before dark I...found that five were missing. ...They had been repairing the trench some distance from where we attacked, and had all been killed by concussion from a very heavy shell. ...The man next to me was hit in the head with a piece of shell...Out of 137 officers and all ranks...[D Company]...had eighteen all ranks left, no officers, but we had captured our Company's front...We captured eight or ten Germans and seven machine guns.*[26]

Portions only of the second and third objectives had been secured, by the 6th and 8th Londons. In the evening the 21st Londons made a desperate attack on the Starfish Line. This was unsuccessful and brought huge casualties, as did a similar attack by the 23rd Londons the following morning.

During the night of 15 September, while enemy artillery pounded the new British positions, burial parties collected the dead who lay mostly in lines just a few yards in front of the trenches from which they had advanced. Padrés and stretcher-bearers picked their way over the scarred battlefield, following the sounds of cries and moans. Not all the wounded were discovered and rescued. At dawn, Anthony French was still lying in a shell crater, his leg shattered. It would be another twenty-four hours before he managed to crawl back. Eric Townsend, wounded in B Company's first wave as he knelt on the German parapet yelling 'Come on, come on', was taken to a field ambulance where he died on 17 September, bringing the number of officers killed to seven.[27]

The remnants, now only about a hundred plus two officers, spent the following day in the new trench, holding out under shell fire. The Adjutant, Lieutenant Ind, came to congratulate them and later led them forward to the Cough Drop (the third objective of the previous day) where they dug in and were temporarily attached to the 6th Londons for their remaining forty-eight hours on the battlefield. The weather deteriorated and men and equipment became caked in mud. On 18 September, three officers and fifty other ranks from the 'non-starters' arrived and a successful advance was made, in conjunction with the 6th and 8th Londons, into the Flers Line. But an enemy party still held a section of trench and several attempts to dislodge them failed. The men by now were exhausted and their guns choked with mud so that when the Germans vigorously bombed down the trench on the evening of 19 September it was found impossible to eject them. In the struggle which ensued, Second Lieutenant Ware of Exchequer & Audit Department was killed in a 'plucky attempt to achieve the impossible'.

'Brilliant success' or 'wanton waste'?

The battalion was relieved early on 20 September. Casualties were reported as fifteen officers and 365 other ranks – a scale of losses mirrored in the other attacking battalions in the wood. Colonel Warrender was said to be broken-hearted as he led the dejected remnants off the battlefield. His pride at the battalion's share in High Wood's capture must surely have been tempered by the huge losses, and by the knowledge that these could have been minimized if senior planners had acted on advice from men on the spot.[28]

The overall ground won on 15 September was about twice that gained on 1 July and with fewer casualties, so there was jubilation at home. In public, much praise was lavished on the London troops for

The Butte de Warlencourt shortly after the war. In 1916 it was strongly held and defended by the Germans. Many CSR men were killed in an attempt to take it on 7 October. Soon other battalions suffered the same fate. The Butte did not pass into British hands until the Germans withdrew in early 1917. Today it belongs to the Western Front Association.

capturing High Wood. Even before leaving the battlefield the battalion received the text of a congratulatory telegram from the King. *The Times'* special correspondent opined, under the headline THE GREAT NEW ADVANCE, SIR DOUGLAS HAIG'S VICTORY...SPLENDID SERVICES OF 'THE TANKS':

> *If our men could take High Wood, as they have taken it, I doubt if there is anything on earth that they cannot take and will not take if they are asked.*[29]

Behind the scenes, however, there were recriminations at the 'wanton waste' of men in capturing the wood. A fortnight later, General Barter was summarily relieved of his command. While none of this was revealed officially at the time, Sir Douglas Haig's diary for 2 October, describing a meeting with the corps commander, indicates where the blame was laid:

> *I went on and saw General Pulteney...The 47th Division failed at High Wood on 15 September and the GOC was sent home! Barter by name. Now Gorringe has taken over command. He arrived on Sunday, so has not had time to make his personality felt. I told him to teach the Div[ision] 'discipline and digging'* [30].

Barter complained that his dismissal was a grave injustice: there was no official inquiry and he had, after all, strenuously argued against sending tanks into the wood and thus denying artillery support for his men. The *Official History* eventually acknowledged this 'tactical blunder'. But by the time this vindication was published in 1938, Barter had been dead for seven years.[31]

The Butte de Warlencourt

After High Wood, the battalion had one night's rest in Albert and less than a fortnight's reorganization outside Henencourt before being flung into action again. Work began on dozens of condolence letters. It must have grieved the surviving officers that in the circumstances they could send only a few standard sentences to each family. Some letters they penned themselves; others were drafted for them by clerks, leaving a space for the casualty's name to be inserted. The person who wrote to Mr and Mrs Cawley of Camberwell had a particularly heavy task: they had lost not one but two sons. Most letters said that casualties had received 'proper burial' but many graves, though clearly marked, did not survive the later fighting. Three-quarters of the High Wood dead now have no known grave. Lieutenant E Fletcher, a former 17th March ranker, was the only one of the seven dead officers whose body was not immediately accounted for. In contrast to the vain hopes that had been held out after Vimy ridge, Colonel Warrender left no room for doubt:

> *I am very sorry...that I cannot offer you any hope of his being*

2118 Pte E W Knell, a 17th March man wounded in the attack on the Butte de Warlencourt, 7 October 1916, and died a week later. His company, D, suffered 98% casualties.

Lt Tom Smith (left) with pre-war friends Capts Leslie Davies and Arthur Roberts. They were photographed in September 1916, shortly before Davies and Roberts were killed at High Wood. By the time this photo reached Smith's family, he too had been killed. Adrian Ray

On the reverse, Tom Smith explains to his father that his two friends are dead: 'Both were splendid chaps but went under on the 15th. Just off up the line again'. Smith was promoted Captain before the attack on the Butte de Warlencourt on 7 October. He was killed that day and has no known grave. Adrian Ray

alive. Nor is there the slightest possibility of his having been taken prisoner. A man in his platoon...saw your son fall as though killed by fire from a machine gun ...Every inch of the ground was so scarred by shells and so covered with shell holes, that it would be possible for the search parties to miss a man.[32]

Some of the survivors were sent on leave, though the shortage of NCOs meant several were kept back for the next attack, which was against the Butte de Warlencourt. The return of some experienced men who had missed High Wood increased the fighting strength but untrained newcomers outnumbered the dispirited survivors. Unlike the eve of High Wood, when most had achieved their peak of fitness and every man knew the plan and had practised it repeatedly, the attack on the Butte was shrouded in uncertainty. There were contradictory rumours and regimental officers were almost as much in the dark as the men.

In the Battle of the Transloy Ridges, 47th Division was ordered to push the Germans back beyond the village of Eaucourt l'Abbaye and to capture the Butte de Warlencourt. This ancient artificial mound some two miles north of High Wood was only about sixty feet high but was highly prized. It gave excellent observation and had been heavily fortified, so that attacking troops would attract devastating fire from above. On 30 September the battalion moved forward via Albert and the Quadrangle near Mametz Wood, where it was held in reserve for 141

Warlencourt British Cemetery. 45 CSR men are buried here, 6 of them in unnamed graves. The distant clump of trees is the summit of the Butte de Warlencourt, which these men were attacking when they died.

Brigade's successful attack on Eaucourt l'Abbaye. The final leg involved an arduous night march over thick mud on the 15 September battlefield, led by guides who repeatedly lost their way. The CSR *History* describes this nightmare journey as 'almost as trying as a battle'. It was a grim initiation for the fresh drafts of Derby men and conscripts, many of whom would be dead in a few days. At dawn they reached the Flers line, which was full of British and German bodies from the earlier action. Two days were spent burying the dead and clearing up these filthy trenches, when the order came at short notice for another attack.

Zero hour was 1345 on 7 October. The plan was for the Post Office Rifles to secure Diagonal Trench, north of Eaucourt l'Abbaye, with the CSR and 7th Londons pushing on to the final objective, the Gird Line and the notorious Butte, some 2,800 yards from the assembly trenches. A Company, again led by Captain Bates, was on the right and made better progress. The three left-hand companies had first to negotiate the village, which was being bombarded by enemy artillery. Those who emerged from the village were swept down by intense machine-gun fire before they had a chance to extend, as planned, into waves. There was no protection from the creeping barrage, which moved forward too fast. 47th Division's attack on the Butte was a failure, as were subsequent ones by other units. It was not taken until the Germans withdrew to the Hindenburg line in early 1917.

Very few details survive of the battalion's action on 7 October. It may be summed up by a phrase in the war diary, 'Battalion badly cut up', and in two sentences in the divisional history, which are remarkable for describing a battalion of which *over half* were recently arrived reinforcements who had never been in a trench before, let alone seen action:

> *Not a man turned back, and some got right up under the Butte, but they were not seen again. Parties dug themselves in where they could.*[33]

Military Medal awarded in October 1916 to 3076 L/Cpl W J Garner, from the GPO. He rescued a wounded man under fire. When he returned to pick up a second casualty, he found he had died. In later life Garner was troubled by this incident: had he chosen to pick up the second man first, might he have lived?

Adrienne Ibbett

Capt G G Bates, the only company commander to survive High Wood. He was in action barely three weeks later at the Butte de Warlencourt and won the MC. One of very few 17th March men to serve for most of the war, he was temporary CO for nearly three weeks in August 1918.

Ione Bates

One of these parties, a mixture of Post Office Rifles and CSR, was gathered together by Captain Bates and dug in along the sunken road from Eaucourt l'Abbaye to La Barque. For this action Bates was awarded the Military Cross:

> *For conspicuous gallantry. He collected men of several units, leading them forward and establishing a position which he maintained without support for two days. He set a splendid example throughout.*

At Mametz Wood the cooks and transport men were once more waiting anxiously as conflicting rumours reached them of the battalion's fate. York Rickard recorded:

> *As all the troops in the line go over the top times out of number it is useless trying to keep a detailed account...Losses are as heavy as the last stunt...Casualties we hear now are over 350. Battalion comes out tonight...Tea and stew, rum and smokes all ready for them.*

After the bedraggled remnants returned, the battalion spent three nights in Albert before leaving on another long journey which would take them to the Ypres Salient. Before setting off, the writing of condolence letters was resumed, those for High Wood being completed before starting on dozens more for the Butte. Casualties this time were reported as 354. There were very few who took part in both Somme operations and survived unharmed. Paddy Brett recorded that D Company went into High Wood 137 strong and came out with eighteen uninjured men and no officers. Brett was sent on leave and learned afterwards that his company was made up to 108, of which three-quarters were new men, and on 7 October suffered ninety-eight per cent casualties. Whole platoons, including Rickard's, were virtually wiped out. Roll calls to establish who was still missing did not help, as many were so new they were not known by name in their platoons.

1916 was a traumatic year for the battalion, especially for the dwindling band of 17th March men (see Appendix 5). Of the two costly Somme actions, it was High Wood which cast the longer shadow over the survivors and indeed over the whole regiment. Some claimed it as the battalion's finest achievement, but recollections were permeated by bitterness about the lack of artillery support and the deployment of tanks and infantry with what Barter had reportedly called 'damned silly orders'. Despite the small number of men remaining in the battalion who had actually experienced it, the battle became deeply etched in the collective memory. As late as 1918 the events were rehearsed to newcomers, who could repeat the story of the tank commander asking Colonel Warrender the way to High Wood.

The fact that so many graves were lost in and around the wood was another source of distress. For the veterans this ground remained forever hallowed. Over the decades they made regular pilgrimages as long as their strength lasted. Perhaps the most poignant proof of the enduring significance of High Wood for the 17th March men was York Rickard's request that after his death his ashes be scattered near the 47th Division memorial. His wish was carried out by family and comrades in 1976 – sixty years after the young cook had waited with hot soup, tea and cigarettes for the pals who never returned.

This memorial to the 47th Division at High Wood, and a previous one on this spot, was a regular place of pilgrimage for the veterans. From a later generation, Doug Goodman remembers his uncle - Alec Reader, killed aged 18.
Roger Goodman

1. *The Times*, 14 March 1916, p 7; Cmnd Paper 76, 1918
2. Army Council Instruction 2427 of 27 December 1916. I am grateful to Charles Messenger for this insight.
3. Anthony French, *Gone for a Soldier*, Kineton: The Roundwood Press, 1972, p 24
4. H V Warrender, letter of 28 April 1916 to Lady Randolph Churchill (CHAR 28/127, Churchill College Cambridge)
5. F W Watts, 'A Night Counter-Attack', in Jon E Lewis (ed), *True WW1 Stories*, 1997
6. *ibid.*
7. French, *op cit*, p 54
8. H V Warrender, letter of 28 July 1916, *op cit*
9. French, *op cit*, p 36
10. Army Council Instruction 1186 of 13 June 1916
11. French, *op cit*, p 42
12. *ibid.* p 67
13. Alan H Maude, *The History of the 47th (London) Division 1914-1919*, London 1922, p 62
14. *ibid.*
15. French, *op cit*, p 70
16. WO 95/2727 (National Archives), 140 Infantry Bde Order No.104
17. The flawed nature of the battle plan is discussed in W M Rossiter, 'High Wood, the attack on 15th September 1916', published (abridged version) in *Tank*, the Royal Tank Regiment Journal Vol No 69, February 1988.
18. WO 95/2727 (National Archives), *op cit*, Schedule
19. French, *op cit*, p 72
20. T P Brett, *Memories of a CSM*, privately published
21. Both the War Diary and the CSR *History* quote zero as 0550, whereas all other surviving sources, including at least one contemporary diary kept by a CSR man, quote 0620. For a fuller discussion, including recollections of the commander of Tank D13, see Trevor Pidgeon, *The Tanks at Flers*, Fairmile Books, 1995, p 105.
22. This was probably Tank C23 - see Pidgeon, *op cit*, p 107
23. Pidgeon, *op cit*, pp 105-106
24. French, *op cit*, p 74
25. *ibid*, p 75
26. Brett, *op cit*
27. *City of London School Magazine,* March 1917
28. Vivian Nickalls, *Oars, Wars and Horses*, 1932, p 135
29. *The Times*, 18 September 1916
30. WO256/13 Vol XI (National Archives)
31. *The Times*, 18 June 1919
32. WO 374/24653 (National Archives)
33. Maude, *op cit*, p 72

Chapter Five

The Ypres Salient and Bourlon Wood 1916-1917

After a brief rest at Albert and Villers-sous-Ailly, the CSR learned with relief that the 47th Division was leaving the Somme for the Ypres Salient. After its heavy losses, the battalion was short of men, especially officers and NCOs. Morale was low. A year later, when the mud and slaughter of Passchendaele was at its worst, the battalion would leave the Salient with equal feelings of relief. But in October 1916, the war there lacked the intensity of the Somme and was viewed almost as a 'rest cure'. Charles Bassett had his first view of Flanders, marching towards Reningholst:

> After the rolling and shattered prairies of the Somme, the peaceful countryside of Flanders was an amazing change. At this distance from the line, not a gun could be heard...The flat country laid out in squares of grown crops, intersected by straight roads lined with feathery poplars...Occasionally there passed a hooded cart, or one loaded with farm produce, driver half asleep on the shafts.

Nearer Ypres the scene was different. The British held the town and a modest salient protruding eastward into German-dominated Belgium. Two years of war had transformed this low-lying, previously well-drained country. Whenever it rained, shell craters filled with water and the ground became a quagmire. The big German offensive of April 1915 (Second Ypres) had failed, as had a less ambitious attack in February 1916. But the enemy still held the higher ground overlooking the Salient and fully exploited this advantage. The front and support lines, roads, light railways and even some of the hutted camps further back were continually under sniper, machine-gun and artillery fire. In June 1917 there would be a British offensive to seize the Messines ridge and Hill 60. But when the battalion arrived eight months earlier, the orders were to harass the enemy locally by aggressive patrolling and raids.

The 47th Division's front stretched from the northern bank of the Ypres-Comines Canal on the right, to the Zwartelen Spur, north of the railway, on the left. The support lines were in sub-sectors known as The Bluff, The Ravine, Verbrandenmolen and Hill 60. The men quickly settled into a routine of about a week each in front and support lines followed by a spell at a reserve camp. When out of the line they could

SUNSET - MENIN ROAD - "GOING UP"
(ANY EVENING)

SUNRISE - SAME ROAD - "THERE"
(ANY MORNING)

MIDSUMMER DAY.
(ANYWHERE ON THE SALIENT)

The Ypres Salient in all weathers.

get to Poperinghe for relief and relaxation in estaminets or at the church club at Talbot House, known as Toc H.

The most severe winter of the war set in. Several measures were introduced to help the men withstand it. Drying facilities were available in the line and the cooks took it in turns to go up and prepare hot meals to be eaten in the trenches. Casualties began almost immediately, mainly from shell and sniper fire. Men on working parties in the Hill 60 sector discovered that the war was being waged by stealth underground. They were impressed by the size and depth of these operations. Mines would play an important part in the forthcoming offensive but for the moment the battalion's main preoccupation was a trench raid.

The raid - 'could not be improved upon'

Planning for the raid was begun under Colonel Warrender, who was shortly to leave after seventeen months in command. Warrender was depressed by the Somme losses and relieved to secure a post away from the front. His successor was Major W F K Newson, on promotion. An employee of the Westminster Fire Office, Newson had enlisted in 1894 and served in South Africa. He was the first territorial officer to command the battalion in France.

Once again there was no shortage of volunteers for a raid. Fifty were selected and trained hard for several weeks under two subalterns: Harry Gosney, of the Board of Trade (a 17th March man recently commissioned), and G F Grove. The raiders were to enter the enemy's front line, inflict as many casualties as possible, secure prisoners for identification and investigate a large and worrying mound of new earth. The raid took place on the night of 22 December, preceded by a two-minute bombardment. The earthworks were found to be harmless and the raiders brought back pieces of German uniform for identification.

96

The enemy had resisted capture and eleven were reported killed. Ten of the raiders were wounded, though not dangerously. Two died: Corporal Geary of the Metropolitan Water Board who was wounded and did not make it back, and Private Pearson. Neither body was recovered and both men are commemorated on the Menin Gate Memorial.

The CSR had long been smarting from the failure of the raid in July 1916. Their relief at making amends is evident from Colonel Newson's report which praised the training, organization and 'spirit and dash'. The verdict – 'I do not think this could be improved upon' – was echoed in a congratulatory telegram from the corps commander. Lance Sergeant H J Steele and Corporal J H Swain were awarded the Military Medal. Spirits were lifted and Christmas, celebrated after leaving the front line on 28 December, was more cheerful than could be expected after such a trying year. Gallantry awards for the Somme operations were announced in January, bringing the total for autumn 1916 to around forty. The Military Cross was awarded to CSM Brett, Captain Ind and Lieutenant Rathbone. There was at least one posthumous award, to Lance Corporal R J B Beazley of the Inland Revenue, who had been commended before for his bravery in bringing in wounded on Vimy ridge.

Reinforcements

During the winter the battalion was gradually brought up to strength, mainly by new men from England. It would be March 1917 before fighting strength once more reached the pre-Somme peak of over a thousand. Colonel Newson, the last 17th March officer, left in February. Newson was succeeded by Captain H Marshall of the Hampshire Regiment on temporary promotion. At least four officers were attached from the Manchester Regiment: Captains A Bowers-Taylor and A D Oliver and subalterns G Hasleham and G F Grove. Captain F D Balfour from the Northern Cyclist Battalion was appointed second in command. Despite all these newcomers, something of the battalion's original character was preserved through the influence of pre-war men still serving in France, particularly among the NCOs and officers commissioned from the CSR's ranks. These included the transport officer, William Craig, and two successive adjutants, Billy Ind and Paul Davenport, both civil servants.

At home, survivors of the Somme battles who had recovered from wounds began arriving at the Reserve Battalion. Some were

'Twicers' were men who returned to France after recovering from wounds. They always had a rousing send-off from Hazeley Down and this unofficial flag was carried to the station. It hangs today in the Drill Hall in Putney of F Coy (Royal Green Jackets) the London Regiment, Mortar Platoon.

commissioned or remained at Hazeley Down as instructors. Others when sufficiently fit were posted back overseas. Like the new recruits, these men sometimes ended up in other units in France, much to their disappointment. Arthur Armfield was at Hazeley Down in late 1916 after a bout of trench fever. He recalled how some of these returned warriors declined commissions, men like Sergeant Levey:

> A peacetime civil servant and original 17th March man back with a wound...now fit and employed as a drill instructor. A very nice type, he refused a commission (for which he was quite competent) for reasons best known to himself – there were many who held a similar opinion – and returned to France.

A common reason for this reluctance was a desire to remain with pals in the battalion where they felt at home. Albert Robins remained a private throughout the war and his view of rankers who took commissions could, if typical, suggest another reason for holding back:

> It might be thought that we would think well of these aspirants and be proud of them, but exactly the opposite was the case. The feeling was that they had deserted their comrades and wanted to lord it over them. This was no doubt unfair, though there is in human nature a love of throwing one's weight about. It was the wiser course when they were not returned to their old battalion.

534291 Pte W J Price, a City bank employee, registered under the Derby scheme in 1916. He eventually joined the CSR in France in April 1917 and served until killed in the advance to victory in September 1918. Joan Price

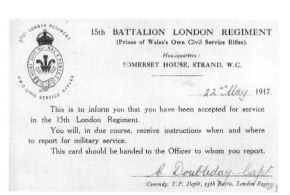

The man who received this postcard was due for call-up but had successfully applied to join the CSR. Usually conscripts had no choice of regiment. But the CSR was allowed to continue direct enlistment until the end of 1917. This was an important factor in sustaining the regimental character.

Civil Service Rifleman at his ablutions in a field. Baths were a rare luxury, often requiring a long march there and back. In 1917, when portable stoves and canvas baths were obtained, Civil Service baths were 'open daily' whenever the battalion was out of the line.

By contrast the NCOs who rejected commissions were respected as 'old sweats'. The continued association of these men with the battalion, both at home and overseas, contributed to morale and perpetuation of 'Civil Service' ways. As late as July 1918, men like Levey were still exerting a benign influence over young conscripts.

Armfield also claimed that 'almost every man' at Hazeley Down in late 1916 was a volunteer. This is probably an exaggeration, since by then Derby men and conscripts were filtering through. It does, however, demonstrate how the special recruiting system made the regiment feel to its members little changed from the early days. The younger Derby men, some of whom had attested while still at school, considered themselves genuine volunteers, like the early members whose behaviour they emulated. Among them were friends, work colleagues and younger brothers of men already serving in France.

The shortage of manpower for the army led to the widening of conscription in April 1917, with men being 'combed out' from previously reserved occupations. The War Cabinet called for the immediate release of 2,000 civil servants and the CSR subsequently enlisted a large group of eighteen year-olds from regional tax offices of the Inland Revenue. Of 'an excellent type', many were sent immediately for officer training. The remainder had up to a year's training in the Reserve Battalion – an unusually long period, which resulted in a supply of high quality recruits who would be of great value in the emergency of spring 1918.

Winter in the Salient

On a draft in January 1917 was Walter Humphrys of the Post Office Savings Bank. He had been under seventeen when the war began and had a long wait before the CSR would accept him for foreign service. Now aged nineteen, he finally got his chance and was sent to the Salient where he joined the reconstituted 14 Platoon. The weather was bitterly cold and sickness levels were high. Walter recalled:

I had frostbite at Ypres, nearly lost my toes. I stepped into an ice-covered shell hole, virtually up to my knees. And when I got back to the trench, the corporal sent me straight out on a wiring duty. I had to lie in no man's land for two or three hours and of course my feet froze. When I came back I rubbed them with whale oil and changed my socks according to orders but it was too late - they were frozen. I had them wrapped in cotton wool for several days and they were looked at every few hours to see they weren't turning black. I lost all the skin on my feet, it came off in slabs. But fortunately they didn't have to remove the toes.

Even though he had been obeying orders, Walter got into trouble for neglecting his feet, a serious offence. Telling this story nearly eighty-five years later, he was still indignant at the injustice:

My feet were frozen and I was 'crimed' for it! I was called to the orderly room and had a charge read out. I said 'Permission to speak, Sir. It wasn't my fault'. He dismissed me.

533990 Pte W Humphrys of Post Office Savings Bank (right) with his pal Pte Fred White. Humphrys suffered severe frostbite early in 1917 but recovered sufficiently to act as stretcher-bearer at Messines in June. He fought at Bourlon Wood and was taken prisoner in March 1918. Pat Welch

Walter's feet took six months to heal fully. Meanwhile he was given light duties, stretcher-bearing and moving supplies by night. Both could be difficult and dangerous. The transport section, usually a 'posh' job, began to attract sympathy from the men in the front line. From their base at Delanote Farm the round trip with water and rations took never less than seven hours and frequently all night. Charles Bassett recalled:

Under fire...the transport driver was at a disadvantage because while the company man could and did seek shelter, the driver had to stand by his horses, which were usually very restive. Those that

were not restive were sometimes worse as they were often curious, especially the mules, who would insist on going to smell the shell holes as soon as they were made. When a mule really makes up its mind about anything, no human power can change it.

Walter's so-called light duties could be grisly and dangerous:

I was just leaving the trench one evening when a fellow appeared with a bundle out of the trench and said 'Drop this off at Woodcote Farm about a mile down' and dumped something on the platform beside me...When I got there I discovered it was a dead fellow in a blanket! That happened twice to me...I was shelled three times. We had a little hut where we slept and we were shelled one day and we just got away from it in time and when we got back the door was half a mile away in a field!

Casualties, mainly from shell fire, took a steady toll. In the first four months in the Salient these ran at approximately thirty per month, of which thirty per cent died. It was wearing on the nerves, as York Rickard's diary reveals. He was still a cook but had long since stopped regarding it as a 'snip' job:

12 January...Lot of men wounded, several killed. I did a bit of stretcher-bearing. Also had a good pull of rum to steady my nerves. They wanted it. Can't stand this shelling as I used to...8 February ...I am cooking by myself in a very low cookhouse outside the stronghold. I have got a 'barmy' chap sleeping in my dugout who tried to do himself in. ...20 February...Hellish bombardment close to us ...My assistant goes temporarily mad while shelling is on and is the worst case of 'wind up' I have seen. Runs all about the trenches like a madman.

On 22 February the CSR began four weeks in the back area as a works battalion. When they returned, a thaw had begun and the trenches were caked in mud and slime. The war intensified, as was customary in spring. Tours in the support and front lines were more costly in casualties, mainly from shelling and enemy raids. In four weeks casualties were more than in the first four months in the Salient.

Battle training

During April the battalion caught a whiff of what the 47th Division historian called 'that indefinable something in the air' which suggested a looming offensive. By mid-May, when they left the Salient for the big training area west of St Omer, it was known that the division would take part in General Plumer's offensive. It took three days to march nearly forty miles to billets around Moringhem. For sixteen days, pre-battle training was pleasantly interspersed with sports fixtures and recreational visits to St Omer. It was here that the battalion began learning new tactics which would prove so effective in later fighting, particularly the difficult defensive operations at Bourlon Wood in November and during the Retreat the following spring. The army had learned lessons in action in 1916. Some of the traditional tactics, such as infantry advancing 'shoulder to shoulder' in waves, were being phased out. The new doctrine called for more initiative by small, well-armed platoons moving in 'artillery' formation behind the main attack.

On return they found the Salient was alive with preparations. A relentless bombardment had begun on the enemy wire and trenches and would continue until just minutes before zero on 7 June. In the 47th Division immediately before this battle, levels of training, morale and confidence were reported to be high. The sight and sound of the artillery was inspiring. Aerial photographs demonstrated to all ranks just how effective the bombardment had been. Confidence was even greater than on the eve of High Wood.

Messines – 7 June 1917

The aim of the offensive was to capture the ridge to the south of Ypres, thereby loosening the German grip on the town and gaining a topographical advantage for a more ambitious offensive to break that

A Coy officers and NCOs just before the Battle of Messines. Back: Ritchings, Lambert, Jones, Browning, Gay, Bickmore, Baird, Armstrong. Middle: Neale, Bigby, Hundleby, Roberts, Rickman, Blanks, Quinton, Banfield, Sinfield. Front: Steele*, Butcher, 2Lt Acworth*, Capt Eccles, Capt Bowers-Taylor*, Lt Morris, Lt Wilson, Jennings. (* Killed on 7 June 1917)

hold entirely. The 47th Division was to attack towards the northern end of the ridge, astride the Ypres-Comines Canal. South of the Canal near Hollebeke, the division's objectives included the remains of the White Château and stables and a section of the *Dammstrasse*. This ground had been fought over in 1914 and the château was now little more than a pile of rubble. The *Dammstrasse* was a heavily fortified trench along the line of the château drive. The well-rehearsed plan was for the 7th and 8th Londons to attack the old German front trench system. After three hours the CSR, with the 6th Londons on the left, would pass through and capture three further objectives about 1,000 yards beyond.

On 3 June the CSR moved forward. At the area known as Café Belge, they experienced their first real gas shell bombardment, though no casualties resulted. After three days of preparations around Swan Château, they moved into assembly trenches on the night of 6 June and began the long wait for dawn. Zero for the first attack was 0310. In a second wave, at 0625, the battalion would advance on a 400-yard front to capture Oak Crescent, Oblong Trench and Oblong Reserve, plus Delbske Farm beyond if possible.

Walter Humphrys was not with the attacking troops. Still recovering from frostbite, he and some D Company cooks were detailed as stretcher bearers. Rickard's jumpy assistant was more badly affected than ever. His nerves were now so bad and his behaviour so bizarre that he was excused by his sergeant from going forward. Before the battle the small party of stretcher-bearers sheltered from the bombardment in a ditch off the St Elooi road. When the mines exploded, that would be their signal to move up to the battle area and follow the attack.

While the CSR attackers waited in the assembly trenches, most of the officers were squeezed into a smelly dugout. The unofficial regimental diarist described the scene as reminiscent of Bairnsfather's sketch, 'An hour before going into the trenches':

> There was the usual 'chorus' generally found hanging round Battalion Headquarters – servants, police, pioneers, signallers and runners. Wallis, the 'head waiter', moved about as unconcerned as ever, with sandwiches and whisky and soda for the guests. ...At 3.10 am precisely, the floor, walls and ceiling began to rock furiously, and we realised that the Australian tunnellers...had not boasted idly when they told us last November that their mine under Hill 60 would one day stagger humanity. A moment later, another big mine went up at St Elooi, and at the same time the most wonderful bombardment there has ever been known was let loose...One could not help feeling overawed by the magnificence... No human beings could possibly withstand such a bombardment.[1]

At this signal, the 7th and 8th Londons advanced. They met little opposition, so effective had the explosions and bombardment been, and

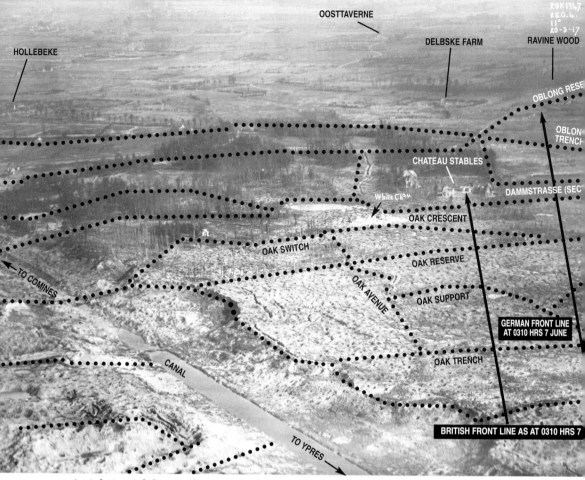

OOSTTAVERNE

DELBSKE FARM

RAVINE WOOD

HOLLEBEKE

OBLONG RESE

OBLON
TRENCH

CHATEAU STABLES

White Ch⁰⁹

DAMMSTRASSE (SEC

OAK CRESCENT

OAK SWITCH

OAK RESERVE

TO COMINES

OAK AVENUE

OAK SUPPORT

GERMAN FRONT LINE
AT 0310 HRS 7 JUNE

CANAL

OAK TRENCH

BRITISH FRONT LINE AS AT 0310 HRS 7

TO YPRES

Aerial view of the attack area on 7 June 1917. Arrows show approximate direction of CSR advance in second wave, 0625 hours. J R Rickard/Ian Passingham

within an hour had taken and consolidated all their objectives. The battalion attackers, prevented from seeing the action by a huge cloud of dust, duly moved forward to the jumping-off trenches. Watches were synchronized. Captain Ind and the Reverend Beattie passed round cigarettes. The enemy's retaliatory barrage was so weak that when the time came to advance the four assault waves were able to line up on top outside the trenches.

The battalion achieved all its objectives. The victory was described in the CSR *History* as a 'walk-over...undoubtedly a cheap one'. Each wave comprised platoons from different companies. This, together with the withdrawal of selected personnel as 'non-starters', prevented any company suffering disproportionate casualties, as had happened at High Wood. In fact the battalion's casualties at Messines were relatively low. The Germans, dazed and demoralized by the twin shocks of mines and bombardment, did not resist energetically and – in the first half of the day at least – their artillery and rifle fire was slight. The battalion took all its objectives and large numbers of prisoners fairly easily.

Army Form B. 104—81A.

Record Office,

_____

_____ 1 6 JUN 1917 _____ .

SIR or ~~MADAM~~,

———— I ~~regret~~ to have to inform you that a report has been received from the War Office to the effect that (No) *532894* (Regd No. *5915*.)

(Rank) *Private* (Name) *J. W. Higgins*

(Regiment) *1/15*TH Bn. London Regt.
P. W. O. Civil Service Rifles

has been wounded, and was admitted to *14*ᵏ *General Hospital Wimereux Boulogne.*

on the *9*ᵗ day of *June* , 1917. . The nature of the wound is *gun shot wound right leg and left shoulder.*

———— I am to express to you the sympathy and regret of ~~the~~ Army Council.

Any further information received in this office as to his condition will be at once notified to you.

Yours faithfully,

C P Stew MAJOR
FOR Lieut.
TERRITORIAL FORCE RECORD OFFICE

Officer in charge of Records.

IMPORTANT.—Any change of address should be immediately notified to this Office.

Telegram to John Higgins' father, seven days after his son was wounded. Processing casualties after a big action like Messines put the medical facilities under great pressure. A W Higgins

532894 Pte J W Higgins, wounded twice at Messines – first by a bullet in the leg then, en route to the dressing station, by a shell fragment in the shoulder. The wounds were serious enough for him to be discharged. Eventually returned to his trade of silk cutter. Despite his wounds, John Higgins lived to be 101. A W Higgins

Most aspects of the well-rehearsed plan went like clockwork. Battalion scouts went forward early on, returning with useful intelligence which was immediately passed down to platoon commanders. The four waves moved at five-minute intervals, observing the new tactic of more space between each man. The artillery support was superb. Albert Robins of A Company advanced in the third wave:

> *It was amazing ground over which we advanced. There were occasionally small sections of shallow trench, but the whole area was a sea of shell holes, very difficult to advance over, being mostly loose earth. It was like the holes in a colander so heavy had the shelling been. There were a few British troops about, and a few unarmed Germans mostly tending their wounded. On we stumbled and our shelling kept up too.*

Largely due to the churned-up terrain and the distances to be covered, the waves at times became intermixed with each other and with the 6th

Londons on the left. The infantry also had some difficulty keeping time with the creeping barrage. While one wave halted and waited for the barrage to lift and move on, more waves came up behind. A large milling crowd developed, resembling to the unofficial diarist 'the field for a big cross-country race'. In some places, however, the infantry got too close to the barrage, as Albert Robins experienced:

> We were led by a new young officer (first time out) right into our own barrage at our halting point. It was just like 'The voice of the schoolboy rallied the ranks, play up! play up! and play the game'. With arm raised, and slightly in front of us, he urged us on. But either we were in advance of our due time, or the artillery barrage was late in lifting and should have lengthened its range. We were in it and caught it. I did not get hit then. The officer had part of his face blown away and fell to the ground. Hot blood gushed from his face over my hand as water from a tap. There was nothing we could do for him.

The attacking troops had strict orders not to attend to any wounded. These would be dealt with by the stretcher-bearers moving up behind. While going forward with his stretcher, Walter Humphrys had a narrow escape. The gas mask on his chest shattered, taking the full force of a shell fragment. As he and his mate hurried to evacuate a casualty over the canal bridge, Walter spotted something strange lying on the road. Peering closer, he recognized a human leg, 'complete with puttee and boot, just on its own'. This and other ghastly sights that day put his religious faith severely to the test. Meanwhile, Albert Robins' platoon had taken its objective, Oblong Trench:

> The advance stopped at a kind of rampart, behind which we stayed for the rest of the day. At one point, in the distance, about 500 yards away, I saw a German walk across an open space. I tried to have a shot at him but, hard to believe, my rifle would not work. I thought I had kept it clean but it just shows how much dust was in the air with all the shelling, for the bolt was clogged...nothing very much seemed to be happening...I would say we were all rather in a stunned condition, Germans and ourselves. I had not seen any officers for several hours.

Once all three objectives were captured, a small party went forward to rush Delbske Farm, which was taken with little opposition and held as an outpost. Towards evening the Germans began shelling heavily but did not counter-attack. Robins, still dug in at Oblong Trench, received a flesh wound in the back of the head from a shell splinter, but was able to walk back for treatment.

The CSR reorganized and consolidated the captured positions. The night was fairly quiet and in the morning the battalion was relieved and moved to a support trench behind the old front line, where they rested for two days. The CSR's success was mirrored across the whole frontage of the attack. In one day, General Plumer's Second Army had captured an important sector of line, impregnable since the end of 1914. There was a general feeling of satisfaction at having taken and held all the allotted objectives and at taking part in what seemed to be a great British victory. There followed two very trying days in Opal Reserve (captured by the 6th Londons on 7 June and now part of the new front line). There was little shelter. Heavy casualties were sustained from enemy shelling as the men dug new jumping-off positions for a planned continuation of the advance in order to consolidate the gains. By the time this advance took place, the battalion was off the battlefield and heading for the customary post-battle rest.

Casualties and awards

The total casualties for 7-12 June were just over 200. The fifty-six dead included four officers – Captains Ind and Bowers-Taylor and Second Lieutenants Acworth and Moran. Over seventy-five per cent have no grave and are commemorated on the Menin Gate Memorial. The most conspicuous casualty was the Adjutant, Captain Ind. He was not in the advance but hit by a stray shell fragment as he followed the attackers up to the first objective in his eagerness to witness the fruits of the training he had masterminded. This 17th March ranker was efficient and popular and his death stands out as another landmark. Next day it was recorded by York Rickard in his diary as 'the greatest loss the Battalion has ever had'.

Though the loss of influential individuals had its effect, the contrast with casualties at High Wood was very marked. The battalion's fighting strength at Messines was lower by about a hundred men, yet they achieved all their objectives for a much smaller proportion of casualties. The difference was partly attributable to the new tactics and to the greatly improved coordination between infantry and artillery, even though the creeping barrage had not kept complete time. About fifteen awards were made, including a Military Cross for 2nd Lieutenant Davenport of the GPO, who now became Adjutant:

> For conspicuous gallantry and devotion to duty. When the officer commanding his company was killed he took command, and by his resource and fearlessness successfully captured the objective, and held it in spite of intense artillery fire.

P.W.O. CIVIL SERVICE RIFLES	
SECOND LIEUT	PRIVATE
NORTHAM J. McC.	FISH A.R.
	GOVER T. J.
SERJEANT	GREENWOOD A. E.
HERTZ A	GROVES L.
SKINNER H. C.	HAINES L.
STEELE H. J. M.M.	HARGRAVE L.
	HARTLEY E.
CORPORAL	HAYER J. J.
FREEMAN H.	HEARD L. V.
SHEPHERD H. A.	HOTTEN W. G. E.
	HOWLETT B.
LANCE CORPORAL	HUNT A. F.
BICKMORE P.	JONES V. G.
BLANKS J. W.	LOVEJOY P. T.
CRONIN G. P.	McADOO T. J.
GEARY A. J. C.	McPHERSON H. F.
WHITE C. C.	MARKHAM F.
	MIDDLETON H. A.
PRIVATE	MUNRO G.
ANDERSON D.	ORAM R.
ANDERSON H. J.	OTTREY J. A.
ARCHARD E. F.	PALMER R. A.
ASHBY A. C.	PANTING E. H.
BARNES F. V.	PARKIN L. C.
BARNETT G.	PEARSON A. F.
BLAXLAND E P	POTTS F.
BRACKING E F.	POWELL A. E. J.
BRAITHWAITE E. C.	RICHARDS B.
BROCKWELL A A T	ROBERTS B. J.
BROWNING S. L.	ROURKE A. F.
COKER F. G.	SAMUELS G. M.
COLVERD S O	SCRUBY A. E.
COURTNEY H	SIMMONDS H. F. R.
CRIPPS F.	STEED W. W.
CUMMINGS W. G.	SUMMERFIELD W. W.
DAVISON R. W.	SUTHERLAND J.
DAY T. W.	TIBBS E. E.
DIBLEY J. J.	TURNER H. S.
Du-FEN J. P	WAGG G A
DUFFIELD H A	WEST G W. A
ENSOR W. A	WESTROP S. B.
FARRIER J. J.	WILKS A. W.

'They are not missing – they are here'. So said Field Marshal Plumer at the unveiling of the Menin Gate Memorial in 1927. Panel 54 commemorates more than 70 CSR men killed and missing in the Salient, over half of whom were killed at Messines on 7 June 1917. Michael Forsyth

A well-earned 'holiday'

After Messines the 47th Division moved back for rest and reorganization and the battalion had a twelve-day 'holiday' near St Omer. The weather was pleasant and the chief diversion was a water carnival, at which the CSR won the 'odd craft' race. Lance Corporal Ralph Thompson had decided to go for a commission. A linguist and employee of the London County Council, he had acted as interpreter for successive company commanders who wanted to retain him as an NCO. In April 1917, however:

> *a feeling of utter weariness at being one of the half dozen or so survivors of the old original [C] Company impelled me at length... to follow the example of others and apply for a commission.*

Thompson's application was approved and he went on leave. On 28 June the battalion began its return to the front. Three days were spent in support trenches called Spoil Bank in the old German front line immediately south of the canal. This was a nasty spot, notorious for heavy artillery bombardments, from which there was little shelter. The discomfort was compounded by appalling unseasonal weather. It was an unlucky period and casualties were high. On 1 July, Ralph Thompson returned from leave and went up the line with the nightly ration party. Most of this party were new men and they regaled Thompson with horror stories about heavy casualties on the ridge. The journey up the line was terrible:

> *I shall never forget the nightmare of that procession of human pack mules plodding its way over open country towards the ridge. Every few minutes an ominous 'pop'...would be followed by a lurid flash and a resounding cr-er-ash unhealthily near us. Each time the ration party heard the warning whine, it made a dive for the ditches on either side of the road. The enemy had the road 'taped' uncannily, and yet trying to walk anywhere but on the road was out of the question, as the ground on either side was churned up, sodden and pocked with shell craters.*

On arrival Thompson was relieved to hear that he would shortly go to cadet school in England. But just before the relief on 3 July, Thompson and half a dozen – mostly from the new draft – were hit by a shell. Six were killed outright and many more, including Thompson, were badly injured. Lying waiting to be evacuated, Thompson witnessed the strange sight of a sergeant major crying over the loss of his men. Later, while in hospital at Bailleul, he heard that the same sergeant had been killed while organizing the burial party. Thompson was severely injured himself, losing an arm and toes.

The casualties in these three days comprised about forty all ranks, of whom nine died. The tonic effect of the recent 'holiday' had been expended in a few days in Spoil Bank. The men marched out of the line on 3 July dirty, tired and downcast. The whole battalion, old hands and new recruits

530176 L/Cpl R J Thompson, of the LCC. Severely wounded 3 July 1917, he was stoic about his lost arm and mangled feet. He wrote to reassure his mother he was 'perfectly fit' and well looked after. 'Each day for dinner I have chicken and a bottle of Guinness am beginning to 'feel my feet' metaphorically speaking'. After a long convalescence in England he married the nurse who had helped his recovery.
IWM (Dept of Docs, Capt R Thompson, 78/58/1)

alike, seemed affected by the malaise. The Reverend Beattie recorded:

> *The men had become rather sulky. They had forgotten how to smile...The discipline had reached a low ebb, the men were dirty and careless in their drill.*[2]

After three days they were back in support trenches. It was at this low point that the battalion was reunited with its pre-war Adjutant, Lieutenant Colonel Parish, who now took command. A man of powerful personality, an advocate of 'spit and polish' and above all an enthusiast for the CSR, Parish was able to achieve a remarkable transformation, with long-lasting effects. He somehow contrived to get the battalion out of the line for four weeks, ostensibly for training in musketry but actually for badly needed rest. Before this, there was one more front-line tour around the gates of the White Château – a very trying ten days which resulted in forty-three casualties including eleven dead. Then on 30 July the CSR – to the envy of the whole division – began its four-week 'holiday' near St Omer. Spit and polish must have seemed a small price to pay for such a break. Parish's popularity evidently did not suffer. York Rickard recorded in his diary:

> *'Gasper' made a speech to whole Battalion...Said this was (when we came out) the finest Battalion in the BEF and it was going to be in future. Wires in caps, etc, 'Civil Service Rifles' in braid on shoulder. Chaps all like him although very hot.*

Officers during Col Parish's short tenure as CO, August 1917, when he revived flagging spirits after Messines. Top row: 2Lts C V Marchant, G M Margrett, T Woods, P Fallon, A Whiteley, G E Tatum, W H Craig. Second row: 2Lts L L Burtt, JAG Falkner, Capt L D Eccles, 2Lts W E Hoste, A W Melliss, P A James, Lt W G Hodge Third row: Capts E H Beattie (Padré), R Middleton, P Davenport, Lt Col F W Parish, Major HFM Warne, Capts F D Balfour, C M Gozney. Bottom: 2Lts R W Illing, W L Ivey.

Unknown to the men, Colonel Parish (nicknamed the 'Gasper') would shortly hand over to Lieutenant Colonel W H E Segrave of the Highland Light Infantry. Parish was suffering from a head wound sustained in 1916 and reluctantly had accepted a staff job. However, he had persuaded the authorities that, before departing, he should lead his revitalized battalion into action.

A useful comparison may be made between the officers of August 1917 and the original cadre of March 1915. Though by 1917 the individuals had changed, they still came from broadly similar professional backgrounds. Over half were teachers, students or from London offices and at least six were civil servants. The half dozen attached from other units were outnumbered by former CSR rankers. The second in command was a pre-war CSR man from the Inland Revenue who had served in France with the 2nd Battalion. Average age had reduced from 34 to 28. The most notable change from 1915 was in educational and social background. Public schools were now outnumbered by grammar and state secondary schools and hardly any officers were graduates. Paternal occupations in 1917 were more mixed and included a surgeon, solicitor, director, merchant, farmer, policeman, salesman, grocer, butcher and railway guard. This change is not surprising. As officer casualties rose and the army expanded, increasing numbers of men from lower middle-class backgrounds were commissioned. What is interesting is that the CSR officers of 1917 were of very similar type to those in the ranks before the war. It had been possible then for junior clerks to rise through the ranks and end up as officers, but the opportunities were few and the most senior positions tended to be occupied by first division civil servants or by second division men from middle-class backgrounds. In wartime there were many more promotion opportunities, with the result that after two years the CSR was still recognizable as the pre-war unit it had been, the main difference being that more junior civil servants held commissions and the officers generally were more socially mixed.

Passchendaele

While the CSR had been brushing up musketry skills, competing for prizes and generally enjoying life in the back area, the British offensive which became known as Passchendaele (or Third Ypres) had begun. The

weather had been appalling. It was still bad when they returned to the Salient on 24 August and learned they would soon join the fight. The battalion was to attack two woods on Westhoek ridge north of the Menin Road called Nonne Boschen and Glencorse. This ground had been captured and lost three times already but according to the latest plan the CSR was to take and hold it.

The training for this attack was apparently framed in the old tactical doctrine which dictated that assaulting infantry arrived at objectives in intact waves, whatever the terrain. Remembering the 'milling crowds' before the White Château on 7 June, the men were sceptical. Nevertheless, feeling that 'something big should be done to justify the recent holiday', they resigned themselves and began practising. The battalion was to advance 600 yards to an assembly point, then navigate some marshy pools surrounded by concrete dugouts bristling with machine-guns. Walter Humphrys, fully recovered from frostbite and now on a Lewis gun team, recalled the task allotted to his section:

> We were supposed to get through all those pools of mud and water and fire in the mouth of the pill box while the rest of the platoon went round the back. We were practising out there and we were knowing it was certain death, which it was, because of the conditions.

In the event Walter was spared from facing 'certain death'. The attack was postponed several times as Westhoek ridge became a sea of mud and was finally abandoned at the last minute. According to the CSR *History*, this provoked 'something akin to consternation' at a lost opportunity to 'prove their worth' at Passchendaele, a battle which later became a byword for the severest trials of the war. Because Colonel Parish was bitterly disappointed, so too were the men. To modern ears, such a reaction seems extraordinary, given the men's recent grim experiences and their scepticism about an operation regarded as bringing 'certain death'. Even allowing for the panegyric tone of this section of the *History* (Colonel Parish had died prematurely in 1921, shortly before its publication), this episode must count as an outstanding example of inspirational leadership. As the Reverend Beattie wrote at the time, the

This panorama depicts the conditions experienced by the soldiers of both sides during the autumn-winter fighting in 1917. Working parties are seen here taking duckboards up to the front. Taylor Library

Hell Fire Corner on the Menin Road, along which supplies were hastily delivered. Taylor Library

battalion 'would have followed him anywhere and done anything for him'.[3]

The CSR endured three further trying weeks in the Salient, including seven days in support trenches around the notorious Menin Road. The cooks and transport section had a particularly bad time:

12 September...had our respirators on for nearly two hours. Eyes nose and throat feel very wobbly...13 September...I missed two 'Blighties' by about a foot each time. The first just missed my left hand. 14 September...Shell on trench three yards from cookhouse...one man both feet blown off, another one leg off. Both died later. During morning one landed on cookhouse. I was not inside but all my equipment and property blown to atoms. (York Rickard)

We...took rations to the ill-starred Menin Road. This gave us good training as circus drivers, for from Hell-Fire cross roads to Hooge Craters we went at a gallop, steering a way through dead horses and mules...At each of these animals our own would shy violently. Arrived at the Craters, we hastily threw the rations off, whether the men from the Line were there or not, and came back at a gallop again. On one occasion we did this between blazing limbers on each side of the road...Quite like a real war this. (Charles Bassett)

112

Casualties in this period amounted to thirty-one, most incurred in an incident involving C Company on 15 September which killed three including Second Lieutenant Northam, a Stock Exchange clerk. Finally, with great relief the CSR left the Salient for good. They also took leave of Colonel Parish. The Padré described the parting:

> The last parade when he said 'goodbye' will always stay with me. He told us to be loyal to his successor and to the name of the Regiment. He hoped that he would come back to us, 'But however that may be I shall never forget these weeks we have spent together. You have shown the best spirit men could show, and I leave you believing that you will uphold the honour and the name of the Civil Service Rifles'. And then we all marched past him and he called me back to him and turned away and wept. God bless him.[4]

Interlude, September – November 1917

Before the next big action, at Cambrai, the battalion enjoyed another 'rest cure' on the Arras front. In the Gavrelle and Oppy Wood sectors the war seemed as quiescent as in the Salient the preceding autumn. Trenches were deep, clean and dry; shelling was almost non-existent. In two months there were nine casualties, including only one death. Charles Bassett recalled it was even possible to drive the ration cart up to the front and hand supplies down into the firing line.

Colonel Segrave, in an effort to reduce the manpower deficiency before the next battle, posted into the front line some fit men from 'behind-the-line' jobs. This account by Bassett, among the men chosen, describes the Colonel's rationale:

> A lot of elderly and otherwise unfit men had been sent back from the line and dumped on us as 'wagon cleaning fatigues', 'spare pack leaders' etc and suddenly the powers-that-be awoke to the imperative necessity of stiffening the very mixed drafts that were arriving with long-service men who were A1.

The batch of young men released from the Inland Revenue in the spring began to reach the front on drafts during the summer. One of these, Douglas Houghton, was dismayed to be sent to the 6th Londons and thus separated from his friend Henry Moore who went to the CSR. Houghton and Moore had both travelled down from the North of England specifically to join a London battalion rather than wait to be conscripted locally. Despite the increasingly varied drafts, the regimental character continued much as before. In a departure from army rules, the issue of rum was not supervised, on the basis that responsible men could be relied on not to hoard it and then get drunk. Albert Robins recalled:

> Within each platoon of the CSR there was a remarkable trust and fellow feeling...I never had anything stolen, a thing that was

not the case in some other situations... There was no need to queue up for...[food]. One man could do that, taking along several mess tins and drawing for 4 or 5 men, because we could trust each other. The same with a tin of jam – one tin might be for 6 or 10...Men could be trusted to take only a fair amount. I am not suggesting that we were perfect, but men did behave very decently to each other.

This distinctive regime was still recognizable when Major Young of the 60th Rifles joined in August 1918. Then, he dubbed his new regiment 'the so-correct Civil Service Rifles' where crime was unknown.

Bourlon Wood

In November 1917 another move was rumoured. The 47th Division was warned to go to Italy, though a pressing need for its services soon arose nearer at hand. Happily expecting to catch a glimpse of the Alps, the battalion set off from the Arras area on 18 November on an exhausting eight-day journey. On the way, they heard of a stunning British success

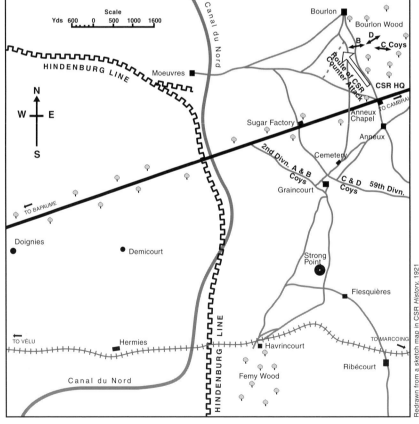

BOURLON WOOD
CSR's
MOVEMENTS
28 NOV -
6 DEC 1917

Redrawn from a sketch map in CSR *History*, 1921

535325 Pte ALND (Douglas) Houghton, Inland Revenue. Enlisted in CSR early 1917 but fought at Passchendaele with 6th Londons. Evacuated with trench fever, he returned to the CSR in England where he and Henry Moore became PT instructors and trained new recruits.

Lady Vera Houghton

at Cambrai. The Germans had been pushed back beyond the Hindenburg Line, built deep behind their front line the previous winter. Third Army had difficulty consolidating these gains and reinforcements were urgently needed. By the time the battalion was moving east across the old Somme battlefield, it was evident that Italy was 'off'. As Private S Chapman, a Lewis gunner with C Company, recalled:

> We knew now that Cambrai was our objective; what part we were to play in the operations we could not tell – whether we were to attack, or follow the 'great push' or were simply there in reserve. ...All next day was spent in preparations that clearly indicated a prospective 'over the top' business. The usual 'small kit' was served out and certain men detailed to stay behind. ...We went [up the line] by motor lorries part of the way, followed by a march with full pack and a blanket, which nearly killed us.[5]

The 47th Division was destined for Bourlon Wood, one of two important features which the Germans stubbornly refused to yield. There was no time for proper planning, let alone rehearsal. They marched straight into a raging battle. As the battalion approached from south of the Bapaume-Cambrai road, signs of recent fighting were evident: dead bodies, scattered equipment, derelict tanks and shell holes which looked alarmingly fresh. A stream of wounded men came in the opposite direction, passing on stories of the 'marvellous advance'.

At night on 28 November the wood was visible in the distance, the trees lit up by multi-coloured flashes of shell fire. A peculiar whistling sound, followed by a dull thud, heralded a gas bombardment. Men fumbled to put on their masks but found they quickly steamed up. Faced with the choice of being blinded by the mask or by the gas, most compromised and just sucked the mouthpiece. Somehow the battalion passed through the barrage and into the wood without casualties. But as C Company moved into its support position, a sunken road about 200 yards behind the front line, Charles Bassett observed:

> Everywhere were dead bodies scattered about and just as we slid down the bank into a sunken road, there was a terrific crash. We frantically dived for shelter, and I found myself gazing into the green face of a dead German, crouched opposite...Up the bank at the other side, and here the ground is covered with shallow holes, dug for protection but which have almost all become graves for either British or Huns. Around us now are crashes that daze the mind, the earth seems to rock with the explosions, soft 'pops' in the air about our heads and puffs of what seems hot air on our faces, tell of gas shells. ...all our faces are haggard and...eyes staring, and nerves evidently at breaking point.

Then came a horrifying incident:

Suddenly...comes a whoosh, and Number 12 Platoon has ceased to exist. My left-hand neighbour, a man who joined with me, is dead. Another ex-Transport man who was on my right is laying in the road with a shattered leg, and is cursing volubly. I myself am down with a piece in the right leg, and all around are men killed or wounded. In front a man is shrieking frightfully. I dragged myself to the bank nearest the line as soon as possible and ripping my trouser leg with a pocket knife (I remember how ill-used I felt because the knife was blunt, although it was a new one) I put on the field dressing.

The battalion's work had not begun and already it had suffered twenty-two casualties. With help, Bassett later reached an aid post. The battalion pressed on and all were in position by 0130. At this stage Third Army's plan was to press home the advance. But before long the Germans showed signs of counter-attacking and the plans were changed. During six of the following nine days the battalion would fight two bitter and confused defensive battles. The second would be fought after only the shortest of breaks and reinforcement by a handful of 'non-starters'.

Apart from one disastrous night on Vimy ridge eighteen months before, the CSR had no experience of a large-scale defensive action. As at Vimy, they were on unfamiliar territory, with no opportunity for reconnaissance. Moreover the men, tired after the long journey, faced new enemy tactics. The German counter-attack was led by fast-moving 'storm troops'. Supported by mobile artillery, these bypassed strong points, leaving them to be mopped up by standard infantry following behind. The battalion thus faced extremely difficult conditions. At times during both phases the situation was critical.

First phase, 28 November – 1 December

Conditions inside Bourlon Wood were ghastly. Unlike High Wood in 1916, where the undergrowth had been trampled down by successive battles and bombardments, Bourlon was still full of thick brambles, harbouring evil smelling gas. Under persistent heavy bombardment, communication was difficult and at times broke down. The battalion became isolated and the training experienced at St Omer earlier in the year now came into play. Remnants of companies, platoons and Lewis gun sections found themselves cut off and had to work on their own initiative. The most critical moment of this first phase came during the German counter-attack on 30 November, when a gap opened between the CSR and the 6th Londons on the left. Colonel

534592 Pte H S Moore. Joined CSR early 1917 and arrived in France in August aged just 19. He became a Lewis gunner and was gassed at Bourlon Wood. Henry Moore's subsequent status as a world class sculptor and artist inevitably aroused interest in his formative experiences. Asked in 1961 'Did the war affect you deeply?' Moore replied: 'No, for me the first world war passed in a kind of romantic haze of hoping to be a hero. Sometimes in France there were three or four days of great danger when you thought there wasn't a chance of getting through, and then all one felt was sadness at having taken so much trouble to no purpose; but on the whole I enjoyed the Army'.

Notice in Daily Telegraph *by P G L Strong in November 1967, 50 years after his close friend D M Taylor was killed by his side. His company went into Bourlon Wood 135 strong, of whom only 14 came back unwounded.*

Segrave gathered together the reserve company plus runners, cooks and officers' servants, and led them across open country outside the wood. After many casualties from rifle, machine-gun and aeroplane fire, this party managed to restore the line. This extraordinary feat was performed just like a training exercise, the Colonel leading with map and whistle. The General Staff later commended Segrave and his counterpart in the 6th Londons for their prompt action in 'a day of high courage and glorious achievement'. This was recorded in a patriotic official publication entitled *The Story of a Great Fight*, which also praised the manner in which Lewis gunners on their own initiative pushed forward and brought cross-fire to bear on massed German infantry advancing on the flanks.

The casualties in this first phase were heavy: a hundred killed, forty-four missing and over two hundred wounded, mainly due to gas. Ten of the missing had been taken prisoner. The battalion had the satisfaction of knowing they had yielded no ground, but elsewhere in the Cambrai salient the Germans had overrun the line. The high command therefore decided to give up ground, including the wood, the defence of which had cost so many CSR lives.

Second phase, 4-6 December

The next phase involved taking up a defensive line south-west of the wood, either side of the village of Graincourt. It was commanded by Major Marshall in the absence of Colonel Segrave who was badly gassed. The battalion was so depleted, it was reorganized into two companies: C/D on the right and A/B on the left. Their job, with the 2nd Division on the left and the 59th Division on the right, was to hold this new line while all troops were withdrawn from the wood and passed through. This manoeuvre was effected so well on 4 December that the Germans did not at first realize what had happened. It was not until 5 December that the enemy sent out probing patrols, provoking several skirmishes.

On the afternoon of 6 December, the Germans attacked in large numbers. They crossed the CSR's front from left to right, leaving A/B Company practically untouched. The position of C/D Company was more vulnerable, as the battalion on its right withdrew and the Germans began working round the flank. A/B Company was able to withdraw in good order, but C/D Company's position became critical. A large group,

117

around a hundred strong, made a fighting retreat over about one and a half miles, seeing off a group of Germans of equal strength on the way. A smaller group of C/D Company which had remained behind near Graincourt was later surrounded. After their ammunition ran out, the survivors were taken prisoner.

Walter Humphrys had been in the thick of the action. He was number five in one of the mobile Lewis gun teams which were commended in *The Story of a Great Fight*. To his dying day, Walter retained disturbing memories of the hell inside the wood and of what happened to his team:

> *The Germans found we had left the wood and attacked us before we had time to retire. ...Number 2 on my [Lewis gun] team was hit in the head while standing by the side of me and later taken prisoner. Then an hour later the Number 1 was killed, shot in the neck, a few yards away from me. Number 4 was shell-shocked. ... Eventually when the order came to retire, I [Number 5] was left on my own...The people in the Lewis gun team were the cream, all educated men. Number 1 was a Bachelor of Arts. Number 2 was a school teacher, a Bachelor of Science ...It was terrible...We lost the cream.*

Casualties in the second phase were 120 killed, wounded and missing, including eighteen officers. Later it emerged that five officers were prisoners. The number of 17th March men killed was five – an indicator of their dwindling ranks. The transport and stores had their share of casualties moving up from Havrincourt and back to keep the battalion supplied. York Rickard's daily diary recounts the depressing news as it gradually filtered through. On 6 December he recorded:

> *Battalion came out at night. Very few left. The whole Battalion could be cooked for on one cooker. All the men very dicky.*

Bourlon village and wood, May 1918. Many CSR men perished in the desperate defence of the wood on 30 November 1917 and in the withdrawal a few days later. Men were still dying from gas poisoning in early 1918. IWM (CO 3440)

Senior NCOs, 1917. At least 3 originals are recognizable. Back row, first and second left: F C Robertson DCM (Board of Education); W H 'Topsy' Turvey (Local Government Board). Middle seated left: T P Brett MC (a chemist). Seated centre is W Richards, the Regular RSM 1916-18, known to one and all as 'Posh Harry'.

There were only 200 left and over the next few days they were further depleted. The shakiness observed by Rickard was largely due to effects of mustard gas. The symptoms were sometimes delayed, as Private Chapman recalled:

> *Gradually the effects...began to tell on us. I developed a cough and lost my voice with my eyes watering. Next day was no better, so the following morning I paraded sick.*[6]

ME

Prisoners of war keeping their spirits up. The photo was sent as a postcard by Capt L L Burtt.

Chapman was discharged as disabled the following April. A number of men died lingering deaths from gas during the next few months. Even the small dose which Henry Moore recovered from involved three months in hospital and left his voice permanently susceptible to huskiness.

The CSR had one further – thankfully quiet – front-line tour before getting the customary post-battle 'rest'. This took place first at Bertincourt, then much further back at Morlancourt, south of Albert. By now there was thick snow on the ground. Here the CSR spent its third Christmas in France. The battalion had fought its defensive action with skill but once more had been massively depleted. It would be February 1918 before fighting strength was fully restored. Then the CSR would face its greatest challenge of the war.

1. The CSR unofficial *Regimental Diary*, quoted in CSR *History*, page 141. The 'head waiter' was Private R Wallis, a civil servant. A 17th March man, he served in the officers' mess continuously until seriously wounded in May 1918.
2. Rev E A Beattie letter of 15 September 1917 (Parish family collection)
3. *ibid*
4. *ibid*
5. QW&CSR *Newsletter*, Vol 8, No.12, October 1976
6. *ibid*

Major Warne (Inland Revenue) and Capt L L Burtt (Stock Exchange) as prisoners of war at Schweidnitz, Silesia. 5 officers and a small number of men were captured near Graincourt in December 1917. After the war the officers were exonerated.

Chapter Six

Reversals of Fortune: France 1918

B y the beginning of 1918, Lloyd George's deliberate brake on the flow of reinforcements for the BEF in France and Belgium forced an organized contraction of the army. Sir Douglas Haig could not shorten the British sector of the Western Front, as the French were still recovering from the mutiny of 1917; and the Americans, though growing in numbers and enthusiastic, were still in large part untrained for front line duties. Moreover the British were forced to take up a further fifteen miles of front in the south from the French army as 1918 began. In responding to these constraints, Haig kept the same number of divisions but spread his resources more thinly. Infantry brigades were reduced from four battalions to three. The CSR remained in 140 Brigade but now served alongside the 17th and 21st Londons. Rumours of a German offensive were rife, and the prospect of facing it in a depleted brigade was not encouraging. At least the CSR survived the reorganization intact, unlike its fellow territorials, the 6th, 7th and 8th Londons, which suffered the ultimate insult of amalgamation with other units.

The freezing winter gave way to a wet spring. For the CSR, the period before the German offensive which was to begin on 21 March was fairly quiet, though enemy shelling and aerial bombardments still occurred daily. Two tours in the line in January at Ribécourt and Flesquières were uneventful. Honours for Bourlon Wood were awarded, including six Military Crosses and also a Bar to Colonel Segrave's DSO. It was not until February that fighting strength was fully restored with the arrival of over a hundred of the disbanded 6th Londons. Only two men were killed in eleven weeks, but sickness from gas was common. On one day alone at the end of February, sixty-three men reported sick after a gas bombardment.

Kaiserschlacht ('The Kaiser's Battle')

Rumours of an offensive had receded by the time 47th Division went back to war on 19 March in the Flesquières salient – ground won during the Cambrai battle the previous autumn. Within thirty-six hours the greatest single attack of the war had begun. The division, newly arrived in unfamiliar territory, was on the extreme right of Third Army, at its boundary with Fifth Army. This was an inauspicious position, for the Germans planned to storm through either side of the salient, cutting in behind and 'rolling up' Third Army northwards. Consequently, over the

German storm troops launch an attack, 1918. Each man is lightly equipped but heavily armed with rifle, grenades in shoulder pouches and plenty of ammunition to sustain the assault. The CSR suffered heavy losses in the German onslaught in March. Taylor Library

next three critical days, it fell to 47th Division to defend the right flank of a whole Army.

Early on 21 March, a terrific bombardment of high explosive and gas shells began along a forty-mile front. In five hours the Germans expended more shells than the British had sent over in the week before the Somme attack in 1916. The battalion sat out the bombardment, huddled in shallow dugouts in support trenches in Lincoln Reserve on Beaucamp ridge. The men wore box respirators continuously for six hours. Many suffered from gas and from nervous strain induced by the incessant screaming shells. Albert Robins of A Company was very sick:

> I had absorbed a certain amount [of gas]. Somehow the others were not affected. The way it took me was at both ends at the same time – diarrhoea and vomiting. As shelling was still going on, one did not go outside but one's pals advised using one's groundsheet, which could be cleaned later, for a lavatory.

Private T C H Jacobs also described his reaction:

> The sense of isolation really got me now. We were trapped in a stinking mud hole filled with gas-laden fog, no adequate fire-step and no protecting wire. All we could do was crouch there in the mud and wait, stunned by noise and concussion. As time dragged on without any let-up in the bombardment, fear was replaced with weary exasperation. I recall thinking 'For Christ's sake, pack it up Jerry. Come over and fight, you bastards'. At the same time I was sane enough to realise that while all those shells were falling we were safe from infantry attack.[1]

The Germans did not plan on this day to 'come over and fight' in large numbers in this sector. They sent aggressive patrols, which the forward battalions of 141 Brigade managed to repel, but unleashed their *Stosstruppen* and massed infantry all along the line to the north and

122

south. So while large amounts of land, prisoners and guns were captured elsewhere on the first day, the Flesquières salient remained comparatively quiet. In the afternoon the battalion was able to evacuate thirty-eight wounded or gassed men and two dead.

During the night of 21 March, the situation on the divisional flanks worsened. The forward battalions were ordered to withdraw to a second defensive line, so that the trench occupied by the CSR became the new front line. The following day was quiet, while the tremendous struggle continued elsewhere. The enemy had made huge advances against Fifth Army to the south, and by the afternoon the battalion's right flank, occupied by D Company, had lost contact with the troops to its right and was 'in the air'. The divisional history records:

> *The 15th Battalion* [CSR], *on the extreme right, had an anxious and heavy task to perform, and the fact that no Germans filtered through the gap throws great credit on the way in which the patrols and machine-gunners did their work.*[2]

By evening the situation in the salient was critical and the battalion was ordered to fall back to a third defensive line – a tricky, unrehearsed manoeuvre achieved successfully overnight. Walter Humphrys, now promoted to Number One on a Lewis gun, took his team out into no man's land for two hours to cover the withdrawal.

'It was a hard day, March 23rd'[3]

By dawn on 23 March most of the battalion occupied half-dug trenches along a line called Dessart Ridge Switch, just west of the Metz-Fins road. It was a precarious position, soon under attack. D Company was once again on the extreme right, facing south, and dangerously exposed by the withdrawal of Fifth Army troops on its right flank. The enemy rushed into the gap, quickly set up machine-gun positions and enfiladed D Company. Trouble then began on the battalion's left, where troops were seen retiring in large numbers. Some of these were rallied by Colonel Segrave and formed into a defensive flank, facing east. Shelling during the morning forced the retirement of more troops on the left and by midday the enemy had established machine-gun posts on this flank as well. The CSR was now dangerously exposed.

When the order came to abandon Dessart Ridge Switch, D Company had been completely surrounded. All its men, including the company commander, were lost, either killed or cut off until taken prisoner. Walter Humphrys, who with his gun team occupied the last position on the right flank, described D Company's fate:

> *German machine gunners had taken the place of the troops which had been protecting our rear. German troops were also bombing us on our right flank and sniping on the left. We were thus completely surrounded. At 2.30pm we, D Company, were given*

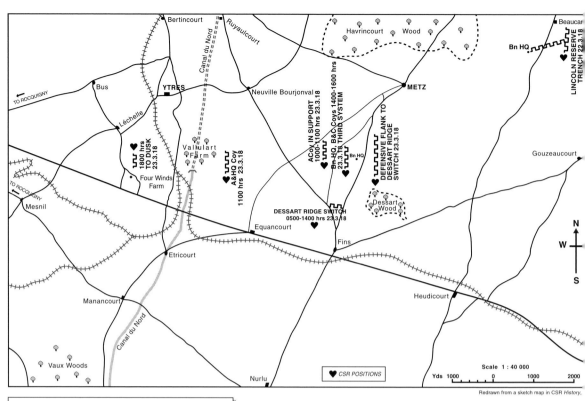

**THE RETREAT 1: CSR's MOVEMENTS
23 MARCH 1918**

Redrawn from a sketch map in CSR History.

orders to charge the German machine guns as the only chance of getting out – an insane idea – but we did it and didn't get far. The few still standing crawled back into the trench, which the main body of advancing Germans attacked about 4.30 pm. Finish.

Waiting nearly two hours for the 'finish' was a severe test of Walter's nerve. Many men lay nearby, cut down during the 'insane' charge. Having crawled backwards and turned a somersault into the trench, Walter found only one other man there. Later this man was shot dead as they both crouched, trying to see what was happening ahead. Eventually, as the Germans entered, Walter retreated along the trench until he found six men of another unit. They surrendered as a body.

For those who managed to retire, there followed twenty-four hours of continuous mobile warfare, demanding wholly different tactics from the rapid counter-attacking manoeuvres practised in recent training. From now on, wrote the division's historian,

...the task of the Division was not to hold definite positions to grim death, but to keep the enemy's advance in check, and at all costs to prevent him striking in behind us, thereby cutting off our troops and subsequently rolling up the flank of the [Third] *Army.*[4]

Colonel Segrave collected a group of fifty and placed them along a ridge about three miles back but at dusk they were forced even further back.

124

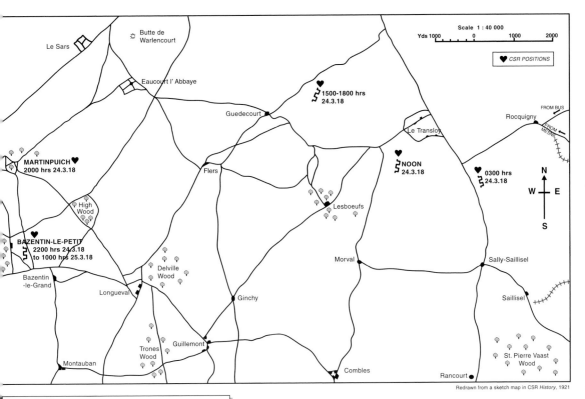

The following text labels appear on the map:

Le Sars

Butte de Warlencourt

Eaucourt l' Abbaye

Scale 1 : 40 000

Yds 1000   0   1000   2000

CSR POSITIONS

1500-1800 hrs 24.3.18

Guedecourt

Le Transloy

FROM BUS

Rocquigny

FROM MESNIL

MARTINPUICH 2000 hrs 24.3.18

Flers

NOON 24.3.18

0300 hrs 24.3.18

N
W   E
S

High Wood

Lesboeufs

BAZENTIN-LE-PETIT 2200 hrs 24.3.18 to 1000 hrs 25.3.18

Bazentin -le-Grand

Longueval

Delville Wood

Morval

Sally-Saillisel

Saillisel

Ginchy

Trones Wood

Guillemont

St. Pierre Vaast Wood

Montauban

Combles

Rancourt

Redrawn from a sketch map in CSR History, 1921

THE RETREAT 2: CSR's MOVEMENTS 24 MARCH 1918

The battalion then split into small parties which lost touch with the command structure; some had not even a lance corporal in charge. A recently commissioned subaltern, Lewis Pickard, described the confusion:

> We started to go back...under fire from each side, and in no particular order, but every man for himself. It was in this period that I received a whiz bang all to myself. Luckily, some of my men found a stretcher and after carrying me some miles, struck a main road. I was loaded on a wagon full of small arms ammo and later found myself in a field hospital.

Pickard was fortunate to get away; many wounded had to be left behind that day. There is no official account of the battalion's fighting retreat until at 0900 the following morning when about 150 men managed to consolidate under Colonel Segrave in a support position six or seven miles back, near Le Transloy. The exhausted survivors briefly took stock. In the previous twenty-four hours there had been more than 300 casualties, of whom two-thirds were 'missing'. Many of these had been taken prisoner but it was months before each man's fate was known. At this stage the missing included many NCOs and at least six officers: the second in command, Major Balfour (killed), Captain Middleton (D Company, captured and died of wounds), Lieutenant Broad (killed), and Second Lieutenants Matheson (killed), Aylmore (killed) and Bright (captured). The fight, however, was not over. During 24 March the

*By the armistice, 213 CSR men were prisoners of war on the Western Front –
the vast majority of them captured during the March Retreat. Here a group of
4,000 British soldiers are waiting to be processed near Arras, March 1918.*
IWM (Q51464)

depleted battalion occupied, then withdrew from, four successive
positions. The retreat took them back across the old Somme battlefield
to Bazentin-le-Petit, past the wood where lay so many of the battalion
who had died capturing it in 1916 – an effort which now seemed in vain:

> *An ironic joke of Fate, surely, to send us back through High
> Wood...The desolation of the Somme
> country was in keeping with our
> feelings. Feet were sore with marching
> over rough country; stomachs were
> yearning for nourishment; mouths
> parched; bodies tired with a heavy,
> numbing fatigue; these things produced
> a desolate feeling akin to the quiet
> sorrow of the surrounding country.[5]*

531876 Lance Corporal C S Amsden
DISTINGUISHED CONDUCT MEDAL

For conspicuous gallantry and devotion to duty
during our retirement when in comand of a
Lewis gun section. Nearly all his detachment
had become casualties: nevertheless, he kept
his gun in action, inflicting severe losses on
the enemy, taking up successive positions as
the retirement developed, and bringing his gun
out of action under fire. Eventually becoming
separated from his Battalion, he attached
himself to another unit which was also in
action, and rejoined his Battalion the next
morning, still carrying his gun and some
ammunition.

---

*Just one example of the extraordinary
courage and determination displayed
during the CSR's fighting withdrawal on
23-24 March 1918.*

At Bazentin-le-Petit the strength rose to
230, with the hurried return of men
from leave and attachments, including
Captain Bates. Next day they withdrew
with the rest of 47th Division to a
strong position along Contalmaison
ridge. There they repulsed a determined
attack, suffering twelve further
casualties. The German attack was not

126

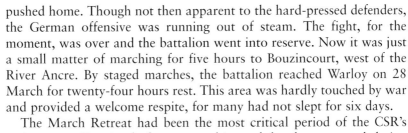

pushed home. Though not then apparent to the hard-pressed defenders, the German offensive was running out of steam. The fight, for the moment, was over and the battalion went into reserve. Now it was just a small matter of marching for five hours to Bouzincourt, west of the River Ancre. By staged marches, the battalion reached Warloy on 28 March for twenty-four hours rest. This area was hardly touched by war and provided a welcome respite, for many had not slept for six days.

The March Retreat had been the most critical period of the CSR's entire career. Despite the heavy casualties and the almost overwhelming German attacks, the battalion had fought on. Officers and men had forced the enemy to contest every yard gained and at great cost. The transport section too had executed an arduous and hazardous withdrawal. Not only did they manage to keep in touch with the battalion and serve hot meals at various points on the way, they did it without losing a man or a horse. In short, the CSR had conducted an exemplary fighting withdrawal with extraordinary courage and determination. For Paul Davenport, writing the account in the CSR *History*, it was the March Retreat, rather than the capture of High Wood, which was the battalion's finest achievement of the war.

Aveluy Wood, 29 March – 6 April

The CSR returned to the front line in Aveluy Wood on 29 March for three days which, though fairly quiet, produced fifteen casualties from shelling. The battalion enjoyed two days' respite, reorganizing at Senlis, then returned to the line on 4 April. The battle of Aveluy Wood was another hard fight, with fifty-nine casualties over three days. By the evening of 5 April, the German commanders recognized that their final offensive was doomed to failure. In sixteen days they had made impressive tactical gains of up to forty miles, but failed in their strategic objectives, not least of which was to split the two British armies. In preventing this, 47th Division had played an important part. The subsequent verdicts of the German commanders on this final day of their *Kaiserschlacht* were 'Our strength was exhausted' (Hindenburg) and 'The enemy's resistance was beyond our powers' (Ludendorff).

While in retrospect this can be seen as a major turning point of the war, it was not generally recognized at the time. The customary period of rest and reorganization during April seemed merely an interval while the enemy paused for breath. The expectation that the fight would soon resume was strengthened by Haig's Special Order of the Day on 11 April ('Every position must be held to the last man...With our backs to the wall and believing in the justice of our cause each one of us must fight on to the end....') and a few days later by a remark of General Gorringe to the effect that more 'dirty work' for the division lay ahead. Accordingly, on 1 May, the men were not surprised to be ordered back

Lt Col WHE Segrave DSO (Highland Light Infantry), an able leader of the CSR in its two big defensive actions. Rowland Feilding said of him, 'He simply worships this Battalion.'

to war. But before then the battalion had been substantially reinforced. At the end of April fighting strength was one of the highest of the war. Over sixty per cent were new men, most of them youngsters who had never been near a front-line trench.

Reinforcements and their effect on regimental character

At home, news of the March offensive caused widespread consternation. The minimum age for sending conscripts overseas was reduced to eighteen. At the Reserve Battalion, now based at Wimbledon, were many partly-trained boys of this age who had enlisted before their call-up. Robert Angel described their reasons:

> When conscription was introduced...it was almost a disaster to me and to many of my friends who were firmly resolved to join the armed forces as soon as we became of age. It looked as if the pride of being a volunteer was no longer attainable and that our eventual embodiment as fighting men would have no merit about it. Fortunately for us ... certain regiments were permitted to accept men who offered themselves at 18.

Angel had joined not the CSR but another of the 'class' corps, the 5th Londons (London Rifle Brigade, or LRB). Youngsters in these units were now hurried onto drafts. Private Derick Haywood captured the fevered atmosphere at the CSR camp:

> 24 March. Large drafts off to France and, since then, three officers and NCOs were taken off parade and warned for France immediately...Pateman spoke on behalf of our platoon and volunteered us...but they said we have to finish training first. Later in the day a second large draft left...Walker, another eighteen-year-old pal who was on the draft...tried to look cheerful, but I could see he wondered what was in store for them out there as the news is so alarming. He is a decent lad. Until now nobody has been sent out until he is nineteen, but things are so grave that we are to go as soon as training can be rushed through. I wonder what will happen to these boys. We're nearly all eighteen, or nineteen at most. ...We went to Wimbledon Station to see them off and came back nearly in tears. Some came into our hut to say goodbye, and others called out as they passed down the lines at 10.30 pm on their way to the station. I wish we could have gone out with that fine crowd. They're mostly boys from jobs in the City, or just left school. They went off singing 'Goodbyee' and other songs. I shall always remember this night.[6]

It seems that the motivation of these boys was as strong as those who enlisted voluntarily in 1914. The difference was that by 1918 they could have fewer illusions about the dangers and horrors they would face.

'Dickie' Sparrow was pleased to be selected for the draft:

> Proceeding to Wimbledon railway station at midnight with our regimental band playing 'Auld Lang Syne' etc at full blast even at this late hour, I spotted two elderly folk, a man and his wife, waving to us from their bedroom window...How proud I felt at this time.

Sparrow had been delighted to be accepted by the CSR, a unit favoured by boys from his school in Cambridge. During training he and his pals had been shown 'respect and consideration by both officers and NCOs' and before leaving for France had been treated to a 'slap-up dinner' and a show in town. It is easy to see why this carefully nurtured sense of belonging to what Sparrow believed was 'an elite...regiment' gave way to bitter disappointment when drafts were split up in France and redirected elsewhere. Sparrow felt fortunate to find his way to the CSR. Many on his draft went to disparate units, badly depleted during the March Retreat.[7]

537334 Pte H H Sparrow, one of the hundreds of 18 year-olds rushed to France after the Retreat. He was wounded near Rancourt on 1 September. 70 years later, he recalled the 'spirit of real friendship' he discovered in the CSR.
Betty Baff

During the emergency the deployment of drafts was haphazard. A group of around 600 reached the CSR on 9 April containing representatives of practically every London territorial unit. Too many for the battalion's requirements, they paraded before Colonel Segrave who picked the best and sent the rest elsewhere. Among those selected were two LRB platoons, including Robert Angel's. Angel was as proud of his unit as Sparrow was of the CSR. Exchanging his cap badge for the Prince of Wales' feathers caused him particular sadness. He was, however, also relieved:

> In the present crisis we were fortunate to find ourselves posted to...the Civil Service Rifles, a unit with much the same tradition and social background as our own.

The new drafts, though young and inexperienced, had been well schooled in England. They arrived with a thorough knowledge of the latest infantry tactics, which the training manuals of 1917 stressed must be 'second nature in moments of

Unusual combination of Military Cross and Albert Medal from the recently reunited medal group of 7 to Capt WLC Rathbone of the GPO. The MC was for leading an attack on the Flers line in the aftermath of the fighting in High Wood in September 1916. The AM was for gallantry in saving life on 6 May 1916. Rathbone and a Post Office Rifles corporal disarmed a mentally deranged British soldier running amok in a trench with loaded rifle and fixed bayonet. Rathbone, originally a 17th March ranker, survived the war but did not live long enough to exchange his Albert Medal for the George Cross. Ian Cook

Officers at Guignemicourt, July 1918. Seated on bench: Capt Rathbone (A Coy), OC B Coy, Capt Bates (C Coy), Col Segrave, Capt Davenport (Adjutant), foreign visitor, Capt Eccles (D Coy).

excitement and tension'. In France, great efforts were made to assimilate the newcomers from the moment of their arrival, when they were greeted personally by Colonel Segrave and posted to companies with their friends. Their training was intensified at platoon and section level in a prescribed system, which emphasized the necessity for them to be confident in their leaders, in their weapons and in their own skills. Even the most junior must be able to display initiative in action.[8]

Capt Eccles and D Coy, July 1918. These are some of the young conscripts who went into battle a few weeks later, wearing khaki shorts. Major Young described them as 'like a lot of boys going to a football match'. Later, Young talked of the 'pitiful trail of dead boys' left behind as the battalion advanced.

The training was supervised by mature NCOs with years of service in the regiment – men like civil servants Levey, Ibbett, W H Moore and W H Wheddon. In the previous autumn, nineteen year-old Henry S Moore, from a large family, had found the older men so paternal that it was 'a bit like being back in the family'. Angel's experience in 1918 was similar. His introduction to the peculiar CSR style of discipline came as his company commander pressed a franc into his hand and implored him to 'buy some hair ribbon'! Angel found this eccentric gesture 'much more impressive than a blunt order to get the haircut which, no doubt, was badly needed'. Later, when he was violently sick on witnessing his first casualty, Angel appreciated Sergeant Ibbett's tolerant attitude: 'He was a fine type of territorial soldier and very understanding'.

Bertie Fereday, an eighteen year-old from the Inland Revenue, had also been relieved to reach 'the good old CSR'. He told his family 'we shall have a better time with the Battalion than with any other'. He was disappointed on being posted to B Company to find very few men he knew and that some were 'rather a washout crowd'. Then his platoon officer intervened, arranging for Fereday and a Wimbledon friend to serve on a Lewis gun section together. The whole regime was designed to make the new arrivals feel at home and engender confidence and pride. In action in August and September these boys would show just how well they had absorbed both their infantry training, based on the hard lessons of 1916 and 1917, and the CSR *esprit*. For the moment, however, they had a fairly gentle introduction to war.

May to July 1918 – many alarms

The summer was quiet, though punctuated by alarms and bouts of associated 'wind up'. The Germans had occupied Albert in March and were expected any day to renew their attempt to reach Amiens. When 47th Division went back to war (as part of Fourth Army) on 1 May, into

positions west of Albert along the banks of the River Ancre, an attack seemed imminent. It failed to materialize, as did a later attack which had been confidently expected on 20 May. The men regularly stood to at dawn. There were also rehearsals for a counter-attack which never took place. Twelve honours were distributed for the March Retreat including a second bar to the DSO for Colonel Segrave, who had become rather popular. A quip current that summer was that the letters 'CSR' stood for 'Colonel Segrave's Regiment'.

In the seven weeks from 1 May casualties were low – only forty-three of whom nine died. Sickness, however, was very high between April and August. This was largely due to an epidemic of influenza, which was brought under control during three weeks in reserve at Guignemicourt, near Amiens, from 22 June. This 'holiday' was notable for hard physical training as well as compulsory sports under the temporary command of Major Pargiter of the 22nd Londons, known as an enthusiast for sport as well as for work. The weather was warm and photographs taken here reveal a youthful looking battalion clad in shorts fashioned from trousers cut off at the knee. On 11 July a memorial service was held for civil servants who had fallen in the war. It was at the same hour as a similar service in Westminster Abbey attended by the King and Queen. Nearly half the battalion attended the voluntary ceremony in France – an indication that its members, though predominantly new men, still considered it the 'Civil Service' regiment.

The Great Advance

Around the beginning of August, there were signs of a major shift in the military situation. News had already arrived of encouraging early successes in the French offensive in the Champagne. On 2 August loud explosions around Albert suggested the Germans were withdrawing. There were other tell-tale signs, such as inspections of equipment and issue of extra ammunition. It was thus no great surprise when, on 8 August, there was distant thunder of guns from the south heralding a new British offensive. This was the opening of the last campaign of the war – the victorious 'hundred days'.

The battalion was not immediately involved, but on 12 August was warned to move at short notice. Other divisions of Fourth Army had made rapid advances between the Ancre and Somme

Track at western edge of Bois des Tailles, near Bray-sur-Somme. The battalion assembled here early on 22 August and, scattered around in shell holes, waited all day for the order to advance.

rivers and on 13 August, 47th Division moved up to take over some captured ground in this area. The battalion went into support positions in the old British and German front lines west of Morlancourt. Robert Angel recalled the journey:

> Plenty of signs of fierce fighting and many dead were still lying unburied. The ground was pitted with shell holes and tangled messes of barbed wire lay everywhere...During a halt we buried several men of the Post Office Rifles including a fine looking sergeant. Limber drivers had a lot of difficulty in getting their pairs past the many dead horses particularly in one place where a complete gun team had been annihilated.

At night on 16 August, they moved to the recently captured front line in the Bois des Tailles, west of Bray-sur-Somme. Colonel Segrave had left to command a brigade and Major Bates temporarily commanded the battalion. Bois des Tailles was an eerie place, with shattered trees and abandoned dugouts. No place to linger, it was dubbed 'Toute de suite' wood. The battalion spent five unpleasant days under more or less constant bombardment, working hard to consolidate the captured ground. On three successive nights patrols went out to establish advance posts, which then had to be fortified. Much digging was carried out under hazardous conditions. Casualties were sixty-five, including fourteen killed and eight missing. It was a shocking initiation into warfare for the youngsters who had arrived in the spring. The battalion then had one day in support positions near Méricourt l'Abbé on the Ancre before moving forward again. Bertie Fereday confided in a letter to his Sunday school teacher some details about the action in the Bois des Tailles which he had felt unable to reveal in a cheery letter to his mother the same day:

537441 A H (Bertie) Fereday, Inland Revenue. Killed in action 22 August 1918. One day earlier he wrote 'If only everyone knew of horrors of this war it wouldn't last another five minutes. But until it's over we have got to 'stick it'...I hope I do my best'. He was 18 years old.

Anthony Fereday

> I have had such a horrible shaking and have not quite got over it...I was digging a communication trench near the front line when Fritz got wind of it. For three hours he shelled us with very heavy stuff 5.9s etc, HE and gas. It was impossible for us to go back to our dugouts...Unfortunately there were one or two direct hits which killed two of our boys and wounded several – one of them, Cansick, was a chum of mine; he was killed. After some time a dug out was found and with some difficulty a few of us left behind managed to get the wounded in safely. I found that while my mind was occupied with work of bandaging up the chaps I was in charge of I seemed to forget the danger and scarcely noticed the hostile shells. It was hell!

Fereday had applied for a commission in the Royal Air Force but the Inland Revenue had held up his papers, and now it was too late. He was killed the day after writing this letter. At Méricourt the battalion was joined by its new commanding officer, Lieutenant Colonel R C Feilding of the Coldstream Guards (and late of the 6th Connaught Rangers which had been virtually destroyed in the March Retreat). With little time for introductions, he led them straight into the resumed Fourth Army offensive, subsequently named the Battle of Albert.

'At it, hammer and tongs'

The CSR moved forward early on 22 August, passing debris of the recent battle, to a sunken road along the western edge of the Bois des Tailles. Scattered around in old trenches and shell holes, the battalion waited in reserve until called forward. The battle was already under way, throwing up clouds of dust and smoke ahead. As usual, three successive objectives were prescribed. The battalion's job was to wait until the third objective had been captured by the forward battalions of 47th Division, supported by cavalry and tanks, then go forward to consolidate it. The third objective was a 'blue line' of defences more than four miles to the east, beyond the misnamed Happy Valley (east of the Bray-Albert road), in the area of Bronfay Farm. The enemy resisted more strongly than expected, and the battalion spent the day waiting for news and preparing for a likely German counter-attack. It was hot and the men spent the time playing cards, writing letters and sleeping.

In the evening fresh orders were received, then cancelled. The enemy had forced a withdrawal from the second of the three objectives and had reoccupied Happy Valley. The situation became threatening and eventually the battalion was ordered forward to fill a gap on 47th Division's right front, east of the Etinehem-Méaulte road. Here they took cover in shelters cut into the side of a low bank. There was a good deal of shelling and machine-gun fire and the enemy was believed to be breaking through. The men stood to till daylight, but the enemy did not come on.

The following day was spent in the same positions, under shelling which Colonel Feilding considered 'more noisy than harmful'. In the evening fresh orders were received. There would be an attack the next morning to retake the second objective of 22 August. The battalion, led by Major Bates, was to follow behind the attackers and 'mop up' Happy Valley, clearing any remaining German gunners from the dug-outs. They moved off soon after 0100 on 24 August. Robert Angel recalled:

> Around midnight a terrific barrage opened up. We lay in our shelter shivering with a mixture of excitement and fright until we were called outside and formed up into small parties. The parties moved forward and down the slight slope into Happy Valley ... In the darkness it was difficult to see what we were doing. Sergeant 'Buster' Brown...hurled a grenade down a gaping hole but hearing it strike, yelled a warning. We flung ourselves flat before it exploded and found that the supposed dugout was no more than a shallow pit. There were many German wounded and we rounded

Lt Col R C Feilding DSO (Coldstream Guards), another inspirational leader. He took command in August and led the CSR on the advance to victory. 'I am with a splendid crowd', he wrote. 'They are like little lions, these London men'.

Caroline Gordon-Duff

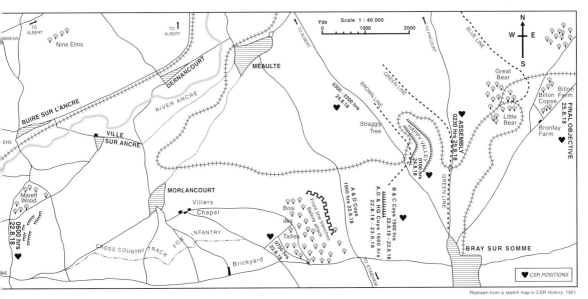

Redrawn from a sketch map in CSR *History*, 1921

up several prisoners during our apparently aimless wanderings. As it got lighter we could see the whole valley, the sides honeycombed with shelters and the wide bottom full of debris of battle, corpses, dead horses, abandoned machine guns and overturned wagons.

The earlier attack had gone well and the mopping up was fairly straightforward. The enemy dead and wounded appeared to be recently arrived, as they had clean clothes and shiny equipment. By this stage of the war, German medical supplies were very poor. Robert Angel found a first aid pouch containing bandages apparently made of crêpe paper. About 300 prisoners were rounded up and arrived at Colonel Feilding's headquarters, 'chattering like monkeys'. As soon as it grew light, the battalion moved to the Bray-Albert road and dug pits along the verge, as shelter from heavy and constant shelling. The overall situation was rather confused. Counter-attacks were expected but did not materialize. Robert Angel was on stretcher-bearing duties:

> *I came across Eland sitting on the ground with a wound in the knee and carried him on my shoulders back to the road where we collapsed into a pit for shelter and a rest. I dressed his wound which*

The misnamed 'Happy Valley', just east of the Bray-Albert road. In August 1918 it was strongly held by the Germans. The CSR advanced on the 24th, behind the successful attack of 175 Brigade, with the job of 'mopping up'. They took 300 prisoners and a considerable number of machine-guns and trench mortars.

was not serious and he was able to hobble with my assistance back to the Aid Post. ...I returned and found the company in a railway cutting. There were dead lying there, mostly Germans, and I shared a hole with one of them during some shelling.

Angel then found his CSM, Christy Ibbett, with a slight shoulder wound. Having dressed it, he sent the sergeant back to get an anti-tetanus injection. Shortly afterwards, Ibbett returned, 'explaining that they were very busy at the aid post and he couldn't be bothered to wait'.[9]

After dusk the Battalion moved back through Happy Valley, in preparation for another action the following morning (25 August). This time the CSR would be attacking, on the right of 140 Brigade, over the Blue Line (the third objective of 22 August) and on to the vicinity of Bronfay Farm. At 0230 the CSR assembled along the Bray-Fricourt road, where lay many recently killed soldiers, British and German. The men were desperately tired, but bucked up when the cooks arrived with food and rum. The barrage started and they moved forward with what Colonel Feilding had already come to recognize as 'their usual goodwill'. They met only light opposition and it was thick fog, rather than the enemy, which prevented them from going straight to the objective. Eventually the farm was located and the correct trench was held as a new front line. Stretcher-bearers spent the morning ferrying the wounded to an aid post in Happy Valley. Their orders allowed them to evacuate seriously wounded men only after the objective had been reached. Until then they could dress their wounds, but had to leave the men on the ground. When the battalion was relieved during the night, spirits were fairly high. The fighting, though drawn out, had not been hard and casualties comparatively light, at about thirty-five. Feilding recorded that most were due to the British barrage. By this stage in the war the accuracy of barrages had been perfected. However, there were occasional 'accidents' as Feilding explained:

530032 Sgt W H Moore, Board of Education. Signalling Sgt and one of the few remaining 17th March men, he was killed early on 1 September 1918. Col Feilding described in a letter to his wife how a shell crashed down outside his dugout, killing and wounding several including Moore and the 17th Londons' American medical officer .

It is surprising how calmly such accidents have come to be regarded, even by the infantry who are the sufferers. ...The infantry commander has often to resist a strong temptation to complain of too close shooting for fear that, next time, the artillery-man in his anxiety to avoid accidents may lift his guns too much. It is generally better to risk a few casualties from our own fire than that the artillery should shoot too much for safety.

There followed three nights' rest around Marett Wood. Colonel Feilding had been on his feet almost continuously for four days and nights. He now found time to write to his wife about his new battalion:

We have been at it, hammer and tongs, the last few days... Things have gone well...We are killing a lot of Germans...[and] capturing large numbers of prisoners. I am with a splendid crowd. They are like little lions – these London men.[10]

136

Major Desmond Young, recently arrived as second in command, got a rather different reaction from Merton, his groom. Merton, like Young, was from the 60th Rifles and had not previously come across the phenomenon of educated territorial soldiers:

> 'How are you getting on, Merton?' I asked, soon after we joined. 'I can't say as how Currie and I are as happy as we was in the old battalion, sir,' he said. 'This mob's all bloody **gentlemen**.'[11]

'At it hell for leather, without rest'

On 29 August the CSR went forward again via the Carnoy craters, north of the Albert-Péronne road, and thence to Maurepas Ravine on the 30th. Once more the battalion was on its old Somme battlefield of 1916, prompting the retelling of disturbing stories of carnage in High Wood. This time however there was something different in the air, which Desmond Young claimed to have recognized even then as 'the smell of victory'. The old static warfare gave way to a continuous advance, slowly but steadily pushing the Germans eastwards. There were no organized reliefs; brigades passed through each other as the front was rolled forward in a constantly moving battle. This new method of fighting posed logistical problems to which the cooks rose with distinction, following in the battalion's wake and serving hot meals after each day's action.

Two nights and a day were spent in Maurepas Ravine, resting in musty huts abandoned by the Germans. Orders were received for an attack on 1 September, when 140 and 141 Brigades were to advance and take part in the capture of the village of Rancourt and a line of trench along the south-western edge of St Pierre Vaast Wood. At 0530, after a short artillery bombardment, the battalion moved forward from the Combles road running south-west of Rancourt. Again, stretcher-bearers followed behind and soon came across casualties. Robert Angel:

> There were several dead including men from the company forming the first wave in front of us. I found one of our runners, Hockridge, lying with no visible mark of injury...Hughes the sanitary man was dead with a shell wound in the chest and as I couldn't find his identity discs I wrote his name on a slip of paper so that his grave might not be unnamed if he ever got one. Burrowes an old school friend and a member of A13 Platoon [LRB] was another killed in this action.

533617 Pte W N Edwards pictured as a student after the war. He enlisted in the CSR straight from school in 1916. Received his second 'Blighty' wound during the costly advance on 2 September 1918.

Eleanor Edwards

The advance was successful and by 0730 all objectives had been reached. The battalion captured nearly 200 prisoners, ten machine-guns, and a motor ambulance complete with two drivers who were immediately pressed into service. Casualties were few but included

Lieutenant E R Lascelles commanding C Company and Second Lieutenant R L Kirk, a South African, whose first day in action in France it was. The day was spent consolidating the gains, during which the Germans continued heavy shelling and attempted to rush through a gap which had opened on the right. At night the battalion was relieved and marched along the Péronne road to the ruins of Bouchavesnes, where the cooks served a hot meal. The following morning there was an ambitious, complex and costly operation.

Moislains: 'Like a lot of boys going to a football match'

On 2 September, the 47th Division was to play a subsidiary role to the 74th Division, which was to make an extensive attack on two villages. The first was Moislains, which lay in the wide valley through which ran the Canal du Nord, and the second was Nurlu on the higher ground along which ran the Péronne-Cambrai road. The 47th Division was to follow closely behind. After Moislains had been captured and consolidated, the CSR would pass to the south of the village, cross the canal, then wheel left to form a defensive flank on the higher ground. Here they would join up with 142 Brigade which was to capture this trench. This ambitious scheme went horribly wrong.

Major Young and Colonel Feilding led the battalion forward in two waves. Immediately they drew artillery and machine-gun fire, which grew heavier and more concentrated as they moved down the valley to the south-west of Moislains. Half the battalion went down, wounded or killed. With great discipline, the remainder pressed on. Colonel Feilding later described it to his wife in horrifying detail:

> Most of the men are very young – in fact, quite boys. They wear khaki shorts with grey hose-tops turned down over their puttees. On their sleeves they have canary yellow hearts as a distinguishing badge. ...Almost immediately the enemy opened with a heavy artillery barrage...soon supplemented with machine-gun fire. In all directions among the advancing battalion the shells started to burst and the casualties very soon began to accumulate. Knox, the American doctor, opened an aid-post in an open trench...where he dressed the wounded throughout the day under shell-fire. The battalion continued its advance. The machine-gun fire grew heavier and heavier. It came from the front and from both flanks. With their khaki 'shorts' showing about 4 inches of bare knee the men went forward, looking, as Desmond Young said, like a lot of boys going to a football match. The runners pushed their bicycles.

This was not the new mobile warfare for which the intensive training had prepared them. The battle plan had failed and the battalion was walking into a death trap. Still they continued:

> It was a truly wonderful sight: – each man with his shoulders

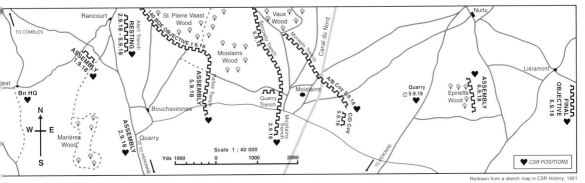

Redrawn from a sketch map in CSR *History,* 1921

squared to the objective, walking with bayonet fixed, apparently unconcerned, through the deadly fire; many dropping; the remainder carrying on; needing no pushing or exhorting; each individual acting as a host in himself. The stretcher-bearers went about coolly, at the walk, from one wounded man to another. I remember one stretcher-bearer in particular – a boy of about nineteen, who was wounded later in the day – and who was really admirable in his utter sang-froid and disregard of self.

The last hundred-yard lap was the worst, and had it not been that the ground was pitted with shell-holes, not one of us could have got across it alive. Towards the end two men fell beside me – not more than a couple of feet away, – one so badly wounded that he died almost immediately. Then we reached the trench.[12]

The trench that the remnants managed to occupy was Moislains Trench, immediately west of and overlooking the village. Other troops of 140 Brigade and some yeomanry had also reached it. Here the horrible truth dawned: the 74th Division had not yet reached Moislains. Germans could be seen in the village and were occupying sections of the same trench to the left and another trench to the left rear. The party held out in Moislains trench all day, beating off attempted counter-attacks from front and rear. It was, according to the divisional history, some of the hardest fighting during the whole advance. Robert Angel described the scene:

The trench was almost obliterated at one point and any observed movement brought instant attention from the watchful machine gunners opposite. There were many dead in the trench, both our own and German. At one point five of our signallers were lying together...It was a place to be avoided and I passed it several times during the day with increasing apprehension. Where the trench deepened we were able to walk upright for a few yards and it was at one of these points that there was a sharp crack of an explosion overhead and England cried out that he was hit.

England, Angel's fellow stretcher-bearer, was now out of the fight.[13] Angel later teamed up with some RAMC men. Together, they tried to move in the open:

We started off and packing up our first customer stood up boldly plus [Red Cross] flag to make our return. The Germans weren't having this and we got such a hail of fire that we promptly went to earth again. In fairness to them, they probably fired as soon as they saw a target without waiting to examine it too closely. Anyway, heroics were out and we tried it the hard way, crawling and dragging the stretcher with us. As...visibility grew less, it was possible to move more freely and everybody who was not otherwise engaged helped to find and bring in the wounded.

Five days later, after this ground had been fully captured, Colonel Feilding examined the battlefield with its lines of dead and established that when the battalion advanced on 2 September, the 74th Division had been *behind* from the start. His description of the dreadful consequences of this error is suffused with admiration for 'these most wonderful men' of the CSR.

Ever onward – Nurlu and Liéramont

On 3 and 4 September the depleted battalion rested in trenches near Rancourt and was reorganized into two companies. Meanwhile the Australians were making progress further south, against Mont St Quentin. There was little activity in the immediate vicinity and at night on 3 September the Germans finally withdrew from Moislains. On 5 September the 47th Division resumed its advance. 142 Brigade held the line of the canal east of the village and 141 Brigade started advancing through this line eastwards towards the Nurlu ridge (which the 74th Division had failed to reach on 2 September). Meanwhile the CSR assembled south-west of Moislains Wood in Pallas Trench, which was full of dead horses plus an abandoned German field battery and two dead gunners. Later the battalion moved forward to Sorrowitz Trench (a continuation of Moislains Trench, where the CSR had held out on 2 September) and waited until needed, being shelled at intervals.

When the call came, A/B Company under Lieutenant Upton and C/D Company under Captain Eccles crossed the canal and took up positions on the far bank. 141 Brigade had met considerable opposition during the day from an enemy post in a huge quarry west of the Péronne-Nurlu road, and from the road and woods beyond. So at 1900 hours the attack was renewed under a barrage. The CSR's role was to protect the right flank. This attack, during a violent thunderstorm, was entirely successful. The battalion resumed the advance at 0800 next morning (6 September). The objective was a north-south line just east of the village of Liéramont. The advance was through thick woods, but was made smoothly. The battalion advanced slightly too far, over a crest and into the view of the enemy who promptly opened rapid fire. From 300 yards away, Colonel Feilding observed:

> *The Battalion, under Captain Eccles, turned and walked some 50 yards back over the crest, and as it reached the reverse slope each man again turned to face the enemy. ...I watched the movement, and the coolness and deliberation with which it was carried out was admirable.[14]*

This was the CSR's furthest point east in this advance. It was barely four miles from the point, between Metz and Fins, from which the battalion had started the Retreat six months earlier.

'A pitiful trail of dead boys'

During the night of 6 September, the battalion was relieved and moved back to bivouacs about a mile east of Moislains, close to the spot occupied during the fighting forty-eight hours earlier. The feelings of satisfaction at having gained so much ground – and the growing realization that an Allied victory was in sight – were mixed with melancholy. As Desmond Young wrote nearly forty years later, they had pushed ahead, leaving 'a pitiful trail of dead boys behind'. Rowland Feilding made a point of inspecting the slope behind Moislains Trench, taking with him the chaplain and some pioneers:

> *We retraced the last lap of the attack ...[on 2 September]. That last exposed slope was a sorry sight. There were our Lewis guns, many of them still mounted and pointed towards the enemy positions – the gunners beside them. The dead lay thick, their packs opened and the contents scattered; their letters and little souvenirs they had carried, thrown out by the ghouls of the battlefield, littered the ground beside them. Beside one boy lay a black earthenware cat, his mascot, which had not saved him. We had certainly paid heavily for this little scrap of trench.*
>
> *We buried an officer and twenty-four men of the Civil Service Rifles there and then, and many others of the Brigade were still left lying. There was no time for anything elaborate, so the poor bodies with their blackened faces were just lifted into shell-holes or into the trench, one or two or three or four together, and earth was put over them. Then a rifle, with bayonet fixed, was stuck into the ground, butt uppermost, to mark each grave...After Farebrother had read the burial service, we left them, and the same afternoon reached the Ancre, in which we bathed.[15]*

Vis-en-Artois Memorial, which bears the name of over 9,000 men who fell in the 'advance to victory' from 8 August 1918. Panel 10 has names of 23 CSR men.

141

The casualties in the advance from 22 August onwards were 389. All the dead were reported as buried but about a third now have no known graves and are commemorated on the Vis-en-Artois Memorial. Earlier, Colonel Feilding had commented to his wife:

> *The standard of courage among these London lads is so high that men who would be considered brave elsewhere do not seem particularly brave here. In fact, they would look like shivering rabbits beside some of them.*[16]

Feilding, too, had made a good impression on the battalion, though admiration was tinged with a certain wariness. Robert Angel explained afterwards:

> [Feilding] *was an elderly man to be fighting as an infantry commander...only recently arrived and already the object of wary admiration. Wary, because his silver white hair and strong dislike for wearing a tin hat made a conspicuous target of him and his runners. In his...book...he comments on the dash and nonchalance of his [CSR] runner on an occasion when they were crossing open ground under fire and the difficulty he had in keeping up with him. It never occurred to the dear man that the runner was putting as much distance between himself and the Colonel as decency would allow.*

Feilding made clear his appreciation of the battalion at the time, but

The brass band which joined the CSR from the 6th Londons in February 1918. Under Sgt Blackmore it became a highly successful and popular institution, adding a touch of class to parades, marches and other regimental occasions. It is pictured here with Lt Col Segrave and Capt Davenport, Guignemicourt, July 1918.

when his letters were published in 1929 the veterans were touched by the extent of his praise. His generous comments had not been written for publication or for any ulterior motive, unlike the more familiar compliments along the lines of 'the men are splendid', which had initially impressed but later lost currency. The 1st Battalion was fortunate to be led by three successive Regular commanding officers who understood the peculiar nature of the educated territorials and appreciated their qualities.

'Abide with Me'

On 7 September, the depleted battalion left the vicinity of Moislains and went north to Auchel, via Heilly and Chocques. The contrast with the devastated Somme area was marked and gradually spirits were restored. A pleasant three weeks were spent enjoying football matches and concert parties. Robert Angel recalled:

> At Auchel....ceremonial guard mounting and a certain amount of 'bull' was the order of the day. There was even an attempt to get webbing equipment a uniform colour by the use of a concoction invented by the RSM which was basically mud. But nobody minded all this.

Awards for the Advance were made, including the Military Medal to Robert Angel and Christy Ibbett. Angel's description of the ceremony suggests that morale was improving:

> My party was commanded by CSM Levey, the senior warrant officer present and a noted humorist, who for want of a proper

collective noun, addressed us by the cautionary word 'Heroes!' before calling us to attention, the command being delivered in tones loud enough to reduce us to laughter but not so loud as to reach the ears of the hierarchy.

Out of the line, the band played at ceremonial guard-mounting. Len Pearson was sufficiently impressed to describe it in a letter home:

Have I ever told you of the posh changing guards we have... every night. ...At first the band plays on the parade ground and then at the end of the piece the RSM gives the 'Fall in' whereupon the whole guards and picket take up their respective places on the ground. After the inspection...the whole stand to attention while Retreat is played. Then the band plays a slow march and marches slowly past the whole lot and then turns and marches back to a quick march. After that they play the hymn 'Abide with Me' and then follows '[God Bless] the Prince of Wales' and the guards etc are marched to their various duties. It's a Guards stunt at Windsor, so they say, but at all events it's jolly fine I can tell you.

Rowland Feilding told his wife how *Abide with Me* always brought a lump to his throat. Nearly sixty years later, Robert Angel was still affected by it:

Banal as this has now become, I rarely hear it without remembering a young soldier standing at the cottage door in Chocques grieving for his lost friends.

Of the ninety-five LRB men who had arrived with Angel in April, one in five were now dead. The CSR had no more big losses in action - only fourteen more casualties in France and only one of those killed. On 3 October, after plans to send it to Italy were shelved, 47th Division advanced through country devastated by the retreating enemy towards Lille. The CSR did not play an active role. Instead, it had a fairly quiet time in support and reserve trenches at Le Maisnil and Fromelles, before marching in stages westwards to Norrent-Fontes, west of Lillers, for ten days training. By then the Germans had withdrawn from Lille and 47th Division was chosen for the victory parade.

Triumphal march through Lille: 28 October

On 26 October the CSR travelled to the western outskirts of Lille. Their arrival caused a spontaneous victory celebration, described by Rowland Feilding:

As we reached the suburbs our band struck up the 'Marseillaise' ...a happy inspiration, and I shall never forget the scene which it provoked. The people came running from their houses – old and young, men, women, and children – carrying lamps and candles. They followed our battalion, clapping and cheering. It was the first time for

144

Official entry into Lille, 28 October 1918. The CSR marched through cheering crowds, led by Col Feilding on a white charger, the band playing Sambre et Meuse *and the* Marseillaise.
IWM (Q9623)

over four years that they had heard troops marching to that tune.[17]

The official triumphal march took place two days later in glorious sunshine. Desmond Young described the march past the line of dignitaries in the Grande Place:

> 'Honour and glory to the 47th Division, our deliverers', said the red, white and blue posters on the walls. The cheering crowds were greatly impressed by Colonel Feilding, mounted on a sixteen-hand white charger...The Civil Service Rifles looked particularly smart, for though we had had no time to paint all their 'tin hats', we managed to paint the right and left sides respectively of those worn by the outside files.[18]

Robert Angel recalled it was difficult to keep in formation, as people rushed forward to thrust flags into hands and equipment. Next day all ranks were allowed to visit the city. After exploring the eastern gate where Royal Engineers were already constructing a bridge across a huge crater blown by the retreating Germans, Angel found a café which looked promising:

> We were utterly confounded by the waitress who enquired 'What's yours?'...We had some very weak tea and a few sticky cakes which cost all of a week's pay but it was worth it for the joy of having it in china cups and poured from a pot instead of ladled from a dixie.

Chasing the Germans across the Scheldt

There remained one further piece of action – to press on to Belgium, where the Germans still occupied Tournai. On 1 November the battalion went into the front line just outside Tournai, among the handsome châteaux and convents of Froyennes, on the western bank of the River Scheldt. This area had been in German hands since the beginning of the war. There were no trenches. The front line consisted of outposts in streets, houses and back gardens of a prosperous suburb still occupied by civilians. It was so unlike the previous four years fighting that Rowland Feilding dubbed it 'opéra bouffe warfare'. It was not all comedy, however. The enemy was still shelling heavily and during five days the battalion had ten casualties including one man – the last – killed. By the time the Germans had finally retreated from Tournai, the battalion had been relieved and moved westwards to Cornet where a bright spark opened a sweepstake on the hour when hostilities would cease. On 10 November the battalion crossed the Scheldt with orders to follow the retreating enemy behind a screen of cavalry. This was an exciting prospect, coupled with hopes of seeing Brussels. But the armistice supervened. The news reached the CSR on the road, as they marched back to Tournai.

Recollections differ as to the precisely how news of the armistice was communicated. But all agree on the manner in which it was received. The full realization did not immediately register. There was a general sense of anti-climax. Then the band struck up a familiar hymn tune to which the following words were sung:

> *When this ruddy war is over,*
> *Oh! how happy I shall be!*

After recovering from gas poisoning, Henry Moore was a PT instructor in England. After the armistice he rejoined the battalion at Ferfay and was billeted with Madame Caron. The young artist, having earlier sketched in the trenches, now turned to lighter subjects. This drawing of January 1919 depicts Moore's monoglot billet mate struggling to explain his urgent need for hot water to shave in. 'To watch Madame and Allen parleying makes me spit blood with laughter', wrote Moore.
Henry Moore Foundation/Wakefield MDC Museums & Arts

FERFAY THEATRE.

Pack Up!

A topical and highly successful revue, produced in January 1919 by Major Desmond Young and featuring the daughter of the Mayor of Ferfay.

1. Quoted in Martin Middlebrook, *The Kaiser's Battle*, Penguin Books (1983), p 162.
2. Alan H Maude, *The History of the 47th (London) Division 1914-1919*, Amalgamated Press (1922), p 154
3. Maude, *op cit*, p 158.
4. *ibid*, p 155
5. *ibid*, p 162
6. Quoted in Lyn Macdonald, *To the Last Man, Spring 1918*, Viking (1998), p 213.
7. *Stand To!*, The Journal of the WFA, Spring 1988, No.22
8. John Lee, 'Some lessons of the Somme: the British infantry in 1917' in Bond et al *Look to Your Front*, Spellmount, 1999
9. Angel's memoir calls this man 'Ibbetson' but no such man can be traced. It is more likely to be 530209 Christy Ibbett, then acting CSM of Angel's company.
10. Rowland Feilding, *War Letters to a Wife*, Medici, 1929, p 290
11. Desmond Young, *Try Anything Twice*, Hamish Hamilton, 1963, p 112
12. Feilding, *op cit*, pp 305-6. Soldiers in 47th Division wore as a sleeve emblem one of the suits of playing cards, those of the 140 Brigade having yellow and the other two brigades having green and red. The CSR emblem was a yellow heart.
13. 548040 Pte EWH England, DOW 4 September 1918. One of the LRB draft accepted into the CSR on 9 April.
14. Feilding, *op cit*, p 309
15. *ibid*, p 311
16. *ibid*, p 291
17. *ibid*, p 332
18. Young, *op cit*, p 114-5

Chapter Seven

Formation, Training, Ireland and France

We've been to Dorking, Watford, Ware,
Old Saffron Walden, we've been there,
One of these days, so please the Lord,
If we're in luck, we'll go abroad.

(Chorus popular in 2nd Battalion, 1916)

'**M**y Battalion was called the Cook's Tourists because of our many travels'. Thus did a civil servant, William Tibbs, inscribe the flyleaf of his copy of the CSR *History* when it was published in 1921. The 2nd Battalion, to which this apt but ironic nickname was applied, eventually served in Ireland, France, Salonika, Egypt, Palestine and Flanders. But for nearly two years it was kept in England and its members worried that they would not get even as far as France.

In August 1914 the rush of former members and new recruits quickly filled up the gaps in the regiment's ranks. A waiting list was opened in the expectation – soon fulfilled – that territorial units would be authorized to raise second battalions. The original CSR thus became the 1st Battalion, or 1/15th Battalion, London Regiment. The 2nd Battalion (or 2/15th) opened its doors at Somerset House in early September. With second-line units of other London territorial battalions, it formed part of 2nd London (Reserve) Division, later renamed 60th Division.

Inevitably the 1st Battalion took priority for allocation of instructors, equipment and even uniforms. The new battalion had a higher proportion of newly enlisted men. In the early days they had a somewhat eccentric appearance, parading in a mixture of 'civvies' and uniform, with a few old rifles shouldered by different men in turns. Two

Four senior civil servants who prepared the battalion for war: E F Strange (Victoria & Albert Museum), R G Hayes (Admiralty), W T Kirkby (Supreme Court Pay Office) and A A Oliver (Inland Revenue). Oliver went overseas as second in command.

newly commissioned subalterns were gazetted to the 2nd Battalion on its formation: Kenneth Wills, aged eighteen and recently passed out from his school officer training corps, and Kenneth Pickthorn, a twenty-two year-old Cambridge don. Both were received frostily by the commanding officer, Lieutenant Colonel Hayes, late of the 1st Battalion. This senior Admiralty official had hoped to maintain his pre-war practice of choosing officers from within the regiment. Wills recalled:

> *On the morning of September 1st, terribly excited and flushed with pride, I got up early and took a bus up the Strand to Somerset House. On walking through the gates of this huge grim building with sentries posted at each entrance I caught my first glimpse of the men with whom I was to serve. Men in civilian clothes being vigorously drilled in small squads by uniformed NCOs, with here and there a uniformed officer supervising. ...I can still feel the sense of pride with which I administered the oath to my first recruits. The squads on the square soon gave place to the formation of companies and these drilled as such and were occasionally marched out to Hyde Park or elsewhere. We had as yet no uniforms, arms or equipment. Still the enthusiasm of those times was wonderful – bowler-hatted clerk rubbed shoulders with the cloth-capped tradesboy and forgot class in his effort to drill more correctly than his new friends*

As Wills' description suggests, the new battalion was more socially mixed than the pre-war regiment. Men enlisted who in peacetime would have been unlikely candidates to join the CSR or indeed any territorial unit. For example there was a group from the East End of London, including a stevedore named Ben Dyer who was soon promoted to sergeant and played an influential role in D Company throughout the war. The admission of 'cloth-capped' members into its 2nd Battalion did not, however, diminish the regiment's image as a 'class' corps. Among new recruits of the bowler-hatted variety was Llewelyn Edwards from the Board of Trade, who joined in preference to 'the ordinary Kitchener's army'.[1] Similar sentiments motivated Edgar Powell, a City clerk:

> *An official in the Staff Department* [at the bank] *asked me what I intended to join. 'The Territorials' I told him. I knew that... Kitchener's Army was already being recruited, but we considered them a non-descript crew. In our view the Territorials had more 'class'...I was somewhat taken aback when I read that I agreed to pay 2 guineas to join and a guinea a year afterwards, but the recruiting sergeant assured us that...the subscription would not now be claimed.*

The Colonel rides upon an 'orse
And doesn't care a [bit] of course
While we poor [blighters] carry packs
Which nearly break our [blooming] backs.
CHORUS: Oh! We're so happy, etc

The Colonel said 'I do believe
You men would all like six months leave'.
Said we, 'Oh no, no [blooming] fear
We're far too [jolly] happy here'.
CHORUS: Yes, we're so happy here, etc

Chorus popular at with CSR in early 1915. More colourful words were substituted for the ones in square brackets, though not in the hearing of Colonel Hayes.

CSR recruits marching up Aldwych, September 1914, on their way to practise manoeuvres in Regents Park. Note the mixture of cloth caps and boaters: the 2nd Battalion was more socially mixed that the 1st. IWM (Dept of Docs, S Pounds 76/146/1)

The 1st Battalion had insufficient volunteers for foreign service. From its earliest days, the 2nd Battalion ranks were combed for fit 'foreign service' men who could be transferred. Lord Arran selected two hundred and fifty in September and in return the 2nd Battalion received the 'home service' detachment and some under-age boys.[2] The 'home service' men were resented in the 2nd Battalion as they had been in the 1st, not only because of their disinclination to serve overseas but also because, being older and more experienced, they gained fast promotion. This reaction by the 'rookies' of the 2nd Battalion suggests that, even early on, it was taking a pride in itself as an active service unit. It was, as Wills put it, 'developing a soul of its own, distinct from that of its mother, the regiment'. Charles Hennessey of the Post Office Savings Bank recalled how recruits had struck up friendships while waiting in the enlistment queue, then asked to serve in the same company. The early comradeship is evident from his description of the first march:

> We had not as yet been issued with uniforms, and, in the varied display of straw hats, bowlers, caps, and clothing of assorted colours and styles, it was difficult to regard ourselves as real soldiers. But in spite of this, we felt proud when we sallied forth

from Somerset House on our first route march, to Regents Park. And as we stepped gaily out, the air rang with the new Battalion's rendering of its first marching song, 'We are the London Boys'.

But the pride was mixed with impatience. Those keen to get abroad realized that their best chance lay in getting drafted to the 1st Battalion or in being commissioned in a different regiment. Many left by both routes during the next eighteen months.

Training in England

After a short period at White City in Shepherd's Bush, the 2nd Battalion moved in the new year to the Dorking area, where it was billeted with the rest of the division. More serious training began. Equipment gradually arrived, including Japanese rifles, raising hopes of overseas service. In February, Colonel Hayes took the battalion on a recruiting drive in London. Intent on attracting at least 300 suitable men, he concentrated on offices in Whitehall, the City and West End.

The 1st Battalion went to France in March 1915 and the 2nd Battalion took its place in the Watford area. Colonel Hayes left to command the 3rd Battalion, formed as a reinforcement unit. When Charles Jones, a young school teacher, joined at Watford he found the battalion still 'seething with discontent' at the 'home service' men who were thought to be holding back their chances of going to war. Hayes' successor was another longstanding CSR personality, Lieutenant

Members of D Coy posing with new Japanese rifles outside their billet near Dorking, early 1915. Standing: Ptes Boyd, Bernard, Cpl Dodd, Ptes Beech, Beer. Seated: Ptes Berry, Batstone, Bastow.

Pay parade at Somerset House after a recruiting march, February 1915. Pay was one shilling a day, hence the very small piles of silver on the table. Guarding the cash is a sentry with a newly-issued Japanese small calibre rifle and sword-hilted bayonet. The paying officer is Capt F Tarver (Bank of England). 2/Lt Wills (later OC C Coy) stands behind. Sheila Parish

Colonel E F Strange, assistant keeper at the Victoria & Albert Museum. Strange immediately set an example by volunteering for overseas service himself. He urged his officers to do the same and left them to tackle their men on the subject. More volunteers came forward though, as in the 1st Battalion, the number varied according to the strength of each officer's appeal.

Colonel Strange was known as a disciplinarian of forceful character. He intensified the training, supported by RSM Freemantle, an immaculate Guardsman with a waxed moustache whose forté was parade-ground drill. Specialist schools taught bombing, sniping and

C Coy group enjoying themselves at Saffron Walden, June 1915. This photograph was made into a postcard with the caption 'Undress Uniform'.

Lt Col E F Strange commanded the Battalion from May 1915 until just before departure to France. An efficient soldier and strict disciplinarian, he welded the new unit into a fighting force. In civilian life he was an authority on Japanese art.

From a photograph taken in 1910

bayonet fighting. Strange was a skilled and efficient trainer. He drove officers and men equally hard and was respected by both. The men hated the 'silly game of spit and polish' but, according to Jones, took a perverse pride in their ability to play it. General satisfaction grew at being turned into 'something resembling real soldiers. We felt that we belonged to the army, not Kitchener's army, but the real army'.

In early June the battalion moved to Saffron Walden. Contradictory rumours, together with periodic departures of the fittest and smartest to France, sapped morale as well as numbers. A feeling grew that the 2nd Battalion might never go overseas. There was thus much relief in the summer when 'home service' and medically unfit men were finally despatched to other units. The resulting gaps, especially among NCOs, were filled by newly-trained, enthusiastic 'foreign service' men. At last, the 2nd Battalion was turning into what Wills called 'a piece of

Sergeants Mess 1916. Of 48 sergeants who went overseas in June 1916, half were pre-war men, 15 were civil servants, 12 were commissioned and 7 were killed. Top: WR Carr, BCL Edwards, AJ Crawford, CJ Quinton, F Lord, EC Frost, HL Pearce, WC Charlton. 2nd row: AEM Pratt, DA Murray, CGO Cross, F King, P Postle, JB Mount, JT Harris, EHT Rowles, Barratt. 3rd row: HC Tubb, BC Dyer, JC McNeill, JC Bowstead, BA Pratt, D Levy, A Silverstone, GF Denton, SAG Nowell, EA Etheridge, WS Pitkin, FH Wagstaff. 4th row: W Bailey, JS Pearce, EJ Stephenson, S Staines, J Wigney, KP Neale, FD Woodward, E Boutcher, VW Grosvenor, HD Settle, H Cook, CW Fryer. Bottom row: E Adams CJ Newman, JC Sale, JS Oldcorn, HT Bassett, AC Gibson, AH Freemantle (Scots Guards), Lt Col EF Strange, Capt AW Gaze (Adjutant), HW Lovelock, HA Syrad, WD Shanahan, AJ Rodd, FG Brockway.

Courtesy of the Director, National Army Museum, London (1981-02-43-2)

mechanism' with each volunteer a cog in the machine.

The battalion moved in October to Bishops Stortford and the following month to Ware. In December Major General E S Bulfin took over the 60th Division and immediately became its champion. Complaining that it had been 'bled white in officers, NCOs and men to furnish reinforcements', he extracted a promise from the War Office that, provided it achieved a satisfactory standard, the division would go to France; meanwhile it would not have to furnish any more drafts.[3] Matters now moved more quickly. In early January the whole division was at last together in a huge camp on Salisbury Plain. Colonel Strange drove the battalion ever harder, as it joined in exercises at brigade and divisional level, interspersed with inspections. Suddenly there was an interruption.

Irish interlude

Out of the blue on Friday, 28 April, came orders for 179 Brigade to proceed immediately to Ireland. The Easter uprising had begun the previous Sunday. Hasty preparations were made and each man was issued with equipment, emergency rations and ammunition. The battalion left Warminster by train early next morning for Wales and camped on a hill overlooking Milford Haven. Here it seemed to the men that the urgency of their mission had dissipated somewhat. After church parade, Sunday was spent lounging in the sun. The next day, the battalion crossed the Irish Sea, to arrive not in Dublin but Queenstown. Charles Jones recalled the reaction of the people of Cork:

> Women shrieked 'City clurrrks' at us...One man mysteriously enquired where we were going (as if we knew!) Another crept up in sinister fashion, took a parcel from under his arm, and produced – a box of cigars. Otherwise Cork was quiet, and our demonstration of force a success.

There followed a week of field training, then a march, in stages, to Macroom, a pleasant market town some thirty miles to the west. Here the four companies each undertook a secret nocturnal operation. The purpose recorded cautiously in the war diary was 'to search certain houses in the neighbourhood endeavouring to find certain persons wanted by the police'. Most of the details returned empty-handed; only three arrests were made. That was the sum of their involvement in putting down the Irish rebellion. Noting how friendly the people had seemed, the battalion left Macroom the following day on another long march, skirting the Bochragh Mountains to Millstreet. From here a train took them to Rosslare, where they embarked on the return voyage.

The battalion was back at Warminster early on 13 May. The Irish adventure had involved a great deal of marching and hanging about waiting for orders which produced a general sense of not knowing what was going on – a foretaste of the typical rifleman's experience on the Western Front. It was now nearly two years since war had been declared and still the 2nd Battalion wondered if it would ever get to France. There was not much longer to wait. General Bulfin had fulfilled his brief to bring his division up to strength and efficiency. When the battalion returned to Warminster, preparations were well advanced. There remained only the final issue of equipment, inoculations, group photographs and an inspection by the King.

Social composition

The Battalion's officer complement was diluted by newcomers but still recognizably 'CSR' in character. Over thirty per cent had served in the pre-war ranks and over half worked in the Civil Service, banks or insurance companies. Four already had experience with the 1st Battalion in France. The ranks were predominantly wartime recruits with no previous military experience, but these too were from broadly similar backgrounds. There was a leavening of respected pre-war men and NCOs. As in the 1st Battalion, many men were related or were office colleagues. Before departure, a number of men 'claimed' brothers from other units who transferred to the battalion. This practice, intended to help morale, rebounded when, as happened several times, one of a pair of brothers was killed. In June 1916 about one in ten of other ranks had enlisted prior to August 1914 – a much smaller proportion than in the 1st Battalion in March 1915. However it was sufficient, together with the officers and the long period of instruction by men steeped in the old ethos, to ensure that the 2nd Battalion developed a similar character and *esprit* to the pre-war CSR.

It helped that the new battalion was brigaded with other second line units of the old Grey Brigade. These units, similar in composition and character and recruited after the outbreak of war, were the 2/13th, 2/14th and 2/16th Battalions of the London Regiment, respectively the Kensingtons, London Scottish and Queen's Westminsters. With the 2/15th (CSR) they formed 2/4 London Infantry Brigade, now renamed 179 Brigade. These new second line units inherited the rivalries that had existed between the first line units as far back as Volunteer days. It was a friendly rivalry, as can be seen from the columns of their own newspaper, *The Grey Brigade*, but it was taken seriously, as is evident in the disappointment of the 1st Battalion at being preceded to France by the other first line units. This rivalry was an important contributor to morale in 179 Brigade throughout its war service.

In the absence of detailed data about the social make-up of other ranks, the thirty-strong sniping section may be taken as representative. It is a small sample (just over three per cent of strength in June 1916) but drawn evenly from across the battalion. Only three, including the sergeant instructor, were pre-war men; the rest had enlisted in or after August 1914. The snipers were predominantly young men (average age in 1914 twenty-two) of whom only eight were married. Of those whose occupations are specified, exactly half were civil servants, the remainder being other kinds of clerk or merchants plus one engineer, a commercial traveller, a tailor's cutter, a gardener, a waiter and a student. By the end

Officers June 1916. Top row: Lt S G Bennett, 2Lt K A Higgs, 2Lts F W Lewis, L H Hart, E E Andrews, H J Spencer, G E Thompson, F W Westmore; Second row: Lts B Peatfield, C H Rimington, H F Rust, 2Lts C M Kilner, F J Smith, Lt & QM A A Joslin, 2Lt A V James, Capts A C H Benke, K A Wills; Third row: Capts C A Bailey, F F Tarver, Major A A Oliver, Lt Col C de Putron, Capt & Adj A W Gaze, Major HFM Warne, Capt F R Radice; Bottom row: Lts J H Randolph, P W Thorogood, F J W Leech (Medical Officer), Capt G R L Anderson, Lt W H Smith, 2Lt F T Bailey.

of the war, only fourteen (just under half) were still in the battalion. Five were dead and eleven had left for various reasons (wounded, commissioned or transferred to other units).

General Bulfin, used to commanding Regular troops, had been struck by the 'extraordinary quickness, intelligence, and alertness of the rank and file' in 60th Division. His initial impressions of territorial officers were less favourable. They 'worked out their problems, and arrived at the same results as Regular officers, but taking totally different and much longer methods'. Accordingly, he instituted intensive training and replaced some of the older officers with younger men already experienced at the front. Colonel Strange was replaced before departure, though this was on medical grounds, as he had been taken seriously ill in Ireland. His successor was Lieutenant Colonel C de Putron, a Regular officer of the Lancashire Fusiliers, with experience of active service in South Africa and more recently at Gallipoli and Salonika.[4]

The battalion left Warminster by train on 22 June and sailed from Southampton that evening on the *Connaught* and *Inventor*, arriving at Le Havre early next morning. They went by train to billets west of St

Pol, then marched about ten miles to Maroeuil, a badly damaged village on the northern outskirts of Arras. The 60th Division was to go into the line opposite Vimy ridge.

'Gunfire and mixed feelings'

Many wrote of their excitement at experiencing the sights and sensations of France after such a long wait. The CSR *History* refers to 'that world of dreams that had for so long evaded us'. The 2nd Battalion would stay only five months – and take part in no major actions – before sailing for Salonika in November. By then they might have different views about this 'world of dreams' but, for now, the general mood was one of excitement and anticipation, tinged with anxiety. On the march, the opening artillery bombardment for the Somme offensive – which would begin on 1 July – could be heard rumbling in the south. As the column approached the front, flashes lit up the night sky. Kenneth Wills, second in command of C Company, was shocked to realize the flashes were distant gunfire. He felt 'a tremendous thrill...and...excited as a child'. The reaction of Private George Bazley, a signaller in Wills' company, was more ambivalent: 'gunfire and mixed feelings'.

The 60th Division sector stretched between Arras and Souchez, directly opposite the high ground of Vimy ridge, where the 1st Battalion had had such a devastating time in a German attack barely five weeks before. From the ridge the enemy had the whole British line and back areas under observation. This was rudely brought home to the 2nd Battalion on the first night, spent in rat-infested ruins in Maroeuil. The cooks carelessly displayed lights while preparing the meal and were immediately rewarded with shellfire. Two men were slightly wounded and a cooker was completely demolished. It was a salutary lesson that villages even two or three miles behind the line were not safe. George Bazley recorded:

> A corporal [was] *slightly wounded and a 'Blighty' too. First blood to the Huns. Didn't like the experience a bit and only 5 days out too.*

Bazley's unease increased the following day when tin hats were issued. Vimy ridge in 1916 was characterized by persistent mine warfare. The whole front was dotted with craters. The 'line' consisted of two parallel defences: a chain of fortified outposts (known as the observation line); and behind it a main trench or firing line, which in the event of attack was to be held to the last. Behind the firing line was the support line, connected to the forward lines by a complex trench network. 179 Brigade was allocated a section in front of the ruined village of Neuville St Vaast. During sixteen weeks in and out of the line, the men became only too familiar with the complicated geography both above and below ground. To avoid observation, the front had to be approached through long, winding communication trenches from villages like Maroeuil and St Eloi.

The observation post in the Paris Redoubt, which jutted out into no man's land. Capt Wills' sketch was drawn from memory in 1917.

On 30 June, small parties went into the trenches for instruction by the 51st (Highland) Division, which was leaving for the Somme. It was an anxious time. The unpleasant experience at Maroeuil had induced some jumpiness and now the Germans were shelling the front line every night, apparently suspecting the changeover in troops. For each man, there was the anxiety of how he might bear up under fire. Private Edgar Powell of B Company was 'very afraid of being afraid'. This fear was common, and possibly worse for officers, who were expected to set an example. Kenneth Wills described his first test as he followed the Black Watch guide up the long communication trench:

> All hell let loose...explosions all round us – thumps and bangs...[It was] not a bad baptism and gave me a fair amount of confidence. If that was the worst the Boche could do I could stick it. ...For ages I had been wondering whether, when it came to the point, I would behave like a coward, or let the men down. It is a horrible feeling, that suspense; and honestly I turned in that night, in the Jocks' dugout, feeling happy.

With his confidence strengthened by this new self-knowledge, Wills felt able to endure the next two years of war without showing fear. It was not until returning to France from the Middle East in 1918 that the wear on his nerves began to show and he found himself getting 'more and more windy and more and more on edge'.

In addition to learning trench routines, the men worked as labourers, maintaining the trench system and attached to tunnelling companies,

158

Not forgotten after 87 years. Ernest Harris' grave at Ecoivres Military Cemetery with photographic tribute, 2003.

Abbey at Mont St Eloi, one of the devastated villages opposite Vimy ridge which the battalion came to know so well in 1916. The Abbey, which was a ruin well before the Great War, dominated the landscape, as it does today.

4354 Pte Ernest Harris, C Coy, one of the first to be killed. His father received letters from Major Warne and five platoon mates explaining he was killed while on sentry duty in an advanced post. Harris was 19, an employee of the South Metropolitan Electric Lighting Company.

Bernard Harris

digging mines. Working parties trudged through miles of muddy trenches, knee-deep in water, to and from their places of work. A particularly nasty fatigue, universally despised, was dragging sandbags of wet spoil to the surface and finding somewhere to empty it, usually in shell holes in no man's land. This 'unsoldierlike' and dangerous activity seemed at times worse than the front line. Private Henry Pope grumbled in his diary:

> We took our turn in 8 hour shifts dragging sandbags full of damp chalk...It was one of the most awful heart-breaking work imaginable – no doubt somebody's bright idea to break in new troops.

The men gradually became acclimatized to trench routine. The CSR rotated with the London Scottish in the right-hand sub-sector of the brigade front, from which the Paris Redoubt jutted out into no man's land. Periodically they went back for 'rest' in the large underground cavern at Aux Rietz or in huts at Bray – two of the few places safe from enemy observation. Intensive training was continued throughout the months in France. In turn, officers and men went to one or more specialist schools to acquire skills in bombing, Lewis guns, sniping, gas, intelligence collection or consolidation of mine craters.

On 1 July, the first man was killed, Private W J Ward of A Company, and on 8 July two men on a working party were hit. One of these, Christopher Pike from the Board of Trade, was evacuated to London where he died six months later. Thereafter casualties ran at roughly eight per week, mostly from trench mortars of various types. Kenneth Wills recalled '...one has a certain amount of fatalistic feeling about [shell fire]. You do not hear it coming and you cannot see it, and you decided that if it is going to hit you it will'. Trench mortars, by contrast, descended slowly and visibly. Their effect was demoralizing, as Sergeant Leslie Pearce described:

> I found the fire trench spell trying: the Bosches had the range of our trench to a nicety and were dropping 'oilcans' (high-explosive bombs slung over from I suppose a sort of catapault) and similar stuff too often for peace and comfort. It is very queer how with those projectiles with short range and high trajectory you can watch the beggar coming and dodge it by getting round a corner in the trench: you're safe enough if there's a good thick bit of earth between you and the explosion.

The raid, 11 September

During the Somme offensive, units in other sectors were charged with obtaining intelligence about enemy troop movements. On 29 July, a patrol of A Company earned plaudits by capturing two prisoners carrying useful papers. In August, the 60th Division began a series of trench raids for the same purpose. Two CSR subalterns, Bernard Peatfield and G E Thompson, planned a raid and began practising behind the line with ten volunteers from each company.

On the night of 11 September, their faces blackened, the raiders crawled out, lugging bombs, ladders and blankets. Immediately they attracted enemy fire and bombs, but no-one was hit. They crept close to the German wire and waited fifteen anxious minutes for a prearranged artillery barrage. The staff waited equally anxiously in the Paris Redoubt as the raiders walked over behind the barrage, clambered across the thick wire on a 'bridge' improvised from blankets, and into the German trench. One party made a block at one end, while another rushed along and

Four pals from 10 and 13 Platoons in France 1916: 5075 C W Clifton, 5078 A P Bartlett, 5080 E J Beard and 5130 A W West. Alfred West is top right. Before enlisting he was a trainee quantity surveyor. Afterwards he regularly visited the battlefields, especially Maroeuil where several of his pals were buried. Janis Croom

4594 Pte A Small of B Company, pictured in the Middle East. 'Lofty' Small was awarded the Military Medal for his part in the raid in September 1916, in which his brother John died.

1819 Cpl G V Knight, Board of Agriculture & Fisheries. He was killed in the Douai sap on 23 September and is buried at Maroeuil.

bombed a dugout, calling for the enemy to surrender. At least two Germans were killed and four were taken prisoner. The party returned quickly, aided by a paper trail thoughtfully laid by Peatfield on the way out.

Several were wounded, including both officers. John Small was later discovered to be missing. Thompson and Small's brother returned to the German trench and brought him back, but he died later of his wounds. The raid was the biggest event of this tour in France and was claimed as establishing the Battalion's reputation as a fighting unit. Sergeant Quinton, who was recommended for an award for his part in the raid, thought afterwards that its importance was exaggerated. Clearly it did not compare with the 1st Battalion's experiences on the Somme, but it gave a fillip to morale, as even Charles Jones' slightly tongue-in-cheek account acknowledges:

The result was a howling success; a DSO and a Military Cross and various other decorations were awarded to the raiders, doubtless 'pour encourager les autres'. The men had been thoroughly trained, even learning a few German phrases...When one thinks of two men standing in a German trench, one at each entrance to a dugout, shouting 'Kommen Sie heraus, you bastards' and at the same time throwing bombs down as fast as they can, one feels that this study of language was a waste of time. But it was evidently a thrilling experience and, like all successful 'stunts', exhilarating. The spirits of the whole Battalion rose as a result.

Before being withdrawn in mid-October, the battalion experienced two nasty incidents. The first, involving C Company on 23 September, was described by Kenneth Wills:

A nasty smash up occurred in the Douai sap...a fellow called Connett came haring down into Company HQ, streaming with blood...[He was] badly wounded but had run all the way round to let someone know what had happened...about 3 or 4 fellows had been laid out and a number wounded...One boy Shelton, who died when being carried down on a stretcher, showed the most remarkable pluck...[He] laughed and joked with me as he was being carried off. The Corporal of the post was sitting in the mouth of the dugout with his head in his hands. I thought the poor chap was overcome with grief, so went up to him and put my hand on his shoulder. As I did so his tin hat fell

Maroeuil British Cemetery has the largest concentration of 2nd Battalion graves (21) outside the Middle East. The veterans regarded it as 'their' cemetery and made regular pilgrimages.

off and his brains flopped down the dugout steps. He had had the whole of the back of his head blown off.

In the second incident, on 5 October, an enormous trench mortar knocked in one of A Company's dugouts. A party of rescuers, frantically digging out the occupants, was mortared in its turn. Seven died, including two who remained permanently entombed and are now commemorated on the Arras Memorial. Leslie Pearce, also of A Company, wrote home:

Sergeant Wigney, poor fellow, is dead...It's sad losing him, but he had the finest death one could have...everyone helping in the rescue knew the risk they ran.

Around this time news filtered through of the huge scale of the 1st Battalion's losses on the Somme. This was an anxious time for those with friends, relatives and work colleagues in the 1st Battalion. Arthur Gaze, the Adjutant, was given ten days special leave when it was learned that his twin brother had been killed at High Wood.

On 19 October the CSR was relieved and went into rest billets before marching to the area around Abbeville. It was an easy trek in good weather and took them through pleasant undamaged countryside and villages. Strong rumours indicated a destination on the Somme but turned out to be misleading. Sir Douglas Haig, under pressure to release troops for Salonika, selected the 60th Division as it was 'fresh, well-trained and at full strength'.[5]

At Abbeville there was a period of reorganization. As in the 1st Battalion in summer 1915, there was a shake-out of officers; some were left behind sick or for other reasons: a few, while efficient peacetime soldiers, had proved unsuitable by virtue of health or temperament for active service. The establishment was fixed at thirty-five officers and 880 other ranks and this was made up by drafts from England. The battalion embarked from Marseilles between 19 and 22 November on *Transylvania, Megantic* and *Menominee.*

2/Lt Ernest Denny, schoolteacher and published poet. Served with the Battalion in France until November 1916. He died of wounds while attached to 17th KRRC in the Salient, August 1917. Triumphant Laughter, a collection of his poetry, was published in 1978. An extract appears at the end of Chapter 11.

Margaret Tims

1. L M Edwards' views are quoted in Chapter 2, p 41
2. For Lord Arran's visit to the 2nd Battalion, see Chapter 2, p 33
3. Dalbiac, PH, *History of the 60th Division*, Allen & Unwin, 1927, p 34
4. *ibid*, p35
5. *Military Operations* 1916, Vol 2, p 46

2nd Battalion casualties: France June-November 1916

Wounded	95
Killed or died	38
Total	133

Dead are buried or commemorated at: Abbeville, Aubigny, Arras Memorial, Ecoivres, Maroeuil and in the UK

Sources: Brigade and Battalion war diaries, CWGC, SDGW, CSR History

Chapter Eight

The Balkans, 1916-1917

In August 1914, Greece, though allied to Serbia, did not formally join the hostilities. At the invitation of the then Prime Minister, Eleftherios Venizelos, a small Franco-British force landed at Salonika in October 1915, as a base for operations in support of Serbia. This move did not, as had been expected, deter Bulgaria from invading Serbia. The force then struck northwards in a vain attempt to assist the Serbs who were being overrun by the Central Powers. It was too small and too late. Hampered by severe weather, the force had to retreat and set up defensive lines in Greek Macedonia.

During the following year, the area around Salonika was built up into a huge Allied camp, with troops from many nations including Russia and Italy. They had some successes in an offensive from August 1916 but the collapse of Romania, another potential ally, changed the balance of power in the region. By autumn the Allies were effectively hemmed in by Bulgarian and Austrian forces. The front ran right across Macedonia from the Struma river in the east to the Adriatic in the west. The supreme commander, the French General Sarrail, pressed for reinforcements. For this reason Sir Douglas Haig withdrew the 60th Division from the Western Front: it was needed to hold a mountainous stretch of front about forty miles north of Salonika port, near Lake Doiran.

The CSR's voyage from Marseilles to Salonika via Malta was pleasant and uneventful. Drilling and vigorous physical training took place on deck and lifeboat practice provided a reminder of danger from enemy submarines. The war seemed far away as they steamed through the Mediterranean, then turned north past the Aegean islands. Salonika, reached on 30 November, appeared very pleasing from the sea: white buildings against green hills and minarets gleaming in the sun. At close quarters, however, it was filthy and smelly. First reactions were unfavourable:

532325 Pte S E Anderson of the GPO enlisted in 1915. An original member of B Company, he served throughout the war and was discharged in January 1919. Unable to tell his family he was sailing to Greece, he sent postcards signed 'M R Sales' and 'M Alter'. The censor evidently missed these rather obvious allusions to the Mediterranean voyage! Janet Gill

> *We only saw the dock quarter and were not impressed. The quayside swarmed with cut-throats of all the Balkan races and the thought struck me, for one, that if I saw Piccadilly again I should be lucky.*[1]

Macedonia was slowly recovering from the Balkan Wars of 1912-13 and conditions remained primitive. Roads were rough and clogged with mud and the most advanced form of transport was an ox-wagon with solid wheels. The battalion marched out of the town. About eight miles to the west they came to a campsite on a desolate rock-strewn plain, along the mouth of the Vardar river. This was Dudular, where the 60th Division was concentrating prior to moving north. Bivouacs were issued: sheets of canvas, about a yard square, each accompanied by a small pole. Christened 'bivvies', these were to be the only protection from the elements for most of the next eighteen months. Charles Hennessey summed up the practical issue: 'Bivvies, soldiers for the use of, and how to make them really comfortable'. Stony ground and deteriorating weather conspired against comfort of any kind. An icy north wind, the 'Vardar blast', swept across the plain, bringing a violent storm. The bivvies were no defence, and the campsite soon became a quagmire.

The transport section grappled with an equally challenging problem: how to break in a string of recalcitrant wild mules freshly arrived from South America. The task took on a pantomime quality as men and animals struggled for mastery. The mules kicked and baulked and escaped in large numbers, shedding their loads as they went. Fatigue parties were organized to help the would-be muleteers, who had had no special training. Some applied lavish amounts of polish to stiff new saddlery. Others struggled to restrain the mules as desperate attempts were made to load them. George Bazley's succinct diary entry says it all:

> 6 December, More mules and more fun for those looking on. Very wet and windy...Disorders in old Greece, Thessaly. Stormy. Touch and go with our tent.

The battalion expected shortly to move north to the Doiran front. Suddenly, 179 Brigade was ordered in a different direction entirely. On 10 December, Bazley recorded:

> Everyone busy packing. Mules loaded after a heavy struggle. Several broke away. Fed up with mules. Moving again. Rumours as usual.

The next day the battalion, minus the transport section and mules, marched to the docks and embarked on HMS *Mosquito*, a destroyer. Each man was issued with 120 rounds of ammunition and two days' rations. The operation was shrouded in secrecy. Kenneth Wills recalled sealed orders being opened once they were out to sea:

> I had wild visions of a second Gallipoli landing, but the whole thing was a most appalling anti-climax. We arrived on a deserted beach sopping wet, with no sign of human life for miles around.

This was Scala Vromeris on the coast of Thessaly. 179 Brigade was being sent a few miles inland to the Greek town of Katerini, in the shadow of Mount Olympus. The reason for this unexpected move lay in the complexities of Greek politics, which were polarized into pro- and anti-

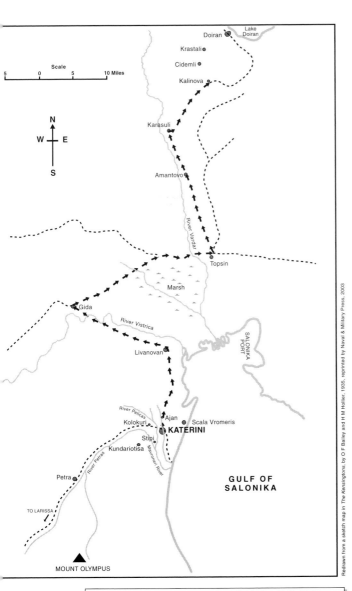

Scale

5   0   Scale   5   10 Miles

N
W — E
S

Doiran ● | Lake Doiran
Krastali ●
Cidemli ●
Kalinova ●
Karasuli ●
Amantovo ●
River Vardar
Topsin ●
Marsh
Gida ●
River Vistrica
Livanovan ●
SALONIKA PORT
River Pelicas
Ajan ● | Scala Vromeris
Kolokuri ●
KATERINI ●
Stipi ●
Kundariotisa ●
Mavroneri River
Petra ●
GULF OF SALONIKA
TO LARISSA ●
MOUNT OLYMPUS

Redrawn from a sketch map in *The Kensingtons*, by O F Bailey and H M Hollier, 1935, reprinted by Naval & Military Press, 2003

THESSALY OPERATIONS DEC 1916 – FEB 1917 AND KARASULI TREK 10-17 MARCH 1917

Allied factions, led respectively by the former Prime Minister, Venizelos, and the King (educated in Germany and married to the Kaiser's sister). Just before the Franco-British landing in 1915, Venizelos had fallen from power, leaving the Allies in the ambiguous position of 'invited but unwelcome guests'.[2] Greece was still technically neutral, but there were fears that the King might yet bring the country into the war on Germany's side.

In September 1916, Venizelos had established a provisional revolutionary government in Salonika and brought over 20,000 soldiers to fight alongside the Allies. Allied relations with the King deteriorated further. In November royalist troops were reported assembling in the Larissa district of Thessaly, threatening the security of the Allied camp at Salonika and thus the stability of the whole Balkan front. General Sarrail decided to establish an outpost line near Katerini to guard the two routes from Thessaly to Salonika - the coastal railway east of Mount Olympus and the road over the Petra Pass. 179 Brigade was selected for the task, with orders 'to act with all military precautions and to place no trust in the inhabitants of the country, but not to provoke hostilities'.[3]

The battalion marched into Katerini on 11 December, in some anxiety over what to expect. Henry Pope recalled:

It was thrilling to march at black darkness into a town peopled by persons who might be hostile to us. There were a number of

165

Former Turkish barracks at Katerini. The battalion was billeted here on first arriving in Thessaly for outpost duty, December 1916. The barracks were filthy and had to be cleaned before deemed fit for habitation.

Sketch by 5088 Pte James Browning, D Company

"The Little Greek Tavern by the Square"

people about looking like black shadows in the darkness.

The café in Katerini's square looked inviting but, like the rest of the town, it was 'extremely filthy'. A party of CSR officers sent their plates back three times before accepting them 'for eating purposes'.

Sketch by James Browning

The natives, on discovering that the British troops were not aggressive, quickly became friendly. General conditions, however, were difficult. Many supplies had been lost during the journey, both in storms at sea and during an epic overland march by the transport column, still struggling with the undisciplined mules. After 'iron rations' had been consumed, the brigade began requisitioning local sheep. The men supplemented their meagre mutton stew with local purchases. Eventually the railway to Salonika was repaired and supplies began to flow. The presence of the troops benefited the inhabitants by boosting the local economy, improving the infrastructure and providing medical services. All this did much to ensure good relations, which remained warm throughout the three-month stay.

The battalions of 179 Brigade were dispersed in and around Katerini. The CSR was billeted first in a filthy former Turkish barracks. After cleaning their new home, parties went out making roads suitable for wheeled transport and constructing bridges across icy mountain streams. On 20 December, the battalion moved a few miles south, and camped for six weeks while building a defensive line along a ridge of hills, between the villages of Stipi and Kundariotisa. It was grim bivouacking on high ground when it rained or occasionally snowed. The work was arduous. On the whole, however, the weather was fine, the scenery was magnificent and there was hardly any sign of the war. Life was not unpleasant:

> This Katarini venture proved to be a lucky break in our active service. Our presence in Thessaly doubtless had an effect. If, however, the Royalists had declared war on us we would have had a very rough time of it. We can look back on our three months... as a pleasant interlude.[4]

Unlike the crude trenches dug under fire in France, the Greek equivalent was quite elaborate. Barbed wire was unavailable. Instead the men used felled trees and thorn bushes to construct barricades, called 'zarebas'. The expertise of a Kew Gardens man in D Company proved useful, though he was heard to bewail the destruction of so many exotic trees.

One veteran recalled:

> We managed to improvise quite a fair defence system, which would not, however, have withstood much punishment. We had lookouts on treetops, patrols and guards galore. All 'locals' coming into the town from the south were stopped, their baggage searched for arms and anything edible snaffled.[5]

When they were not digging or on guard duty, there was the usual programme of training, inspections and compulsory sports fixtures. The battalion celebrated its first Christmas overseas:

> Our first memory of Christmas Day 1916 is of crawling out of the usual canvas bivouac at the edge of a beech wood into a bitter dawn and watching the rising sun transform the majestic mass of Mount Olympus...into a riot of gorgeous colour...After breakfast we made ourselves 'posh' and sauntered into Katerini to watch the Battalion sports meeting...Unfortunately we missed most of the proceedings by dropping off to sleep under a large oak, somnolency being induced by the hot sun and a certain amount of the red wine of Samos...in the little Greek tavern by the Square. We woke in time to hear the band play 'God Save the King' and found we had a 'head'. This was cured...by...wading out to...the middle of the Mavroneri [river] and allowing the ice-cold stream to flow completely over us! Thus restored, we were able to do justice to our Christmas dinner...of roast beef (local brand), potatoes and Christmas pudding (the real stuff from England), washed down by Army tea.[6]

In the new year the defensive line was completed and working parties once more turned to road and bridge making. On 15 February the

In France the men had dug trenches under fire. In Thessaly, with no sign of the war, they graduated to digging roads. This photo of CSR 'navvies' taken in January 1917 appears to show timber supports for the approach to the bridge they helped to build over the icy waters of the Mavroneri river. IWM (Q.32676)

battalion was withdrawn from the outpost line. For the next two weeks C and D Companies occupied positions around Kolukuri, just west of Katerini, with the other companies in barracks. Throughout the whole time there was no indication of hostility from the Greeks, except for two isolated visits by aeroplanes, apparently on reconnaissance. It was indeed a quiet war, as an incident recalled by Wills and Jones demonstrates. Parties from C and D Companies were sent on a special operation, not stalking an enemy, but acting as beaters for the Brigadier's game shoot! According to Jones, the novelty soon wore off:

> Going through the woods in open order banging tree trunks and shouting 'Cock! Cock!' was amusing at first. After a time we found it wearisome…and when Corporal 'Loder' received a few pellets in the face … the last vestige of pleasure disappeared. We were paid to be shot, it was true, but we expected to be able to shoot back.

Salonika was the unhealthiest major theatre of the war. Almost from the first day, the battalion suffered outbreaks of impetigo, dysentery, jaundice and nephritis. Later, in the hot weather, malaria was rife. The sickness rate was consistently high. Up to March 1917, officers were admitted to hospital at the rate of one per week; several were evacuated to Malta 'for change of air and return', the more serious cases to England. One happy by-product of a bout of sickness was the formation at a convalescent camp of a talented concert party. Christened the *Roosters*, it had among its star performers Private Percy Merriman of the CSR. For the rest of the war the *Roosters* (along with another party, the *Barnstormers*) entertained the 60th Division when out of the line. Indeed the *Roosters* continued for another twenty years, with many appearances on the BBC.

At the end of February 179 Brigade concentrated outside Katerini and prepared to move north. By then the royalist troops were no longer considered a threat, most having withdrawn south of the Gulf of Corinth. General Sarrail was planning a spring offensive and the Brigade was needed on the Doiran front.

'No man who did that march will ever forget it'

The 'Karasuli trek' up the Vardar valley was the battalion's worst collective experience to date. The journey of about a hundred miles from Katerini to Kalinova took seven consecutive days. This was well within the men's capabilities, even with full packs. Yet the journey warrants seven pages in the CSR *History* and looms large in all the memoirs. What made it so testing was the combination of inhospitable terrain with extremes of Balkan weather. As Charles Jones declared, 'No man who did that march will ever forget it'.

Local inhabitants and the French garrison gave the men of 179 Brigade a warm send-off on 10 March. During the first four days the

This photograph is labelled 'Battalion headquarters, Topsin'. The CSR passed through Topsin on the fourth day of the epic Karasuli trek in March 1917.

weather was fine. The going was rough and the mules tended to shed their loads, but steady progress was made, via Tuzla, Livanon, Gida and across the Vardar to Topsin. Day five was excessively hot and the first man fell out in a dead faint. It was then, according to Henry Pope, that officers began to show concern:

> *Lieutenant F W Lewis tried on a man's pack to 'see how it went' and had to admit that 'he did not know how the poor devils did it'. Woe to us.*

On day six, north of Amantovo, the column came within view of enemy balloons and lookout positions. Movement by day was deemed dangerous, so a temporary halt was made, with orders to move again after dark. By then the weather had deteriorated. In heavy wind and torrents of blinding rain, the column struggled forward over uneven ground for six hours continuously. This was agonizing, as Kenneth Wills explained:

> *A man carrying 95 pounds keys himself up for a fifty-minute march and looks forward to the ten-minute halt as the limit of his endurance and his goal. If the ten minutes does not come he is liable to snap.*

Certainly some individuals 'snapped' and berated their officers. Charles Jones, for example:

> *It was in fact one of the hardships of the march that the distances were always understated by our officers...I remember turning fiercely on a very new and very inoffensive subaltern and telling him what I thought of the policy of lying to men in order to get them to march all the way. He murmured apologetic agreement, but he looked rather scared; evidently the answering of angry and eloquent corporals had not been included in his training.*

Finally, after six hours, a halt was called at Karasuli. The men were further dispirited however at being forbidden to smoke in case this alerted the enemy. The next leg was on a road and promised to be easier. But it was not and, as Jones recalled, the men abused even Colonel de Putron to his face:

> *Our troubles were not yet over; for at frequent intervals the road dipped into nullahs. Usually dry, they were now raging*

torrents, two or three feet deep; and at one of the worst stood our Colonel himself, shining a torch on to the rushing waters to guide us through. Though we had never loved him, nobody could blame him for that night's work. Yet as we passed man after man turned to fling an oath into his face.

At last they reached a soggy campsite of sorts. So many mules had stumbled and lost their loads, there were not enough blankets or bivouacs to go round. Rum was issued haphazardly in the dark and some of those most in need received none. They simply fell into the mud and lay there, more or less unconscious. Many of these were sent to hospital before the march was resumed on the seventh and final day. The order to move off came suddenly and took the cooks by surprise. The men watched in anger and disbelief as dixies of half-cooked stew were emptied into the mud. The route was now along a road, which was easier going, but the weather became even worse. Jones remembered:

The wind grew stronger and stronger, colder and colder; we were meeting the 'Vardar blast' whose local fame is great. Then came the snow, blinding us, and adding to our load. Men who had started out exhausted failed to survive this new attack, and fell by the roadside, often with a pal to look after them; one man's life was undoubtedly saved by a corporal and private who lay one each side of him giving him the warmth of their bodies. The mules were slipping and falling, their loads were doing likewise; and the monotonous cry 'Fall out four men' [to reload mules] brought curses from men who could only just keep going.

533765 Pte W J Tibbs, a civil servant. Enlisted in 1916 and joined the battalion at Salonika in early March, just in time for the Karasuli trek ('easily my toughest army experience'). He served in Palestine and France and was among the last to return home in September 1919. His comment on the war: 'When will the peoples of the world ever learn?' Evelyn Kench

So done-in were the men that even the ten-minute halts did not help, as Kenneth Wills explained:

After ten minutes halt [Company Sergeant Major] Oldcorn and I went round literally kicking men up and forcing them to get on. Some were so dead beat that all they wanted to do was to be left to sleep and to die in the snow. I have never had such an experience of slave-driving in my life. We forced them up by poking them with a bayonet and threatening them, and kicking them. They were absolutely done to the wide, and turned round and cursed us to our face, cursed everything, God included – the only time I have seen such abject misery in my life. Finally we got them all up and going again and I determined that whatever occurred I would not let them halt again.

At about midnight they reached Kalinova and made camp. The trek was over. Next morning, 17 March, the cost was counted. Fifty-two men and one officer had been admitted to hospital in the last two days, suffering from exposure or injuries to legs and feet. It could have been worse: a man of the London Scottish had collapsed and died of exposure before medical aid could reach him. In the decades after the war, there were many survivors who, like William Tibbs of D Company, regarded the trek as their lowest point:

> This march...was easily my toughest Army experience. At Karasuli, I actually fell asleep standing up leaning on my rifle for support. Others did the same; we were so exhausted and dare not sit or lie down, because of the mud and slime.

It was claimed that the trek affected men long afterwards:

> There is little doubt that seeds were sown on those nights which shortened the lives of many who appeared in 1918 to have come through the war without harm. [7]

Soon after arrival at Kalinova a small party of officers and NCOs went forward to reconnoitre the new positions. They had the unexpected and pleasant experience of celebrating St Patrick's Day with the outgoing battalion which happened to be the London Irish. Thereafter 17 March had double significance: the day in 1915 on which the 1st Battalion left for France and the day two years later on which the 2nd Battalion finished the epic Karasuli trek.

'The quietest war we ever had'

The 60th Division was responsible for a ten-mile section of the Doiran front running westwards from the lower slopes of the Pip ridge (held by the Bulgars) to the river Vardar. On 19 March the Battalion took over the sector running from Wagon Hill just east of the village of Reselli, westwards to Bekirli. The contrast with their experience opposite Vimy ridge could not have been greater. The opposing forces were ranged along lines of hills three or four miles apart. Even at its narrowest, on the extreme flanks, no man's land was at least a mile wide. The scenery was hardly affected by war. Kenneth Wills described it:

> No man's land...was intersected by a number of little streams with here and there a deserted village, and here and there fields of opium poppies, apricot orchards and mulberry groves. Macedonia in spring [was] very lush, rich country with plenty of wildlife...It was the quietest war we ever had.

Hill 535, on the Pip ridge. From the towering crest the enemy had excellent observation and could target long-range shells at British positions. This sketch from Capt Wills' album is labelled 'The Bugbear of the Balkans'.

The depth of no man's land meant there was no risk from rifle or trench mortar fire. Instead of creeping along communication trenches keeping a careful lookout for incoming missiles, the men could walk upright when behind the line. Charles Jones recalled walking back 'along a beautiful rocky ravine with a streamlet running through and

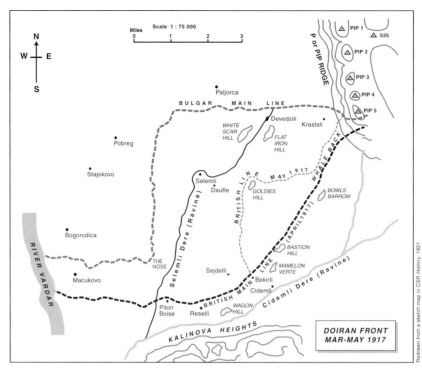

Scale 1 : 75 000

Miles
0   1   2   3

N
W — E
S

P or PIP RIDGE
△ PIP 1
△ PIP 2
△ PIP 3
△ PIP 4
△ PIP 5
△ 535

Paljorca

BULGAR   MAIN   LINE

WHITE SCAR HILL
Devedzili
Krastali

Pobreg

FLAT IRON HILL

Stajokovo

Selemli
Dautle
BRITISH LINE MAY 1917
GOLDIES HILL
WHALE BACK
BOWLS BARROW

Selemli Dere (Ravine)

Bogorodica

THE NOSE

BASTION HILL
(APRIL 1917)

Macukovo
Sejdelli
MAMELON VERTE
Bekirli
Cidemli

Cidemli Dere (Ravine)

Piton Boise   Reselli
BRITISH MAIN LINE
WAGON HILL

KALINOVA HEIGHTS

RIVER VARDAR

DOIRAN FRONT
MAR-MAY 1917

Redrawn from a sketch map in CSR History, 1921

Capt C H Rimington, from the Bank of England. Commissioned from the ranks in 1915, he served throughout the war and commanded A Company.

bushes in full bloom on the sides'. Apart from occasional visits by German aeroplanes, the principal aggravation derived from the topography. The Bulgars possessed the higher hills. From their strongly entrenched positions along the western slopes of the formidable Pip ridge they could observe British positions and even some back areas. By daylight, no more than two or three men could gather in the observed area without presenting a target for artillery. Forward positions were therefore manned lightly during the day. Most of the men stayed further back and, when not on working parties, whiled away the daylight hours sleeping, reading or playing cards. At night the trenches were strongly held and patrols regularly criss-crossed no man's land. Occasional shots were exchanged with enemy patrols but there was no serious fighting. Sergeant Leslie Pearce summed it up:

> *Thank God, we are out of range of trench mortars – and of rifles and machine guns too, just here – so we have only shell fire to reckon with. ...If friend Bulgar's hill overlooks yours, he is very apt to be interfering with your mealtimes and general welfare. But what he can't see he usually doesn't waste shells on.*

The weather began to warm up. Summer kit and helmets were issued and work was halted during the middle of each day. A special 'mosquito squad' was formed with responsibility for prophylactic measures to reduce the risk of malaria. All the memoirs include some appreciation of

British troops bivouacked on the plain beside the Vardar river.

532990 Pte C F Spencer, employee of Westminster Bank and member of A Coy. The 2nd Battalion had a much lower casualty rate than the 1st and many more men, like Charles Spencer, served throughout the war. Judith Gibbons

A shower rigged up from perforated petrol cans at Tetre Verte, April 1917. All CSR men were ordered to take a very public shower, which caused much amusement.

Capt KWM Pickthorn, one of the original officers of D Coy. Later he commanded B Coy. In Salonika he transferred to the Royal Flying Corps as an observer. Seriously wounded in May 1917 when his 'plane was attacked and shot down by the German ace Eschwige. After recovering, he worked in military intelligence in the War Office. H G R Pickthorn

the flourishing wildlife. Leslie Pearce, for example, wrote:

> *You would scarcely believe how for miles and miles on end you tread on wild thyme; and now it is all in blossom, and very lovely. Endless variety of wild flowers here. ...Natural history's interesting here with a marten or two in our ravine, and stoats and hamsters and tortoises and lizards eighteen inches long and snakes up to five feet. Several sorts of hawk.*

When General Sarrail's spring offensive began on 24 April the Pip ridge was among the objectives, since from these peaks the Bulgars could enfilade any outposts that might be pushed forward. The main attack on this front was to be made by the 22nd and 26th Divisions further to the right. The 60th Division was to relieve the pressure on the main attackers by raiding a strongly fortified position known as The Nose. This difficult task was given to 180 Brigade, while 179 Brigade was held in reserve. Thus the CSR did not participate directly. They witnessed the three-day preliminary bombardment and the covering fire for the attacks which took place on the night of 24 April. Even when the action had started, the difference from the Western Front was still noticeable, as Jones recalled:

> *I remember...when the war had 'warmed up', watching a fierce bombardment...the crashing and coughing of the guns never stopped and the bursting shells lit up the night; yet in the valley below the nightingale was singing and the scent of wild thyme came on the breeze.*

On the CSR's left, the 2/20th Londons gallantly raided The Nose, sustaining a high number of casualties in what was intended only as a diversionary attack. On the right, the main attackers captured the two most southerly peaks of the Pip ridge, also with heavy casualties. There was then a fortnight's pause. The battalion was relieved on 27 April and the companies were sent to different locations behind the line. It was a relief to be able to move around freely without fear of observation, but there were also tough working parties.

The offensive resumed on 8 May. Once again 60th Division was to play a subsidiary role. The 26th Division was to renew the main attack on the western edge of Lake Doiran and the 22nd Division would simulate another attack on the Pip ridge. The 60th Division, further west, would advance its line to encompass several small hills in no man's land, including one called Goldies. None of these small hills had been permanently occupied by the enemy, though he sometimes manned posts on them at night. If successful, this advance would result in the front line running across lower-lying hills than those held previously – a gain which appeared to be of questionable value. The task of capturing this partly-contested ground was allotted to 179 Brigade and was carried out successfully by the Queen's Westminsters and London Scottish. CSR's D Company participated in support of the London Scottish (sustaining a few casualties) while the other companies stood by, ready to turn out if called. It was a fairly easy victory because in each case the enemy had either withdrawn from his post or offered only token resistance.

Goldies

On 10 May, the battalion took over the newly advanced line from the London Scottish and Goldies hill from the Queen's Westminsters. The following three weeks were the most hazardous for the battalion of the whole Salonika tour and accounted for the majority of its casualties in action there. The task was to consolidate the new positions, digging trenches and erecting wire on the forward slopes of three of the hills including Goldies. The ground was virtually solid rock; even the shallowest of trenches had to be blasted out with heavy explosive and the debris shovelled out. All work was done at night under cover of strong fighting patrols, to guard against enemy incursions. During the day most troops were withdrawn, leaving only a small number of sentries who, if wires were still intact, could communicate with headquarters by telephone. The enemy objected strongly to losing command of these hills, especially Goldies, and shelled them repeatedly at night, causing casualties and playing havoc with the wires.

Goldies hill was a long spur running out as a salient from the new line. It had three peaks known as GI, GII and GIII. New British trenches were dug and successfully held on GII and GIII. Possession of the forward

peak, GI, was still contested. A steep ravine ran between it and the enemy front line. The Bulgars now threw a plank bridge across the ravine and sent patrols each night to contest possession. Kenneth Wills recalled one particularly bad night going up the ravine which led to Goldies to meet a D Company party struggling down with several casualties. It poured with rain and the stretchers were difficult to manoeuvre along the muddy paths. The party eventually reached the regimental aid post, where Captain Leech (known to all ranks as 'John Willie') attended to them:

> *Luckily only about four were really seriously injured, and the others were to be sent on next morning to the Field Ambulance. I helped John Willie as far as I could with the badly wounded and this was a pretty ghastly job. One fellow was absolutely hopeless: he had over 30 wounds in him which were dressed one by one. Both legs were shattered and I cut off one of his feet with a pair of scissors. The extraordinary part of it was that he did not seem to feel any pain at all. I gave him a cigarette and before he died he coherently dictated a letter to his wife. Luckily the poor devil died before the pain really came on.*

Daily life was now closer to the regime on the Western Front. Patrols often approached close enough to the enemy to be at risk from bombs and rifle bullets. Among the casualties were three sergeants: Leslie Pearce was killed by a sniper on 24 May as he went out to check his sentries; Frank Wagstaff died of wounds received on Goldies; and Sergeant Platt was seriously wounded by a bomb. Pearce was a pre-war territorial and, like Wagstaff, worked at the Board of Trade.

The contrast between the front line and the surrounding countryside was an enduring characteristic of this sector. When not in the line, the battalion camped in the quieter hills on the former front line. One of these camps, Gully Post, was particularly beautiful. The men bivouacked under trees, surrounded by wild flowers and trilling nightingales. It was here, after an unexplained shot rang out, that a rumour circulated of a soldier committing suicide. The story was not verified but Jones' reaction to it is interesting:

> *I can well imagine a man successfully steeling his soul against war and its ugliness and finding all his defences broken down by the sudden contact with so much beauty.*

For those whose emotional defences were still intact, there were opportunities for dangerous work, especially for adventurous junior officers. Lieutenant Andrew and his batman Private Joines, a D Company sniper, were commended more than once for daylight intelligence-collecting missions. Lieutenant Cribbett of B Company was mentioned for leading a night raiding party on 31 May to attack the enemy bridge over the ravine at GI. In an unusually colourful official report, his company commander stated:

530454 Sgt Leslie Pearce, pre-war territorial from the Board of Trade. His last letter home on 24 May ended ' I'd give lots for dear old England again... Well, I've to get my rifle done before doing a patrol tonight, so must close now...' Pearce was killed that night, by a sniper.
David Langford

175

Karasuli Military Cemetery, Polikastro. Nine CSR casualties are buried here, including two Board of Trade men, Leslie Pearce and Frank Wagstaff. The design is noticeably different from the cemeteries in France, with flat gravestones and a regional variation of the Cross of Sacrifice. Alan Wakefield

> *The raiding party...made a bold dash for the bridge – two planks only across the ravine – these were at once pulled down – a live bomb was picked up here and is forwarded herewith (the detonator was taken out by Mr Cribbett). The Bulgar eats eggs and his shells were the only signs of him...The Bulgar has not been seen on Goldies at night since Lieutenant Cribbett fought with him a few days ago.*[8]

George Bazley, the signaller, spent much time on these hills in the early mornings struggling to mend broken wires before withdrawing to safety. By the end of May, as the battalion was about to be relieved, he had had enough:

> *Goldies has quite got on my nerves. Little sleep and never sure how long lines are going to last. Thank goodness we can hand over good lines.*

On 1 June, 179 Brigade was withdrawn from the line. Though it was never announced officially, the 60th Division was bound for Egypt. The battalion returned to the coast, marching about fifteen miles each night. They bivouacked at Uchantar, close to the campsite of the previous December, while training and refitting took place. Courts of enquiry had been held into losses of animals and equipment on the journey to Thessaly and during the Karasuli trek. As a result, fines were imposed on all officers and men. Powerless to object, the men showed their contempt by adapting a popular song:

> *Pay up your tanners, for the Army's broke*
> *And smile, smile, smile!*

The CSR left Salonika on 20 June. On the voyage celebrations were held to mark the first anniversary of departure for France. Despite the attrition from sickness, turnover in the first year was much lower than in the 1st Battalion. Ten original officers were still serving. There was general relief at leaving Salonika, which is recollected in the memoirs with some cynicism. Fourteen men were left behind in cemeteries there

'Nobody was allowed to go down below to the animals, though we could hear them screaming'. 960 animals were lost when the Cestrian, torpedoed by a German U-boat, sank off Mudros, 24 June 1917, en route from Salonika. She was carrying the Sherwood Rangers Yeomanry and the CSR's transport section to Egypt. Paul Whitehead

'TH   PEARSON
ER BEING TORPEDOED

Two members of the transport section, pictured in Egypt after being torpedoed on the Cestrian. *Note their motley clothes.*

and the losses in other London units were much higher. It was hard to see what purpose their deaths served. The advances on Goldies, in particular, seemed tactically worthless. Charles Jones summed up:

There was an unsatisfactory feeling about the Salonika front. There was apparently no hope of any successful advance, and one stood an excellent chance of getting killed quite uselessly, on some futile errand without hope of result. The casualties from sickness, too, were very great...Added to these disadvantages was the lack of mail, cigarettes, rations of all kinds, and leave – all due to the action of enemy submarines ...In short, there was a general air of futility and neglect about the front, a feeling of being cut off from home in more ways than one.

In the Middle East the battalion would be still further from home. But the offensive they were destined to play a part in would be more decisive in the prosecution of the war.

1. 'ECC', B Company, in QW&CSR RMA *Newsletter* Vol 7, No 9, April 1969, p119
2. Falls, C, *Military Operations Macedonia*, HMSO, 1933, p129
3. *ibid*, p228
4. 'ECC', *op cit*, p119
5. *ibid*, p119
6. 'DED', in CSR *Gazette*, Vol 14, No4, February 1937
7. 'Sigs Loo', in *The Mosquito*, No 165, May 1965
8. WO 95/4928 (National Archives)

2nd Battalion casualties: Salonika December 1916 – June 1917

Wounded	42	
Killed or died	14	
Total*	56	*includes only deaths in Salonika, not elsewhere

In addition, there were numerous casualties due to sickness.
Dead are buried at:
Karasuli and Salonika (Lembet Road) Military Cemeteries

Sources: Brigade and Battalion war diaries, CWGC, SDGW, CSR History

---

Chapter Nine

The Middle East, 1917-1918

The 2nd Battalion reached Alexandria late on 22 June 1917. It was exactly a year since they had landed in France. Arriving at their third front in twelve months, some wondered if they were destined to spend the war going from one 'side-show' to another. In fact the 60th Division was reinforcing the Egyptian Expeditionary Force at a crucial point in the war in the Middle East.

At the start of hostilities, Britain's main concern in Egypt had been to protect the Suez Canal, which was vulnerable to attack across the Sinai desert from Ottoman Palestine. Britain remained on the defensive during 1915 while attention focused on the Dardanelles campaign, for which Egypt was the base. Then, in 1916, the British began pushing the defences eastwards across Sinai. This was done in stages, while a railway, water pipes and 'wire' roads were constructed. This impressive infrastructure was slowly extended along the Mediterranean coast. Turkish forces were gradually pushed out of Sinai and by early 1917 were dug in along the frontier of Palestine between Gaza and Beersheba. British attacks on Gaza in March and April had failed, with many casualties. Now an autumn offensive was planned and General Allenby had just arrived to lead it. On leaving London, Allenby was told by Lloyd George 'the Cabinet expects Jerusalem before Christmas'.

The battalion, knowing little of the strategic picture, went by train from Alexandria to Ismailia on the Suez Canal. It was height of summer and they were given several weeks to acclimatize at Moascar camp. Ismailia was clean and pleasant with good facilities and leave could be taken in Alexandria and Cairo. The only drawback was a relentless Regular army style 'spit and polish' campaign. Henry Pope was not alone in grousing:

Bathing parade at Ismailia. Capt Wills and C Coy appear to be wearing water bottles for modesty!

'Heat and dust' – C Coy marches out from Moascar Camp shortly after arriving in Egypt, summer 1917. The heat was intense and the men had to acclimatize before moving into the desert to train hard for the autumn campaign.

> Hate this camp! Old bits of brass and worn-out leather require continuous cleaning and fellows were given extra parades in the heat of the day (with tunics on) for the slightest offence – worse than Warminster. …Colonel's daily inspection of lines with all kits outside cleaned and polished in glaring sun to decide which of us might have a pass into town. How we must impress the natives!

Towards the end of July, the battalion left for desert training. They made the long journey from Kantara in open coal trucks along the railway to Deir el Belah, then marched inland. Now they must learn to survive intense heat with minimal rations and water. The transport section, newly equipped with camels, would operate independently, travelling far and wide to draw daily water supplies. Keeping up with the battalion during mobile desert warfare would be a challenging task. The transport section, especially Lieutenant 'Sparrow' Gearing, consistently rose to it.

Into the desert

The first desert trek took two consecutive nights. Even after sundown the heat was fierce. Henry Pope recalled:

> It was 'some' march. Trudging along with huge packs (carrying blankets), feet sinking into soft sand at every step and exerting every ounce of strength to keep up with the pace. Fellows cursing and swearing everywhere. So thick was the dust that if a person had been shaking a cork mat in one's face it could not have been worse. It got in our nostrils and down our throats and covered every exposed portion of our bodies with thick dirt.

The 60th Division was taking over the Shellal-Gamli section of line, held as a chain of small outposts with the main body of men bivouacked nearby. The enemy was at least twenty miles away and the front was protected at night by cavalry patrols. The battalion spent twelve days here from 1 August. The CSR *History* gives the flavour:

> An average day…was…early morning company drill in front of the wire, breakfast, and then utter collapse and seeking the shade until about 4pm. The only joy of the hot day was the arrival of the camels with water…Everyone lay down and put pieces of muslin over their faces, hands and exposed knee caps, so that the flies should not be too irritating. Each afternoon a hot wind, called the 'Khamsin', blew regularly and brought with it a sandstorm. Drifting sand found its way into every nook and cranny.

Training hard for the attack

After a fortnight in support and training at Tel el Fara, the men were judged to be acclimatized. Over the following two months, training was intensified at El Shaulth. It was apparent there would soon be a 'great attack' and preparations were thorough and demanding, with long night marches and practice attacks. It was fairly monotonous, though the officers had some variety from navigating by compass and riding for reconnaissance purposes towards the Turkish lines.

Battalion Headquarters at El Shaulth, where the men had tough desert training. The campsite was in flat, monotonous desert scenery. Sand and flies were the chief features.

The battalion was reinforced by drafts from England and in 1917 it received, like the 1st Battalion in France, young civil servants released in a batch from regional tax offices. One of these, Vic Blunt, described his fellow recruits as 'a delightful crowd to know'. Blunt joined at El Shaulth on 22 September and was posted to B Company. He felt immediately at home:

> It was a great thrill to be among friends, educated, well-spoken lads so different to the many I had met since leaving England.

Blunt lacked the benefit of slow acclimatization and was thrown straight into desert training, for which his twelve weeks at Hazeley Down had hardly prepared him:

> 1 October: Had another attacking stunt early this morning. Only got in the way of another brigade on manoeuvres. Battalion marched back to our base camp at El Shaulth in the full heat of the

Everyone enjoyed visiting Cairo. Second right is 530872 Pte Percy Eels who with another stretcher bearer 531201 Pte F R Davey was later awarded the Military Medal for 'conspicuous gallantry and devotion to duty', bringing in wounded under heavy fire in the battle for Jerusalem on 8 December 1917.

BLUNT. — TOOTILL. — JENNINGS. — BOWEN --- FINCH ;

Pte F V 'Vic' Blunt (Walsall tax office) and pals about to leave Hazeley Down, August 1917. Two months later they went 'over the top' at Beersheba. Tootill and Jennings were wounded. Blunt saw more action at Sheria and Jerusalem and later transferred to the Royal Flying Corps. Kathryn E W Blunt

day. [It] nearly killed me, I was absolutely beaten when we arrived at camp...Oh this war is a bugger...4 October: Reveille 3am. We marched about one mile then watched...an exhibition of trench wire cutting by artillery. We went out again in the afternoon on a Brigade field day – attacking up the Wadi. Finished absolutely beat, never had a worse day in the Army...lots of 'buggering about'. 6 October: Feeling jolly rotten from the effects of the exercise during the last two days. Absolutely fed up with everything.

Leadership and morale

Morale during this period was not high. Perhaps not surprisingly, the CSR *History* gives no hint, but in 1934 an officer recalled the battalion as 'a mass of good fellows but disgruntled soldiers'. In 1967 another veteran went further: 'our keenness had been dulled and we were not doing well'.[1] According to Wills, the malaise was so pervasive that several officers applied for transfers. This could be attributed to the hard desert conditions or even to lingering disappointment at being withdrawn so quickly from the Western Front. The veterans, however, favoured a different explanation: that since going overseas they had been subjected to harsh discipline and a gulf had been forced between officers and men.

In common with other territorial units, the CSR had a tradition of friendly relations between officers and men, who came from similar professional and social backgrounds. It relied on self-discipline and peer pressure among its members, rather than direction from above. Colonel de Putron, a Regular, made no concessions to this liberal view and his lead was followed by his second in command (albeit he was a territorial officer) and by the Regular RSM. Junior commanders like Wills and Benké tried to operate the more traditional system within their companies whereby NCOs dealt with misdemeanours quickly and effectively. While de Putron's regime may have produced results in a Regular unit, it had the opposite to the intended effect in the CSR. Thus there was general relief when, after de Putron left for a training post near Cairo, he was succeeded by an informal, cheery young Regular captain on promotion. Tom Bisdee, from the Duke of Cornwall's Light Infantry, arrived three weeks before the battalion's first real challenge. Overnight, friendly officer-man relations were restored, without detriment to military discipline:

> He realised very early the type of men of whom the Battalion was composed, and was content to lead and guide rather than to drive. Destructive criticism had no place in his armoury.[2]

The immediate transformation in morale was probably due to a combination of Bisdee's refreshing leadership style and the prospect of getting some 'action' after the long period of hard training. A few weeks earlier another change had taken place. General Bulfin left on promotion and was succeeded as divisional general by Major General Shea. A rather theatrical character, Shea bemused the men on his first inspection by standing on a bully beef box, gazing cheerfully at the assembly and remarking enthusiastically, 'I like you! I like you!'

Lt Col T E Bisdee DSO MC, the youthful and popular CO who 'worked wonders' and led the battalion through the successful Palestine campaign. Bisdee died in a riding accident in 1934, aged 46.

Capture of Beersheba, 31 October 1917

General Allenby planned the main thrust of his attack against the Turkish left flank Hareira-Sheria. This was waterless country and it would be necessary first to capture Beersheba and its wells. From the high ground north of the town it would then be possible to attack the Hareira-Sheria line, 'rolling up' the Turkish line from its left. Preparations could not be totally concealed, especially with so much reconnaissance on the ground and by air. The plan was carefully devised with ruses and feints to delude the enemy into thinking that the attack would come around Gaza. The deception, sustained right up until the actual attack, worked well.

The Turkish line ran south of Beersheba, forming a stronghold around the outskirts. The 60th Division was to attack a section of trenches cut across the Beersheba-Khalasa road. On the division's right were troops of the Desert Mounted Corps, who were to envelop the Turkish left flank. Over ten nights, all units moved progressively and stealthily into position. General Shea addressed 179 Brigade and wished

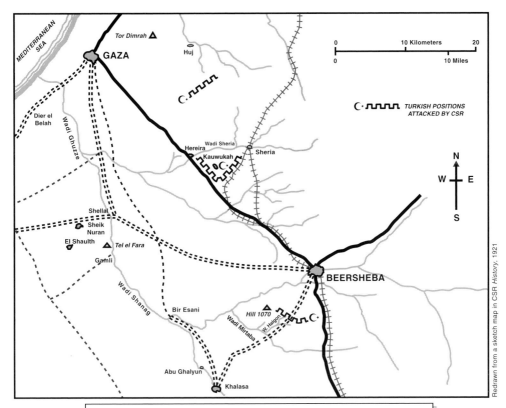

BEERSHEBA & SHERIA OPERATIONS, OCT 1917

everyone luck. He reminded the men that he would be 'carrying ribbons in his pocket' to reward gallantry on the spot.

The CSR began moving forward on 20 October, having left behind a number of 'non-starters'. While waiting several days south of Bir el Esani everyone had an enforced rest. Many wrote 'last letters' to be sent if they were killed. Captains Wills and Benké were given three days leave to Egypt, casually referred to as 'death leave'. On 28 October the battalion moved forward to Abu Ghalyun. Aerial photographs were studied and final orders issued. Colonel Bisdee's stirring eve of battle address brought loud cheers. Morale had never been higher:

> *Our one idea was to take the Turkish trenches and satisfy ourselves that our long training had not been in vain, and that we were worthy to rank with the 1st Battalion whose exploits in France had long been our secret envy.*[3]

That evening the battalion moved off towards the assembly positions. On the last section along the Beersheba road, absolute silence was observed. The column turned stealthily into Wadi Halgon, taking up positions in stony, broken ground criss-crossed by shallow gullies. C and B Companies under Captains Wills and F W Lewis were to make the assault, with A under Captain Rimington in reserve. D Company under Captain Benké was to go forward and secure the start line for the attack.

Vic Blunt, the twenty year-old from the Walsall tax office, only ten weeks after leaving England, was uncomfortably aware of the test he faced:

> Here we got our baptism of fire and a taste of fighting 'wind up'. Rifle fire opened up and enfiladed us from neighbouring hills. It was a rather terrifying experience in the dark hearing bullets whizzing about all over the place with no idea from where they came. We had one or two casualties and a camel and a horse were knocked out close to us. The numerous little wadis and gullies made excellent cover and we were able to lay down and await the dawn in comparative safety. In spite of the rifle fire I managed to get an hour's sleep. Oh, how I awaited the light of dawn – thinking, wondering and praying.

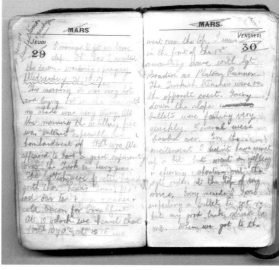

Vic Blunt's diary entry for 31 October 1917, the night before the attack on Beersheba: 'Oh how I awaited the dawn – thinking, wondering and praying'. Kathryn E W Blu

While B and C Companies waited in their gullies, spattered by intermittent machine-gun fire, D Company pushed forward to positions above and to either side of the line of the planned attack in the morning. Their job was to form strong defensive lines on the ridges overnight and to provide covering fire during the attack. They were very exposed and would suffer as a result. Corporal Jones spent the night lying on the ridge top. As light came he could make out lines of Turkish bivouacs about 500 yards distant. As the enemy troops began moving about, 'the opportunities for sniping were too good to be missed, and we got some splendid shots'. This attracted machine-gun fire and some D Company men were hit.

Before the assault could begin, Hill 1070 on the left had to be taken. An artillery bombardment began at daybreak and 181 Brigade soon after 0830 took the hill, the Turks having been taken completely by surprise. The artillery then bombarded the main Turkish line in preparation for the attack. The men breakfasted on tea and rum and awaited orders. In the advanced positions D Company, acting on a report that the enemy was already retiring, opened up with rifle and Lewis gun fire. Corporal Jones recalled:

> We got down in line, as we had done so many times in practice. For myself, I was completely calm and collected, and even enjoying myself (it was not always thus). …I was calm enough to notice that not even constant practice produces results in action, for the line 'bunched' badly in places. I walked up and down, spacing the men out…We maintained a brisk and steady fire, forcing the Turks to

keep their heads down; though none of them seemed to be retiring! For 20 minutes hardly a shot came over. Then, however, finding that no attack materialised, and that we made no attempt to advance further, Johnny Turk began to take courage, and before very long he got busy with rifle and machine gun.

The report had been wrong: the enemy was not retiring. One by one, men in Jones' line and in a nearby Lewis gun team were hit. With no sign of the battalion advance, the D Company remnants withdrew into what shelter could be found in the valley bottom. The three-hour wait which followed was agonizing. Meanwhile in the assembly positions the tension among B and C Companies was rising. 'Strange to think that this may be my last entry in this diary', scribbled one man.[4] Then the order came to attack in half an hour. Vic Blunt of B Company recalled:

We lay quietly waiting for the time. Was I frightened, I don't know. All I knew was that over the ridge in front of us were the Turkish lines and these had to be taken…At 1215 we went over the top. I was in the front of the first assaulting wave as platoon runner to Sergeant [Bowstead]. We were in a little wadi behind a ridge. It was necessary to get over the ridge, and off the skyline as quickly as possible. Once over the ridge, it was a rush down the valley and a charge up the opposite ridge where the Turkish trenches were at the top.

As he rushed over the ridge, Blunt noticed little scattered groups of D Company in 'suicide positions' among the rocks. They were 'real heroes', he felt.

Bullets were falling everywhere. Several of our lads were hit and I noticed one or two bowled over. In the excitement I didn't have the 'wind up' one little bit. I just went on running, yelling, cheering and shouting out the Sergeant's orders at the top of my voice. Every minute I was expecting a bullet to get me but my good luck stuck to me. …When we got to the Turkish trenches we jumped straight in and shot or bayoneted or took prisoner all that were there. I was lucky, the section of trench I jumped in was empty.

From his exposed position in the valley, Jones had witnessed B Company advancing:

It was a wonderful sight; they came down the hill at a run, keeping splendidly in line. My chief impressions…were of a Lewis gunner laden with a huge pile of ammunition drums yet running as fast as anybody, and a company commander waving his stick and grinning like a schoolboy. I dragged my men up to give covering fire as they passed, but

---

**530275 Private E J Cook, C Company
Distinguished Conduct Medal**

On 31 October 1917, for very conspicuous gallantry and devotion to duty. Having reached the enemy's work with his Lewis gun, the remainder of the team being casualties, he came under enfilade fire from an enemy machine gun. Grasping the situation, he turned his Lewis gun on the enemy gun. A duel ensued in which Private Cook was wounded and knocked into the trench. He recovered, crawled along the trench, seized another magazine and opened fire again, putting the enemy machine gun out of action and wounding two or three of the team – the remainder being killed or wounded immediately afterwards. This enemy machine gun had undoubtedly caused us many casualties.

Unusually graphic citation. Seven medals were awarded for Beersheba including a DCM for the CSM of C Coy, 'Joe' Oldcorn of the Inland Revenue.

before I had fired half a dozen rounds the attackers were racing up the hill in front, and soon came the inevitable roar at the end of the charge.

Further to the right C Company, led by Captain Wills, advanced across a valley swept by machine-gun fire. The Turks remained firing until the very last moment before throwing up their hands. Wills discovered his men were highly excited:

Bringing in Turkish prisoners after capturing the Beersheba defences. The battalion captured 3 officers, 50 other and a machine-gun.

> *Most of the Turks threw up their hands and I believe that some of them were bayoneted in cold blood. Everyone seemed absolutely berserk with excitement and madness and men were abnormal. When a bit of sense came to me I realised that the first thing to do was to extend our gain to the right of the trenches which had now been captured. ...I had a devil of a job to get the men to come out of the trench; they were all mad with excitement and apparently did not hear my orders. I had finally to prick one fellow with a bayonet to get him to take any notice of me and then haul him out hanging on to the butt of my rifle. Finally I got two or three out and then the rest came.*

Within half an hour, the battalion had captured all its objectives and cleared the last pockets of resistance. Most of the enemy had fled and the work of consolidation could be done with little risk. As planned, the Kensingtons pushed through to take the high ground overlooking Beersheba, capturing two guns as they went. The cavalry worked round the flank and occupied the town in the evening, securing the precious water supplies before the Turks could destroy them.

While casualties numbered seventy-five, including sixteen dead, these were not considered heavy given the strength of the positions attacked. But they were the most the 2nd Battalion had yet suffered and the shock to the survivors was great. Vic Blunt was distressed to learn that six from his draft had been killed or wounded. The men knew they had done well, even before Colonel Bisdee came up to congratulate them, and this knowledge appears to have sustained them during the night as they huddled for warmth in evil-smelling captured trenches. Kenneth Wills summed up the mood:

> *In spite of our losses and the beastliness after the show, everybody was in the most wonderful spirits. We felt we had at last proved ourselves.*

Attacks on the Kauwukah and Sheria defences, 6-8 November 1917

The attack had been successful but was only the beginning of a long, hard campaign. The victory must now be exploited quickly, before the enemy could recover and regroup. With the wells at Beersheba secure, Allenby's aim was to capture the Turkish main line of defences about

Capt Wills leading C Coy on 'Mustapha'.

Hereira and Sheria. The 60th Division was to attack strong defences on high ground near Kauwukah on 6 November, in concert with the 74th Division on the right and 10th Division on the left. So after only a short lull, the mobile warfare would be resumed. In the next sixty-two hours the battalion would push forward over twenty-three miles, attacking three times on the way.

Before moving off, the men spent two days bivouacked on the battlefield. It was in a disgusting state. They cleaned the trenches, collecting and burying many enemy dead. Good as his word, General Shea pinned the ribbon of a Military Medal on the chest of Private Joines of D Company for running with messages through heavy fire. Other awards took longer to come through. The battalion was then allowed one rest day north of Beersheba. It was a relief to be away from the filth and flies. Kenneth Wills, who had joined the battalion straight from school in 1914, described his reaction to leading men into action:

> *I do not think I have ever been happier than I was that morning riding out at the head of the company, feeling frightfully proud of the men and with new confidence in myself, for I knew in my heart that we had done well and that the men thoroughly trusted me.*

At night on 4 November the battalion made an unpleasant march of about eight miles over thick sand to the area of the next attack. The dust and lack of water was almost unbearable, as Private Cyril Hull of B Company recalled:

> *November 5th* [was] *the worst day I have ever spent…It was burning hot, and we had no water, and several fellows nearly went mad with thirst. Fortunately…we found some nice green water, of which I drank about a gallon. It was better than all the wine I have ever tasted.*

By early morning on 6 November, the battalion had assembled and was awaiting the result of the 74th Division's attack. The CSR was in support, with the Queen's Westminsters and Kensingtons leading. The plan was that after the first Turkish lines were captured, the CSR and the 2/19th Londons would push forward and take the rest of Kauwukah system. The men spent an anxious morning waiting while heroic teams of horse artillery cleared the Turkish wire for them. Wills addressed his men:

> *I remember making a little speech before we started on the consumption of the water supply…exhorting them to put up as*

good a show as they had at Beersheba, telling them not to forget their dead when they met the old Turk again, and that the souls of the fallen marched with them.

At last the CSR advanced behind the Westminsters, who captured the first objective. Then, as planned, the CSR and 2/19th Londons pursued the enemy over open country. Many lines of trenches were captured with little opposition. The enemy was given no chance to develop any counter-attacks. Soon, the whole of the Kauwukah and Rushdi systems were in British hands. Vic Blunt described the advance:

> *We advanced through miles over open country before we came to the enemy trenches. Bullets and shells were everywhere. I saw a good many poor fellows bowled over. I was very near one chap who seemed to have his shoulder blown off. I could do nothing to help him but I was pleased to see him picked up by a stretcher party. We captured the trenches taking many prisoners.*

179 Brigade, including the CSR, handed over the captured positions and went into reserve for a brief reorganization. The following afternoon, the brigade was off again in pursuit, this time to high ground above Wadi Sheria which, because of its water supply, the Turks defended tenaciously. The battalion crossed open ground under heavy shellfire. For the first time they deployed in 'artillery formation' – small 'blobs' of men at intervals, rather than in line, so as to present a smaller target for gunners. It proved effective. B Company, led by Captain F W Lewis, formed the advance guard and established an outpost against considerable opposition. The rest of the Battalion followed and spent the night digging in. Patrols were pushed out but there was no sign of the enemy. Vic Blunt, in the advance guard, described the action:

> *We attacked the enemy positions at night, charged up the slope and over the skyline. We managed to get over without much loss and then tried to dig in…We were no sooner over the ridge when enemy machine gun fire opened up. This made us dig in 'like all hell'. The bullets were whizzing everywhere and seemed to be trained on the ridge…I dug as hard as I could with my entrenching tool, trying to get as low as possible into the ground. The bullets were so close that I felt I was bound to get hit – don't think I have ever been more frightened. Out in front was a wounded Turk who was crying and yelling; this made me feel more frightened. Our Sergeant was*

531214 Sgt C F Jones, a schoolteacher, served in D Coy throughout and was awarded the MM. Jones was deeply affected by the war and it coloured his later life. In his memoir, 'NCO', he pays tribute to the 'extraordinary sense of companionship' in the CSR. F B Jones

shouting 'Keep your heads down'. When dawn came, what a relief we could not see a single Turk. They had, apparently, all retreated during the darkness.

Next morning the advance was resumed towards Huj. The CSR and London Scottish were in the lead as 179 Brigade pushed forward over open country and deployed for an attack on the village of Muntaret. C Company led by Captain Wills formed the advance guard and had about twelve casualties. It was tough going, especially for those carrying Lewis guns. Wills afterwards declared, 'no troops without good discipline could have done it'. The rest of the battalion followed C Company onto the ridge. Jones, in D Company, recalled:

Again we were off in artillery formation. This time we made a better target and it was definitely unpleasant to find shells falling so close; we saw a headless body, black against the sun, go twisting up and up from the platoon on our left; and one of our own corporals collapsed with a mixture of sunstroke and shell shock – a stout fellow too. However 'Bernardo' [Flynn] and I, bringing up the rear of the platoon, carried on pleasant casual conversation, both pretending hard that we weren't afraid, and knowing perfectly well that when next we were in bivouac we should discuss which incidents caused us to 'have the wind up' most. For though there may have been fire-eaters to whom fear was unknown, I never met them; the men I knew always confessed to it when the show was over.

Further advance across the plain was impossible because of shell fire. At this point General Shea came up and ordered the most famous cavalry charge of the war, by the Worcestershire and Warwickshire Yeomanry using sabres to knock twelve guns and their Austrian crews out of action. It was a spectacular sight but the yeomanry casualties in men and horses were very heavy. The way was now clear to push on. With the London Scottish providing the advance guard, the CSR went forward again, finally coming to rest at Tor Dimrah near Huj. This marked the end of this phase of fighting. The Turkish high command had ordered a general withdrawal northwards from the Gaza-Beersheba line. From the evening of 8 November the 60th Division was given a rest. Bivouacked on grassy slopes at Tor Dimrah, Vic Blunt had time to reflect:

What a time we had been through during the last ten days. Rations nothing but bully beef, biscuits and jam. No cigarettes. Not one night's proper rest and continually on the march – having marched and fought from beyond Beersheba to the sea. The Battalion owing to casualties etc is only just over half strength. Everyone is absolutely beat. I am as weak as a kitten, feeling done up all over. My face is covered with septic sores and my feet are all blistered. Today I had my first wash for a week. ...As I go to bed tonight I hope that never again I shall have to go through such a

*period...What with no water, fighting, marching, and short rations
I thank God I am alive and well.*

The battalion had marched sixty-six miles in eight days, making several attacks on the way. So deeply embedded was the 'trench warfare' mentality acquired in France, it was hard to believe that the ultimate objective was Jerusalem, another fifty miles away.

Capture of Jerusalem, 8 December 1917

On 19 November, the battalion set off along the fertile coastal plain between Gaza and Jaffa. It was a hard march. The autumn rains had begun and already the stubble fields had turned to sticky mud. Supplies of food and water remained meagre, but could now be supplemented with fresh food from local villages. En route they heard that British troops were within ten miles of the holy city and preparing to capture it. As they reached Junction Station, on the Jaffa-Jerusalem line, there were signs of recent fierce fighting in which the Jerusalem's rail link with the coast had been cut. The city lay only about twenty miles to the east but was surrounded by the Judean Hills - steep, rocky and inhospitable. The column turned inland and soon joined a partly metalled road which wound upwards, following a precipitous path through the hills. It was a long, arduous climb and the hard surface produced worn boots and sore feet for even the hardiest veterans.

Eventually they halted at Kuryat el Enab, a village set in pleasant terraced hillsides with olive and fig trees. Here the men were rewarded with almost two weeks' rest. The weather turned cold but no winter uniform was issued. Charles Hennessey recalled, 'we kept in our bivvies and got all the fun we could from a good grouse and some friendly bickering'. Vic Blunt's diary is more graphic:

Went sick with a septic finger. Told that over 200 men in the Battalion are dressed daily, with sores. We are still living on mobile

Captured Turkish positions immediately west of Jerusalem. The official caption read 'Nothing can give a finer idea of the nature of the obstacles that our troops had to encounter during their victorious advance on Jerusalem'. IWM (Q12874)

rations – tinned stuff, no vegetables – which is no doubt the cause of this bad blood. ...Everyone is getting very lousy. I am alive with lice and Hewer just cannot sleep for them.

Colonel Bisdee announced there would be one more 'stunt', to capture Jerusalem, and then a rest for the winter. Even this popular officer aroused cynicism when congratulating medal winners. According to Blunt, 'this did not impress many; opinion just a lot of 'all balls' nonsense'.

General Allenby's strategy was to compel the Turks to evacuate Jerusalem by completely encircling it, thereby avoiding fighting around the holy sites. This called for a complex plan, in which the 60th Division would attack eastwards, then wheel to the left, while the 53rd Division would guard its right flank and occupy the city. However the 53rd was still fighting its way up the Hebron road from the south and might not arrive in time. 179 Brigade was given an important and difficult task on the right flank: to attack the Turkish defences west of Jerusalem, along the Jura Heights and above the village of Ain Karim. These had to be captured before the general attack all along the front.

On 7 December, 179 Brigade concentrated near Soba, from where Jerusalem could clearly be seen. After an uphill march in heavy rain and cold wind, the men waited miserably for most of the day. Still dressed in shorts, they suffered from cold, wet and lack of sleep. In their communal singing that day, George Bazley detected a note of hysteria. General Shea, who visited the brigade there, afterwards vouchsafed that he had seriously wondered how men in this condition could attack the formidable mountain positions with any chance of success.[5] At night the brigade deployed near a watch tower above Ain Karim. The approach was along a winding path down a precipitous hillside. In driving rain the entire brigade, complete with mules carrying Lewis guns, stumbled along in single file. There was no preliminary barrage; it was to be a surprise attack. However, it soon became clear that the enemy's strength and readiness had been underestimated. During the morning local commanders had hastily to adapt the plans. For the CSR the first indication of Turkish wakefulness came in the faint glimmerings of dawn, when machine-gun fire from the direction of Ain Karim forced everyone to take cover.

While the rest of the battalion waited, C Company under Captain Wills went to assist the Kensingtons, who before daylight had captured the Jura Heights to the south of Ain Karim but were now engaged in a desperate struggle to consolidate it. In confused fighting on the ridge several counter-attacks were repelled and the enemy finally retreated. The CSR's medical officer Captain Leech and the stretcher-bearers did excellent work evacuating and treating dozens of casualties, including seven from C Company, of whom two died. While the struggle ensued on the Jura Heights, the rest of the battalion was in close support to the London Scottish, who ultimately overcame determined resistance from

Turkish trenches around Ain Karim. By 0400 all the brigade's objectives were gained and the main attack along the Lifta road could begin. Later the CSR pushed forward to the high ground overlooking the main Jerusalem road. The 53rd Division had, as feared, been delayed. As a result the right flank was exposed to enfilade fire from artillery on high ground south of Jerusalem. C Company suffered further casualties from this fire on rejoining the battalion. A new advance was ordered, then cancelled. The battalion ended the day bivouacked in outposts on the outskirts of the city, having had sixteen casualties in all.

Operations were suspended until the next day, but the Turks had already started evacuating Jerusalem. Rumours to this effect reached the battalion soon after dawn on 9 December, when orders arrived to be ready to move. A crowd of civilians with a white flag tried several times during the morning to surrender to junior members of the 60th Division. Eventually General Shea formally

General Allenby's entry into Jerusalem, 11 December 1917. The battalion marched into Jerusalem two days earlier to cheering by residents celebrating the end of Ottoman rule. Before long the Turks made a determined counter-attack, which the Londoners repelled at heavy cost. IWM (Q12616)

accepted the surrender around midday and General Allenby made his ceremonial entry two days later. This was the first time a European army had held sway in Jerusalem since its loss by the Crusaders in 1187. The resonance was not lost on the British press or the government's organs for propaganda. However, none of this was known to the CSR on 9 December as they set off towards the city, wondering if they were in for another attack. After more delays, they eventually marched into the suburbs. Henry Pope recalled the welcome:

> We had a glorious reception. All residents very excited and enormously glad to see us and one actually threw flowers at us.

Cyril Hull wrote home:

> They certainly seemed pleased but I have a shrewd suspicion that it is our money they want, not us. We must have looked a ragtime selection. Unshaven for days, some in drill, some in serge, one and all wet through and rain sodden, we all sang as loud as we could 'We are some of the London boys', and several other choice selections, not psalms as some people imagine.

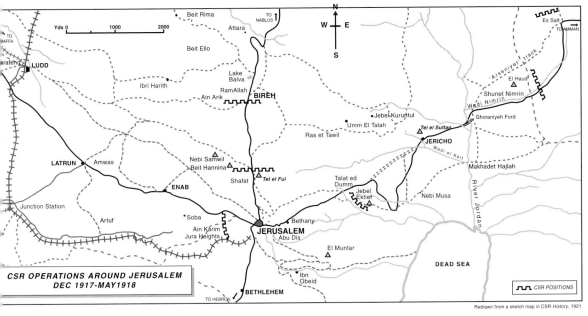

CSR OPERATIONS AROUND JERUSALEM
DEC 1917–MAY1918

Redrawn from a sketch map in CSR *History*, 1921

There was enormous excitement when the men discovered they had a dry billet in a German school – the first time under a proper roof since leaving France. Jones recalled:

> *Its floors were mostly stone, and had been fouled by the Turks; there was a dead body in the well; we had no rations, no overcoats, and no blankets; yet as I sat in a 'sergeants' room' lit by one solitary candle I felt thoroughly happy – as we all did. To be together in a room was truly a unique experience. [It was only] one night, but it was enough.*

Defence of Jerusalem: Tel el Ful and Beit Hannina, 27 December 1917

Next day the battalion moved out for five days in an outpost line at Shafat, on the Nablus road. It was still cold and wet and all companies were depleted by casualties and sickness. Captain Wills was suffering from dysentery and shortly afterwards was evacuated to hospital in Alexandria. At Shafat there was a call for volunteers for a raid. Wills was surprised:

> *It shook me that so few men volunteered from C Company. I suppose the men were as tired and fed up as I was.*

By 15 December the battalion was back in Jerusalem, with time to explore the sites. Christmas in the holy city seemed a pleasant prospect when suddenly they were ordered back into the hills. The battalion was to occupy support positions behind the line Beit Hannina-Tel el Ful astride the Nablus road – the main approach to Jerusalem from the north. Allenby's plans to renew the offensive, already delayed by the weather, suffered a new setback. Intelligence indicated the Turks were bringing fresh troops from the Caucasus to try to snatch back the city and inflict a severe blow to the Allies' prestige in the Middle East. Christmas was cheerless, as Henry Pope of D Company described:

193

Battalion headquarters at Tel el Ful, north of Jerusalem.

> *Christmas Eve!! Raining hard. Pack up and marched to hills in support as attack by Turks expected. Awful night, perishing cold and soaked through once more. Spent half the night carrying Lewis gun equipment from one place to another. Christmas Day - spent day in 'prehistoric stone cabin' or rather an alcove in some rocks with bivouac sheet for roof. Stay all day propped up on a stone because floor was a lake. Pouring with rain all day. Rations – 3oz of bully and about two biscuits. What a Christmas dinner! Half starved and shivering with cold.*

The Turkish attack from the north finally came on the night of 26 December. It lasted eighteen hours and was staged with great determination around two small but strategically important hills, Tel el Ful and Beit Hannina, held respectively by the Queen's Westminsters and Kensingtons strung out in defensive positions behind stone sangars. As the attack developed, CSR platoons went to the aid of both battalions. In desperate and prolonged fighting, the onslaught was finally beaten off. The Turks were prevented from breaking through into the outskirts of Jerusalem, but at tremendous cost in lives of Londoners.

Between midnight and 0800 there were no fewer than eight assaults on Tel el Ful. Lieutenant T H E Clark and two platoons of D Company went up and fought alongside the Westminsters. It was a grim struggle, ending with a sharp bayonet fight. The two CSR platoons suffered fifty per cent casualties. Just before dawn the Turks managed to gain a footing. The situation now was critical. Two more platoons (11 and 16, under Second Lieutenant Harris and Sergeant Jones) were ordered to 'eject the Turk with the bayonet'. This final counter-attack, made under severe shell fire,

Tel el Ful, scene of bitter fighting on 27 December 1917 as the Turks made their last desperate attack to break through and retake the city. The battalion suffered very heavy losses here.

Graves of Londoners on Tel el Ful, killed fighting off the Turkish counter-attack on 27 December 1917. It was a grim struggle, ending with a sharp bayonet fight in which two CSR platoons suffered 50% casualties. Ptes A G Long and F V Bolton were buried here but their graves are now in Jerusalem War Cemetery. Bolton enlisted with his brother, who was killed in France in 1916.

finally pushed the Turks off the hill. But the two platoons became surrounded and cut off, with disastrous results. Bernard Flynn later summarized the whole operation:

> *The call in the morning for everybody out. The first enthusiastic close-quarter encounter with the Turks; my chagrin at missing a retreating Turk at 25 yards when firing from the standing position. The later realisation of our precarious position, surrounded and exposed to enemy fire with men being killed and wounded around us. Barely adequate cover behind an outcropping of rock...'Tiny' Warren congratulating me on the prospects – remote they seemed to me then – of getting back to hospital...'Tiny' being killed instantaneously on raising his head to get a better sight to fire a rifle grenade. 'Bulldog' Harris a little to the left behind some rocks, exuding confidence. A fatuous signal to retreat from a runner up the hill – how the hell could we? The Turks coming on again and a last desperate bayonet charge led by 'Bulldog' and Charlie Jones. That was the last I saw of Harris.[6]*

2/Lt R H Harris, killed at Tel el Ful. A pre-war territorial from the Stationery Office, he had served in both battalions and was popular and highly respected.

Harris was the only officer to be killed before the battalion returned to Europe in July 1918. Meanwhile the Kensingtons, reinforced by the CSR's A Company under Lieutenant Andrew, had been under equal pressure at Beit Hannina. Wave after wave of enemy was beaten off. The Kensingtons' regimental history describes how, with Turks swarming up the slopes, the situation became critical:

> *With the assistance of the valuable company of CSR... [Colonel Mackenzie] judged the moment opportune to stake all by taking the offensive against the odds...The order was given for the whole front line to charge over the top of the ridge it had defended so stubbornly. The bold move succeeded, and the panting Turks, unable to face the oncoming bayonets, broke and bolted down the boulder-strewn hillside, followed by a fusillade of rifle fire and bombs. At this moment the remaining three companies of the CSR arrived post-haste and were thrown in...This settled the issue beyond all doubt.[7]*

The CSR's casualties were fifty-five killed, wounded and missing. It was some time before bodies could be recovered and numbers confirmed. Stretcher-bearers did magnificent work recovering the wounded under fire. One, Private Reginald Martin of the GPO, was recommended for the Victoria Cross. (He received the Military Medal, and was later killed by gas in France.) Charles Jones, badly wounded, managed to reach safety but most of 11 and 16 Platoons were killed, wounded or captured. Several, including the badly injured Flynn, were rescued some days later and only four were taken as prisoners of war to Turkey. The story of 'Bulldog' Harris, prominent pre-war soldier and school of arms champion, and his heroic death in a last desperate bayonet fight within sight of the walls of Jerusalem created an indelible impression on the regiment's communal memory. It was ranked alongside Vimy ridge and High Wood as examples of selfless courage against impossible odds.

German submarines haunted the Mediterranean. HM Transport Aragon *was torpedoed and sunk off Alexandria on 30 December 1917. A destroyer, HMS* Attack, *picked up survivors but was also sunk. Over 600 lives were lost, including 17 reinforcements on their way to the Battalion in Palestine. This photograph was taken by a deck officer who survived, Mr J F A Thompson.* Bob White

This was the enemy's last determined effort to retake the city. There remained some work for the 60th Division, pushing the line out north-eastwards as far as hills around Bireh. This was successfully achieved by 31 December. The CSR had been relieved on 28 December and was in support while this took place. It was not called upon to fight again until mid-February. The intervening period was spent in and around Jerusalem, reorganizing, road-making, doing outpost duties, training new drafts and preparing for the next attack.

Jebel Ektief, 19-20 February 1918

General Allenby had instructions to renew his offensive, with the aim of forcing Turkey out of the war. The Turks had retreated in two directions: northwards to Nablus and eastwards to a line which crossed the Jerusalem-Jericho road at Talat ed Dumm and extended northwards to Ras el Tawil and southwards to El Muntar. From Jerusalem to Jericho is only about sixteen miles but down 3,000 feet, then down another 800 feet to the Jordan river. The ground immediately east of Jerusalem is extremely difficult – steep hills with narrow gorges and inaccessible ridges. No more difficult terrain had yet been encountered in the campaign.

The next operation began on 19 February 1918, led by the 60th Division with the Anzac Mounted Division attached. The object was to advance on Jericho and drive the Turks east of the Jordan. 179 Brigade was again on the right flank, with the task of attacking the southern end of the Turkish line, specifically the hills of El Muntar and Jebel Ektief. On the first day, the London Scottish captured El Muntar. The CSR and Kensingtons were to assault Jebel Ektief the following day. This operation, ultimately successful, was fraught with difficulties and delays. Due to the almost impassable terrain, the Kensingtons were held up and could not arrive in time.

The CSR moved forward slowly to be in position by dawn on 20 February. D Company as advance guard had to get up a steep track (the Pilgrim's Way). The CSR *History* describes the terrain:

> *Probably of all the country over which the Battalion had passed throughout its stay in both Salonika and Palestine, none could compare with the deep ravines and precipitous cliffs over which the advanced guard had to pass ... To move forward a matter of three miles occupied a full six hours of hard climbing over ridges and difficult descents down precipices.*

Nevertheless D Company got into position. Then the main body of the battalion moved along the wadi bed. They found the place of deployment sprayed by machine-gun fire. Unable to move forward, they had to find another way, climbing up the steep wadi sides – complete with Lewis guns, first aid post and signalling mules – and down into the next wadi. Twenty years later, an 'ordinary platoon-man' gave his verdict:

> *Great credit is due to those who led us...when halted in the bed of the wadi, unable to move forward on account of the heavy fire, although the ordinary platoon-man probably did not realise this at the time. In fact some of us were half dozing while waiting for a way to be found out, partly due, no doubt, to the effects of the rum we had had some time earlier...It was a good example of leadership and dash overcoming great obstacles...a fine achievement of the Battalion.*[8]

Capt K A Wills served as OC C Coy for most of the war. He was recommended for awards for fine leadership at Beersheba, Jerusalem and Jebel Ektief and mentioned in General Allenby's despatch. He received the Military Cross in April 1918.

Down in the next wadi, machine-gun fire raked across from the left. With no sign of the Kensingtons, C Company was ordered to take that battalion's place on the left and fire on the enemy guns. The prearranged artillery bombardment fell behind the enemy's lines, leaving his guns undisturbed, so the battalion was unable to 'trickle forward', as ordered for the assault at 0800. After a second and better-aimed barrage, the battalion attacked not one but three successive ridges, each one strongly held. The attack was by A and B Companies and half of C. Captain Wills (now back from sick leave) and CSM Oldcorn led the charge. The Turks eventually gave way and fled into the Jordan valley. Casualties were between seventy and a hundred, including twelve dead. The CSR spent the night and next day perched on the precipitous cliff, from where Jericho could clearly be seen on the plain below.

The battalion remained on Jebel Ektief while Nebi Mousa and Jericho were captured and the enemy retreated across the Jordan. It was a relief not to be fighting but there were difficulties bringing up supplies. On 23 February they had a day's rest, then moved to outposts in hills near Umm et Talah, just in front of Jebel Kuruntul. There followed another period of comparative peace and delightful weather, during which the battalion reorganized and did more road-making. From now on, reinforcement drafts contained more varied types of men. As Jones recalled:

> *A large draft of boys had arrived. They were a cheery lot, and splendid material; but we hadn't seen anything quite so youthful or as unversed in the ways of the world as they were for what seemed like many years, and one had to adjust one's ideas and one's methods a little, for fear of disillusioning them too soon; for their boyish cheerfulness was an asset too valuable to be thrown away. Therefore I defended them as a lioness its whelps from the overweening demands of the Orderly Sergeant.*

First Jordan raid: Es Salt, 21 March – 2 April 1918

From their outpost at Umm et Talah, the troops could look down 3,000 feet to the plain and see the Jordan river and Dead Sea in the distance and the Mountains of Moab beyond. The valley was considered uninhabitable for white men and the troops assumed the war in that direction was over. Thus when the order came to descend and cross the Jordan, it was greeted with disbelief. General Allenby had decided to send a division of infantry across the Jordan and up into the Moabite hills as far as Es Salt. Cavalry would press on to Amman and attack a tunnel on the Hejaz railway, which ran northwards from Medina. The idea was to cut the railway and thus support the northward advance of the Arabs with Colonel T E Lawrence.

On 21 March, the CSR concentrated with the rest of 'Shea's Group', the raiding force of 60th Division and Anzac Mounted Division plus support units. The river was unfordable and, as expected, the Turks had destroyed the bridge at Ghoraniyeh. The river was swollen and it was only with the greatest difficulty and heavy losses that 180 Brigade established a bridgehead further south at Makhadet Hajlah. On 23 March, the battalion crossed this new bridge, passing through the scattered bodies of men of the 2/19th Londons, shot as they hauled over the first rafts. A mile-wide belt of thick scrub extended from the river bank, ending in flat ground from which hills rose steeply. The plan required using two routes from Ghoraniyeh to Es Salt, fifteen miles up in the hills. The first was the partly metalled road to Amman, entering the hills at Shunet Nimrin. The second, known by the troops (incorrectly) as the Arseniyat track, was a precipitous path north of the road which followed Wadi Abu Turra. El Haud, the highest point in the foothills, commanded these routes and had to be captured.

After bivouacking overnight in Wadi Nimrin, 179 Brigade received orders to attack El Haud. The CSR and Kensingtons were in support and had an uninterrupted view of London Scottish and Queen's

Westminsters creeping up amid shell and machine-gun fire to take the hill, which they did with little difficulty. The Turks retreated further into the hills. With El Haud captured, the way was clear to advance on Es Salt. On 25 March, the battalion set off as advance guard up the Arseniyat track – another trying journey over difficult terrain in appalling weather. Fortunately there was no sign of the enemy. By the time they bivouacked, drenched and exhausted, outside Es Salt, they had ascended nearly 5,000 feet in two days. Lieutenant Andrew and 16 Platoon cautiously entered the town, to discover the Turks had left and the locals shooting in celebration. The rest of the division moved off towards Amman, leaving the CSR guarding the town, where it remained for seven days until the whole raid was called off.

When the Turks left Es Salt, serious disorder broke out. Ethnic and religious rivalries erupted into violence and there were outbreaks of looting, even of the hospital. It fell to Major Gaze, as 'administrative commandant', to restore order. Gaze, a clerk from the GPO, had his work cut out. His first act was to settle a dispute by returning a valuable horse to its owner. When Gaze declined payment, he immediately gained a local reputation, according to Wills, for being 'just, but a little mad'. Gaze's prestige increased when he obtained supplies for the hard-pressed hospital and this enabled him to maintain order inside the town.

The security situation further afield was worrying. The raiding force was a long way from its base and there were difficulties with supplies. News arrived of a likely Turkish attack on Es Salt. The battalion quickly constructed sangars and took up defensive positions north-west of the town. Enemy firing began on 28 March (Maundy Thursday) and continued throughout the day but no serious attack materialized. A feeling of uneasiness grew, fed by alarming rumours that the operation against Amman was going badly. It appeared that if Turkish cavalry attacked at

Pontoon bridge across the Jordan at El Ghoraniyeh for the first 'raid', in March 1918. The Battalion crossed further south, struck across the scrub of the river valley and made a difficult ascent to Es Salt in the Moabite hills beyond. IWM (Q12604)

Es Salt, the brigade would be outnumbered. Other battalions of 179 Brigade returned to Es Salt. An indication of the anxiety is that one platoon was ordered to march backwards and forwards repeatedly over the skyline, trying to look like a continuous column of reinforcements.

At night on 30 March the enemy attempted to rush a post but was driven back. In two days there had been seven casualties including two deaths: one from a sniper and one from sickness. Captain Randolph of B Company was seriously wounded. As Jones' put it, things were getting 'very lively'. He still had the young boys under his paternal care:

> I had put my bombers behind a machine-gun sangar, and had my youngsters strung out to the left. This was their first time under fire, and some of them were quite nervous – which does not mean frightened; and I found that the most useful work I could do was to lie down beside them one by one and talk as if nothing unusual was happening – the cream of the joke lying in the fact that I was shaking like a leaf the whole time. ...After a brisk little engagement, the enemy withdrew. No doubt the shelling had shaken his nerve; the machine gun had done some good work; the boys, once they realised that this was all in the day's work, were as cool as veterans

Captain J H Randolph, badly wounded at Es Salt. An employee of Coutts Bank and pre-war territorial, he was bombing officer in France and later OC B Coy in Palestine.

Many of the 'old soldiers' found it hard to acclimatize to mountain temperatures and suffered, like Jones, with 'the shivers'. Some of them destroyed their sun helmets, which they resented having to carry in cold weather – an impulsive act they would soon regret. Early on 1 April (Easter Monday) it was clear that the attack on Amman had failed and the whole force would withdraw. The Armenian population of Es Salt, having welcomed the British so warmly, realized it was unsafe to remain and fleeing refugees impeded the evacuation. The CSR was among the last to leave. The journey down was even worse than the climb up. With enemy cavalry known to be close behind, it was inadvisable to halt and rest. Many arrived at the river stumbling with fatigue. The battalion crossed the new pontoon at Ghoraniyeh on the afternoon of 2 April, having marched about thirty miles virtually non-stop. The Jordan valley was at

Men of 179 Brigade and 3rd Australian Light Horse at Es Salt, March 1918. The battalion remained here for 7 days guarding the town while the raiding force went on to Amman.
IWM (Q12608)

its steamiest and most oppressive and during the climb up to Jerusalem some of the men were bordering on total physical exhaustion; some, according to Wills, were 'almost weeping with fatigue'.

After a short rest in billets on the Mount of Olives, the battalion had a period in reserve west of the Nablus road near Wadi el Jib. It was a pleasant respite bivouacked on a terraced hillside in warm weather. On 23 April, Colonel Bisdee left, to universal regret, to command the Kensingtons. Major Gaze succeeded him on temporary promotion. There were rumours of a return to the Western Front, where the situation was critical following the massive German offensive on 21 March. Thus the news of a second Jordan 'stunt' was greeted with more amazement than the first.

Second Jordan raid: El Haud, 28 April – 5 May 1918

Less than a month after struggling up from the plain, the battalion was once again marching down. After the British retirement in early April, the Turks had reinforced and reorganized their forces on the east bank. After abortive pre-emptive strikes on British positions in the Jordan valley, the enemy withdrew to Shunet Nimrin and held it in strength, constructing new defences on the slopes of El Haud. In this second 'raid' General Allenby aimed, using cavalry and two brigades of the 60th Division, to retake Es Salt; cut off and destroy the force at Shunet Nimrin; and eventually link up with the Arabs who were still advancing northwards. So far as these short-term objectives were concerned, the raid was a failure: the force was back across the Jordan again within a few days. But the venture had one important long-term consequence. It thoroughly deluded the Turks into thinking that this would be the direction of Allenby's final (and ultimately successful) offensive. At the time, however, it appeared to the London troops to be a futile operation. For the CSR it would be an unpleasant coda to their Middle Eastern expedition, costing forty-five casualties including four dead.

The battalion crossed at Ghoraniyeh on 28 April and spent the following day bivouacked in thick scrub on the plain, sweltering in the heat. While the cavalry moved on Es Salt, 179 and 180 Brigades were launched against the Shunet Nimrin defences including El Haud, the hill captured by the London Scottish with such relative ease in March. This time, the enemy – though taken completely by surprise – defended fiercely. On the night of 30 April the London Scottish and Queen's Westminsters captured the foothills with heavy casualties (the London Scottish alone had forty-eight per cent casualties), but were then held up. Renewed attempts on 1 May were unsuccessful. The CSR and Kensingtons took over the captured ground on the night of 1 May.

In what seemed to local commanders to be an impossible task, the CSR was ordered to make a final daylight attempt on El Haud in conjunction with the London Irish on the right and Kensingtons on the left. Wills, who judged it to be 'absolutely hopeless from the outset', was in command of the attack and set off at 0630, after artillery preparation. A and B Companies were leading, with C in close support. Wills described an incident which is interesting for being the only one of its kind he recalled:

> On our way up the little wadi I twice overtook a man of another Company who was lying in the bottom of the wadi. He informed me he had a strained ankle but I diagnosed it straightaway as 'wind up'. The first time I tried to cheer him up; the second time I made him go on at the revolver point, the first time I had ever threatened anybody in this way.

Returning from the second Jordan raid in May, the men were astonished to find these lorries waiting to take them up the steep road to Jerusalem. They tumbled in like excited schoolboys. Soon they would be on their way to the Western Front.

Reasonable progress was made up to the first spur but the higher slope was strongly defended by sangars, from which issued the same murderous fire as had mown down the London Scottish. Worse, the enemy poured fire from the right, where the London Irish were held up, due to being enfiladed in turn from their right.

The CSR pushed forward about 500 yards, forcing a small salient into the enemy's lines. A and B Companies incurred heavy casualties before going to ground. Captain Wills and C Company were further back on the crest of the small salient. They posted Lewis guns and spent an anxious day, acutely aware of the wounded lying in front but unable to go forward to assist them. The slightest movement brought forth a hail of machine-gun fire. The heat was intense and the hillside swarmed with flies attracted by dead bodies. To the left, the Kensingtons were in a similar predicament.

At dusk, stretcher-bearers crept out and helped the wounded in, leaving the dead where they lay. The remnants of A and B Companies withdrew, leaving C strengthening the positions in the little salient, where they remained for two more days. It was fairly quiet except for occasional exchanges of machine-gun and rifle fire. Alarming news filtered through that the raid further north was going badly. Then, on 4 May, the Turks counter-attacked the London Irish on the right, exposing C Company to enfilading fire. The situation was temporarily critical but saved by a signaller, Private Freer. Though wounded, he was able to pass a message calling for artillery support which enabled the London Irish to repel the attack. On the evening of 4 May orders were received that the whole force would withdraw. D Company was left in the uncomfortable position of rearguard, holding the positions on El Haud till the rest of the battalion had withdrawn. They kept up Lewis-gun fire for an hour, then hurried down to Ghoraniyeh.

After a brief rest near Jericho, the men were amazed to find lorries waiting to take them up the steep road to Jerusalem. El Haud turned out to be the battalion's final action in Palestine. The crisis on the Western Front demanded that every available man now be sent to France. The 60th Division was to release seven battalions, to be replaced by Indian troops. Allenby was starved of reinforcements and unable to launch his final, victorious offensive until September.

Ten days rest was allowed at Ain Arik, north of Jerusalem, where sports and entertainments were organized. There was then a short period furnishing working parties at Beit Rima before saying goodbye to the Kensingtons who alone of the Grey Brigade would remain in the Middle East. The men set off for Egypt with mixed feelings. The prospect of home leave from France was attractive but the break-up of the 60th Division was unsettling. Henry Pope recorded of the move to France, 'very pleased to hear it, I don't think…We apparently are going to lose our identity.'

On 17 June the CSR left Alexandria on the *Indarra*, arriving at the Italian naval base at Taranto on 23 June – exactly a year since arriving in Egypt and two years since going to France. On board, seven of the original officers sat down to a celebratory dinner. They were lucky to eat it for only a few hours earlier the *Indarra* had been attacked by a torpedo which missed by yards. The battalion had lost a significant number of men in Egypt and Palestine – not just as casualties but also to commissions and to other units which remained in the Middle East. However, in contrast to the 1st Battalion at this stage of the war, it still contained many more of its original officers and men. The return to the Western Front would bring a larger scale of casualties and many original men would perish in the last few months of the war.

1. J L Hutchison, CSR *Gazette*, Vol 12, No.2, July 1934, p2; QWR&CSR RMA *Newsletter*, Vol 7, No.4, June 1967, p 59; and Vol 7 No.5, October 1967, p 71
2. Hutchison, *op cit*
3. 'DED', B Company, CSR *Gazette*, Vol 13, No.2, July 1935
4. *ibid*
5. O F Bailey and H M Hollier, *The Kensingtons*, 1935, p 312
6. QW&CSR RMA *Newsletter*, Vol 9, No.5, April 1979 p 57
7. Bailey & Hollier, *op cit*, p 326
8. CSR *Gazette*, Vol 14, No.3, p 4

2nd Battalion casualties: Egypt & Palestine July 1917 – June 1918

Wounded	283	
Killed or died	99	
Total*	382	*includes 17 drowned from HMT *Aragon*

In addition, there were numerous casualties due to sickness.
Dead are buried at:
Alexandria, Beersheba, Cairo, Deir el Belah, Gaza, Jerusalem, Kantara, Port Said, Ramleh

Sources: Brigade and Battalion war diaries, CWGC, SDGW, CSR History

Chapter Ten

Return to the Western Front, 1918

Oh, we're the boys who tour the world, who've been on many a front.
We've sampled every kind of war and every kind of stunt.
We've seen the East, we've seen the West, we want to see no more.
But some old blighter's sent us back to where we were before.

(Marching song, 1918)

By June 1918, after seeing action on three fronts, the 2nd Battalion's self-deprecating nickname 'Cook's tourists' had begun to catch on. Continuing the joke after the war, ex-Lance Corporal Cyril Hull MM insisted to his family that, having spent so much of the war on a train, he had had 'a very easy time'. The week-long journey from southern Italy to northern France was hardly comfortable but by now the men were inured, as George Bazley recorded at the time:

> We entrained...[in] cattle trucks...and looks like an uncomfortable journey. As it happens we are used to this style of travelling. As usual the officers travel in comparative luxury in coaches. Got down after a bit of a struggle and managed to get a more or less decent sleep. After two years, feel as if I could sleep on a sword edge.

When the train stopped there were opportunities for leg-stretching and buying food and even souvenirs. Sergeant Jones was indignant at having to mount a guard on these occasions:

> Fortunately there were no serious attempts at robbing the train and our fellows did not attempt to get out of the stations; for while

Taranto, Southern Italy. The battalion spent a day here in June 1918, after the voyage from Alexandria. It was rumoured they would fight on the Italian front. Orders were received 'not to refer to our gallant Allies... as 'Italianoes', 'Ice-creamoes', 'Chip Potatoes' etc'. Next day they boarded a train for France.

their morals may have been no better than those of other units and their thirsts were of the largest size they always had sufficient decency to keep their appetites in check where the honour of the Regiment was concerned – a quality which was shared by the whole Brigade.

The run through Italy and along the Riviera was pleasant but as the train crossed France, Jones thought he detected a general war-weariness even in the countryside. Inevitably, there were mixed feelings about returning to the Western Front. The prospect of home leave was enticing, but the general outlook seemed bleak. The German offensive in March had not succeeded in splitting the British forces and cutting them off from the coast, but it had forced a humiliating retreat and the surrender of up to forty miles of territory. In April, the enemy had crossed the River Lys, forcing the evacuation of land desperately hard won in 1917 on the ridges of Messines and Passchendaele. The front line in the Salient was now almost up to Ypres itself.

On 1 July the battalion detrained at Audricques and went into billets near St Omer. Henry Pope recorded his misgivings on returning to 'this land of slime and slaughter':

> *Marched about 14 miles via St Omer to La Nieppe. Seems like old times to march over the cobbled roads crowded with military traffic. It has a certain fascination but we do not feel eager to know what the future has in store.*

Their future, it transpired, was in Flanders, where further attacks were expected. Along with the London Scottish and Queen's Westminsters, the battalion now formed 90 Brigade in the reconstituted 30th Division. Before going into the line near Mont Kemmel on 25 July, there was a period of reorganization, spent in billets west of Cassel. Special courses brought the men up to speed with developments in infantry tactics since they had left France in 1916. There was also field training and practice in the counter-measures to be taken if, as expected, the Germans attacked on the Kemmel-Hazebrouck front. Home leave was opened up – for many, their first in two years. According to Jones, 'one and all declared...that the people at home did not know there was a war on.'

The battalion was now subject to its first big personnel changes. Major Gaze was promoted, becoming the first civil servant to command the 2nd Battalion overseas. Later, during the Flanders operations, command was given to another civil servant and pre-war man, A C H Benké, who for two years had led D Company. A number of NCOs left for officer training. While in the Middle East they had resisted applying, perhaps not wanting to leave their pals and the battalion. However on return to France the prospect of four months' officer training in England must have been very tempting. The general manpower shortage resulted in haphazard posting of reinforcements. The battalion received drafts of variable quality, including young conscripts intended for other units and older men 'combed out' of non-combatant jobs. Training these mixed drafts and inducting them in 'Civil Service' ways required some effort. Another noticeable change was the relative inexperience of new subalterns. Some of these required much support and guidance from their sergeants as well as their company commanders. The following comment by Captain Wills is revealing, even after making allowance for regimental pride:

> *In the fourth year of the war I was sent three subalterns none of whom had ever seen a shot fired...[None was] as fit to command a platoon as practically any man in the ranks of those same platoons, and certainly not half as fit as any of the NCOs, a great many of whom could have got commissions easily but would not do so as they knew it meant leaving the Battalion which they loved.*

The military situation in the Cassel sector, astride what had been the France-Belgium border, was dictated by a series of 'monts'. These were hardly real mountains, but assumed significance due to the flatness of the surrounding plain. The Germans possessed the highest, Mont Kemmel, which gave enormous tactical advantage. The British held Mont des Cats. They also looked down on the Germans from a line of hills between Mont Noir and Mont Rouge. The Germans possessed Dranoutre ridge, which ran down from Mont Rouge through the ruined villages of Locre and Dranoutre.

What a reintroduction!

From 25 July the battalion spent five days in support trenches near Mont des Cats. It was virtually impossible to move around during the day. Until the Germans were forced off Mont Kemmel at the beginning of September, no rations, reliefs or anything else requiring movement could be organized during daylight. The CSR *History* records that nothing of interest occurred in the battalion's first five days 'beyond the usual unpleasantness of trench warfare'. In his diary Henry Pope of D Company was more expansive:

> *What a reintroduction to the western front! Very 'uncomfortable' – no trenches. Position very exposed and the only cover a few small shelters built into the side of the road. We stayed here for the day and in the evening took over the front 'line'. There was no line. Only a few shell holes 'improved'. Travers, Fullager, Hawley and I formed one Lewis gun post. It was a fairly deep shell hole with a piece of corrugated iron over one side as a shelter - water at the bottom and the sides loose mud. Of course it rained all night. There was continuous shelling and machine-gun bullets flew very close every now and then. We were like shipwrecks on a lonely isle except that the platoon was **somewhere** about and we knew there were more troops **somewhere** behind – about every hour or so an officer and man would come round to see if we were*

awake. In a heavy bombardment towards dawn Pibworth's gun team was knocked out and several were killed and I heard afterwards Pibworth had lost a leg. Eventually we were relieved from this post and went back to the roadside for 24 hours.

Pope and his team were not the only ones to feel isolated. Captain Wills of C Company was in the support line in a tiny coffin-shaped headquarters, with no telephone and unable to get to the front line except at night. This was 'defence in depth', whereby one company held a small section of line – two platoons in front, one in support, one in reserve, with headquarters in the 'line of resistance' in the rear. Used to leading from close quarters, Wills hated this new arrangement:

> *I was very worried now, for the two officers in command of the platoons in the front line were both of them new, neither of them had seen a shot fired and I was not impressed by either.*

The casualties in this first tour numbered about fifteen, of which at least three were killed. After a week's rest the battalion spent seven days in support in the Locrehof sub-sector, followed by two further days in the front line

Dranoutre Ridge 21-28 August

The German offensive in Flanders – so confidently expected and so feared – did not materialize. Further south, the tide in the war was already turning and this affected the whole Western Front. The Germans had to divert troops away from the Salient, which gave the British the opportunity to seize the initiative there. The 30th Division was ordered

HQ officers at Boesinghem, late 1918. They claimed to be exhausted after entertaining the village priest to a liquid lunch, whereas the priest toddled home apparently unaffected! Standing: Major RBW Andrew, Capt & QM A A Joslin, Capt & Adj S C 'Sammy' Hall, Lt J L Hutchison. Seated: Lt THE Clarke, village priest, Lt Col A W Gaze, and the chaplain the Rev R Edwards. Jennifer Gaze

Medals awarded to Lt Col A C H Benké. He won the MC at Beersheba and the DSO as CO in Flanders. The group also includes the Defence Medal 1939-45 and the OBE awarded for his civilian career as a prison governor. Family of A C H Benké

Lt Col A C H Benké, in 1939-45. A civil servant at the Home Office, Benké joined the CSR in 1910. He served briefly as a 17th March officer before joining the 2nd Battalion, in which he played a prominent role. An inspiring OC D Coy, he eventually commanded the battalion in Flanders in 1918.
Family of A C H Benké

to take Dranoutre ridge on the night of 21 August. The London Scottish took the lead. The CSR was in reserve and eagerly awaited news, which was encouraging: the Scottish achieved all their objectives, though suffering heavy casualties, and the ridge was won.

In the immediate aftermath came fierce enemy shelling and determined counter-attacks. The CSR relieved the London Scottish in the newly captured line on the night of 22 August, beginning what Captain Wills described as 'three days...of absolute misery'. In heavy shelling during the relief, Captain H J G Back of Prudential Assurance, newly promoted to command D Company, was severely wounded, both legs being badly smashed. The battalion occupied positions close to Locrehof Farm, forming an unpleasant little salient into the German line – a likely target for a counter-attack. The line was just a few scattered shell holes near a slag heap, and the men began digging to try to connect them up. Patrols went out to watch for any sign of attack and Lewis gun teams were posted at key points, including a B Company team on the slag heap. The first counter-attack soon came but was beaten off, as Wills described:

> Down came their barrage in an inferno of first gas shells and then HE, luckily most of them bursting beyond us. Then the sound of bombs exploding. My men fired furiously, then absolute quiet...

Fearing a second attack, Wills organized a wire entanglement across the neck of the salient:

> In the ordinary way one wires with a covering party in front but we had not the men and so had to chance it...The men worked like Trojans and Kelly worked like three men. We all tore our hands on the wire but nobody minded.

Leaving a gap in the wire so that the advance Lewis gun team could get back, they then set about wiring in front of the slag heap.

530247 L/ Sgt P J Kelly, C Coy. In his memoirs Capt Wills described the desperate action on Dranoutre ridge on 22/23 August 1918. He and Kelly were attacked by two German machine-gunners. Kelly's quick thinking and decisive action saved the day and he was awarded an immediate Military Medal.

532753 L/Cpl Victor Dark, a schoolmaster originally from Devon, joined the Battalion in France in August 1916 and served in Greece and Palestine. Was wounded at Beersheba and recovered, only to be killed in the fight for Dranoutre ridge on 23 August 1918. Arthur Dark

Time was getting short and it was only a question of minutes now before the next attack might develop...Corporal Kelly and I approached the slag heap from the rear carrying a roll of barbed wire on a stake between us. Both of us had on wiring gloves...As we approached...a couple of men came round the left-hand side of the heap. I thought that they were part of my wiring party and shouted at them asking what the hell they were doing. A second later a German stick bomb burst some few yards away and I realised that they were Boche. I am afraid I lost my head, tried to tear off my wiring gloves and get to my revolver. Not so Kelly, the Ulsterman, who kept his head and did not try to get off his gloves, but took out a Mills bomb, pulled the pin out with his teeth and threw it. The bomb exploded and got them both. Afterwards we discovered that they were Boche machine-gunners and had brought their machine gun along with them. If they had kept quiet and had not attacked us at once they would have lived to tell the tale and we should not.

The two Germans were the advance party for the next counter-attack, which now came on. Again it was repulsed by frantic firing, after which all became quiet. The enemy did not attack again, but Wills discovered many casualties including Private Ellis of C Company. The entire B Company Lewis gun team on the slag heap were casualties:

They had received, I imagine, a direct hit from a shell and were one horrid pulp with the Lewis gun smashed in their midst.

Total casualties were fourteen deaths and about thirty wounded. The dead included several original members of the battalion and Second Lieutenant E Jones of D Company who had been with the Battalion barely six weeks. While on Dranoutre ridge, Captain Wills suffered badly from dysentery contracted in Palestine, where he had nearly died from it:

The line was primitive in the extreme; there were, of course, no dugouts, no sanitation. One could not leave the trench; rain fell incessantly; Boche aeroplanes came over and dropped bombs and we were continuously shelled. My dysentery came on me again and I felt sick and the skin on my legs sore and painful [from mustard gas]

Shortly afterwards Wills was evacuated to England and did not return, having played such a prominent role in the 2nd Battalion's war and in this account of it.

From Mont Rouge to Wulverghem: 30 August – 3 September

On 28 August, fires were burning all day behind the German lines from Kemmel southwards as far as the eye could see. A withdrawal seemed imminent and on 30 and 31 August the battalion stood by, ready to move at half an hour's notice if the enemy was seen to surrender any ground. On 1 September the Germans began to draw back, evacuating Mont Kemmel and retreating to a line on Messines ridge. The 30th Division was ordered to advance across the devastated area left by the enemy and push forward the front line as far as possible. A full-scale attack on the ridge was not planned immediately. Meanwhile the tactic was to harry the Germans as they settled on their new line of resistance. This kind of warfare required men to work in small, often isolated patrols, probing the enemy's new defences and setting up small outpost positions. It gave rise to opportunities for leadership and initiative at all levels, including the most junior NCOs and privates. This is reflected in the divisional honours list for this campaign, in which the CSR shared.

On 3 September, the battalion relieved the London Scottish near the ruined village of Wulverghem beneath the enemy position on Messines ridge. Here they spent a very difficult two days and three nights under heavy shellfire but continued to probe and push forward. Some modest progress was made – advancing the line about 200 yards – but there were twenty-four casualties of which six were killed including another young subaltern who had only joined the battalion on 8 August. Of five men reported missing believed killed, three were never found, and are commemorated on Tyne Cot Memorial. The other two were discovered alive on 8 September and one of these, Private Cleaver, was awarded the Military Medal for staying out in no man's land with his wounded comrade until help arrived.

The CSR now qualified for almost two weeks 'rest'. This was spent chiefly at Mont Vidagne, with working parties at Westoutre on road making and other heavy duties. There were also memorable performances by a concert party formed from men of the transport and stores. On 12 September there was a parade at which the corps commander presented ribbons to a group of men decorated for the Dranoutre operations, including Sergeant Kelly. On 19 September, the battalion marched about ten miles to Neuve Eglise, and the companies split up for separate duties. This was a comparatively quiet period, though the positions were exposed to enemy observation from Messines ridge and any movement by daylight would provoke heavy shelling. There were five casualties, including three killed.

Recapture of Messines Ridge and on to the River Lys, 28 September – 3 October

The CSR's 1st Battalion had lost many men in the wresting of Messines ridge from the Germans in June 1917. The ridge had remained in British hands until April 1918 and some feelings of satisfaction might be expected as the 2nd Battalion helped to recapture it. But, as the 30th Division historian noted, the ridge provided 'neither time nor the place for philosophizing'. The operations in which the two CSR Battalions took part were markedly different – a fact which demonstrates how far by late 1918 the balance of advantage had turned in the Allies' favour. Whereas in 1917 a major action had been necessary to wrest Messines ridge from German possession, in September 1918 it was retaken in an operation supplementary to a much larger attack further north beyond Ypres. This time the ridge would remain in British hands for good.

The first objectives were very limited – roughly the first line position of the enemy. This was a series of ruined cottages and farms, fortified with machine guns, which were to be taken by fighting patrols rather than a staged attack. This, according to the CSR *History*:

> ...called for a good deal of initiative on the part of company, platoon and subordinate commanders in rushing and getting around machine guns when even the mere covering of the ground alone presented considerable difficulties.

With the Queen's Westminsters on the right and the 2/17th Londons on the left, the CSR was to attack in the general direction of the main road from Wulverghem to Messines. The principal objective allotted to the battalion, called Big Bull Cottage, was heavily fortified. After it was taken, if the corps on the left advanced successfully, then the CSR and 2/17th Londons would make good a line over the ridge, and even further as the situation might develop.

At 0530 on 28 September, British artillery opened up – not a creeping barrage but falling on selected areas to cover the work of the fighting patrols on the allotted objectives. The CSR *History* records the action:

> Both our attacking Companies [A and C] got well off the mark under this artillery preparation and possessed themselves of all their objectives, the greatest resistance coming from Big Bull Cottage, where most of the occupants were killed, and before 0700

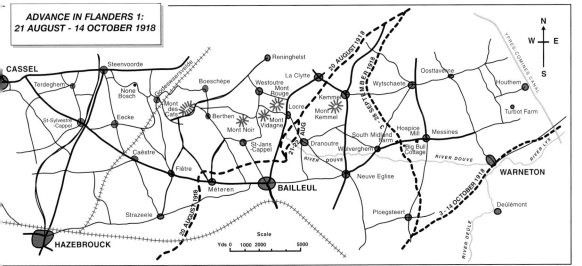

ADVANCE IN FLANDERS 1:
21 AUGUST - 14 OCTOBER 1918

Redrawn from a sketch map in CSR *History*, 1921

Charles Quinton as a patient at Netley Hospital (seated, second left). He was ill for two years but was able eventually to resume his Civil Service career. Family of C J Quinton

530127 Sgt C J Quinton, Exchequer & Audit Department, had served throughout the war and on his first leave home, August 1918, he married Ethel whom he had known since Sunday School. Quinton was dangerously wounded in early October and had his leg amputated in hospital in France. Family of C J Quinton

the Battalion had claimed seventeen prisoners and nine machine guns....All the enemy strong points to be attacked had the armaments of machine guns, Captain Peatfield's company, A, our left attacking company, accounting for six, Second-Lieutenant Pittam leading the platoon that captured them. Lance-Sergeant P Mason of A Company mopped up a post of four with no little dash and skill, helped by the daring reconnaissances of the previous night, in which Private J Volke had a notable share.

C Company (Captain F H Du Heaume) had also pushed forward and captured a network of trenches known as Rome Alley, driving off the garrison and killing a few of the enemy while their patrols afterwards pushed towards Gabion Farm, which was strongly held by the enemy. Against this strong point C Company had to form a defensive flank, as the 2/16th Battalion [Queen's Westminsters] had not advanced in the first stage of the day's operations. No determined counter-attack was made on our front, although the enemy was active with his snipers and machine guns.

B and D Companies moved up to support positions and the new front line was held, while news was awaited of other attacks taking place, both to north and south. Eventually the enemy, facing attack from two directions, began to retreat over the ridge. This opened the way for 30th Division to push further forward. The battalion advanced in the dark,

Telegrams to Ethel Quinton. On 11 October her husband was classified 'seriously ill'. The following day he was 'formerly seriously ill now dangerously ill' and permission was denied to visit him.
Family of C J Quinton

Two pages from Charles' remarkable letter to Ethel, just days after his leg was amputated. He had lost many friends killed and his relief at having a 'Blighty' wound, even such a serious and disabling one, is palpable: 'Oh! How great it is to be able to look forward to a future. Surely, in spite of the pain I am in at times, God has been good to us both. How happy we shall be when we meet.' Family of C J Quinton

meeting some resistance from German rearguards. One Company (A) actually reached the ruined village of Messines that night, but had to fall back owing to slower progress of other troops.

The battalion was ordered to continue advancing the following day to secure the canal crossing at Houthem, some three miles beyond Messines. In preparation, A Company was relieved in the front line by

D, which, according to Jones, was no longer the well-oiled machine it had been in Palestine:

> We took over the line and soon a runner came with some orders. They were rather mixed...Obviously the old company was not itself. Captain Andrew was on leave and we were commanded by an officer who, though courageous and experienced, was badly out of practice, his recent service having been with the transport. In addition to Mr 'Lindmore' we had one subaltern borrowed from another company; and we had only two sergeants. One can hardly imagine orders like those in the old days.

'Lindmore' was Jones' pseudonym for one of the new type of young officer, of which the battalion received several at this period. He was inexperienced and unsure how to lead his men: 'Will you see to it, Sergeant', was his too ready response when ordered to take Messines. Worse, he openly criticized the battalion, regarding it as poor discipline that privates addressed corporals by their first names. He did not stay long. At dawn on 29 September the CSR advanced in a heavy mist. There was little resistance and Messines village and the ridge were taken easily. Jones recalled:

> Messines [was] a ghastly chaos of bricks, mud, water, filth of all descriptions, the whole covered with an impenetrable thicket of barbed wire. A dozen machine guns could have held it against an army. Fortunately there weren't a dozen machine guns; there was not a Boche for miles. Our only casualties in the village were due to wire, for hardly a man came through unscathed. I reached the other side with my puttees in shreds and one thigh exposed from groin to knee.

After sustaining some casualties going down the eastern slopes of the ridge, the CSR made rapid progress across open country towards Houthem. Linking up with troops of 89 Brigade, the battalion then assisted the advance on the left of the 41st Division, which had already got across the canal. At night the CSR formed a defensive flank to the 30th Division, near the canal and facing south.

The River Lys now formed a new and formidable defensive line for the Germans and on 30 September there was no further advance on 30th Division's front. The battalion marched back to Messines ridge and occupied old German dugouts and pill boxes. This fluid form of warfare was very tiring. Sergeant Jones in particular showed signs of fatigue:

> It had been a very wearing 'stunt'; for in addition to the sheer fatigue of advancing over muddy and broken ground, there was a considerable nervous strain about the whole affair, a lot of time spent waiting for things to happen, even if they never did; and when I got back ... I had a day of complete exhaustion – another sign, though I did not realise it, that I was showing strong signs of wear and tear, that my powers of resistance were declining.

During the successful Messines operations, casualties had been comparatively light: twelve killed and forty wounded, due mostly to heavy artillery fire. The biggest casualties came from a shell on battalion headquarters which killed, among others, 'Doodle' Lovelock, a Bank of England official prominent in the pre-war regiment. Lovelock was well known as an original of the 2nd Battalion who in Egypt had become its first 'home-grown' RSM. He was succeeded by another original, Ben Dyer of D Company, who himself was killed a fortnight later. The deaths of original men after four years' service were deeply unsettling and feature in all the memoirs.

After an unpleasant stay on the ridge, which was still being heavily shelled, the battalion moved to support positions in flooded pillboxes and dugouts in Ousttaverne Wood. A less unpleasant respite followed near Wytschaete. Jones was gratified when Mr 'Lindmore' was replaced by 'a real subaltern – young but not too boyish, full of energy, complete with Military Cross'.

From the Lys to the Scheldt and beyond: 11 October – 11 November

The CSR moved forward on 11 October, for what turned out to be its last action of the war. The twelve-mile march to America Corner (just north of Wervicq, which was then in German hands) was extremely trying. The advance party was gassed and had to be evacuated. The positions around Wervicq were drenched in gas, littered with dead horses and overlooked by higher ground south of the nearby River Lys. It rained heavily. The attack was set for 14 October, allowing two days for familiarization. There was continual gas shelling, and all reconnaissance had to be done at night.

The River Lys presented a formidable defensive line for the Germans as they retreated from Messines ridge at the end of September. These Scottish troops are crossing at Halluin on 18 October. Two days earlier the CSR managed to get across about 3 miles downstream near Wervicq. IWM (Q7131)

The plan for the next attack was to push forward to the River Lys and if possible get across and onto high ground beyond. 90 Brigade was to attack on the left. On the brigade front the CSR would attack on the right and London Scottish on the left. The attack was timed for 0535, preceded by a four-minute barrage. Sergeant Jones took his platoon up to the jumping off line an hour beforehand, established the men in shell holes and issued rum. He felt sick and miserable, having caught a mouthful of gas, but somehow managed to sleep for the final half-hour. He was woken by the start of the barrage, which was like nothing the battalion had experienced before.

Some of the 30th Division gunners realized this was their last big barrage and gave it everything they had. 'It came down along and in front and behind the Lys with all the cumulative fury of four years of war – machine gun bullets, shrapnel, smoke, gas, thermite and high explosive'.[1] The effect on the enemy was devastating. The battalion advanced behind the barrage in clouds of smoke, rushing pillboxes, capturing machine guns and taking prisoners. Accounts of this action exude excitement, almost enjoyment:

> *The smoke cloud was the thickest I've ever seen...We just pushed on...I forgot all about my dose of gas in the excitement, and just went on like mad. The boys were fine, and some of them had some funny experiences.* (Charles Jones)

> *We immediately got word to go forward so – me with the encumbrance of a Lewis gun – we started. We were very excited and there was a lot of noise. [I] kept expecting to be knocked out by a shell but wasn't. We went across ditches and through wire, getting more wetted and torn. Occasionally we stopped at a pill-box to collect prisoners but there was no resistance. Feeling 'don't care' we lighted cigarettes as we went forward. Mash threw a bomb in a place in which we thought were Germans but instantly a big firework display started – it was a Verey light store. The place, made of thin timber, caught fire. In one dugout Palmer found a Jerry parcel containing a very nice cake so we devoured this going forward. It was good. Very heavy mist this morning and we lost direction a bit and went far past our objective so had to sort ourselves out.* (Henry Pope)

> *Prisoners kept emerging in a state of sheer terror, some crying bitterly, others cursing the Kaiser. Our chief difficulty was that they imagined – not without reason – that it was safer to stay with us. We had to drive them towards the rear with threats and even kicks ...We arrived at our objective without difficulty and my officer and myself took a stroll to find the next Battalion.* (Charles Jones)

There was similar success all along the line. The Germans began to fall back, surrendering ground all the way from the coast in the north down

534313 Pte C R Honychurch enlisted when just 17, having travelle from Barbados wit an older brother in 1916. In France h trained as a Lewis gunner and was attached to 7th KRRC. Gassed and evacuated to UK when still under 18. Spent the rest of the war at home in Royal Defence Force. The CSR was one of several London 'class' unit favoured by white Barbadians.

Doug Honychurch

to La Bassée in the south. On 90 Brigade's front, the attacking troops paused for consolidation, and the artillery on both sides exchanged fire. Over 300 prisoners passed through battalion headquarters in half an hour. CSR casualties were forty-two, including seven killed.

By evening the enemy was falling back across the River Lys, destroying bridges as he went. But he still held the high ground on the far bank from where his guns could interfere with any attempted crossing. At night on 15 October A Company managed to get across near Wervicq on a bridge which was not quite destroyed. Under Captain du Heaume, they moved eastwards and formed a bridgehead at Bousbecque, providing cover for Royal Engineers to construct a pontoon. The remainder of the battalion crossed in the morning and occupied Bousbecque. The village was cleared and a defensive line formed on the outskirts. Henry Pope took up residence in a German pill-box:

> *Very snug and comfortable places they were – apparently belonged to Hun officers. Furnished with beds and dressing tables and various nick-nacks...Jerry's barrage fire was interesting to watch from our safe position...He shelled every road and street and practically every likely billet for troops.*

By evening it was clear that the enemy was again retreating and would not make his next stand until reaching the River Scheldt, about fifteen miles further east. From now on the nature of the terrain changed dramatically, as Charles Hennessey noted:

> *We began to find ourselves moving forward into a countryside untouched by war. The contrast between this undamaged line and the tortured earth in the Messines area was unbelievable, and the outlook gave us a feeling of elation.*

French and Belgian civilians began emerging with friendly greetings, and hung flags from the windows of their undamaged houses.

The Queen's Westminsters and London Scottish continued the advance, encountering little opposition until reaching the Scheldt, where the Germans made a stand, causing a temporary hold-up.

**ADVANCE IN FLANDERS 2:
15 OCT - 8 NOV 1918**

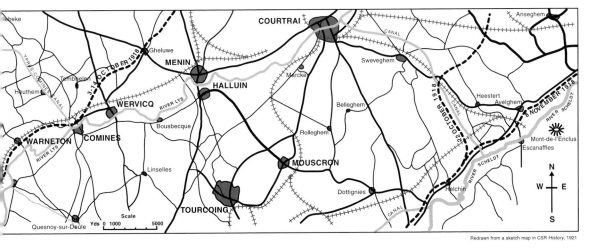

Redrawn from a sketch map in CSR *History*, 1921

90 Brigade was given a rest until the end of October. This was spent in comfortable billets around Tourcoing in the undevastated area. The men enjoyed sports, football and entertainments.

The battalion had just one more period under fire – three days from 1 November at Avelghem, beside the Scheldt. Most of this they spent underground, while German artillery across the river reduced Avelghem to rubble around them. The battalion was relieved on 4 November. By now there was uncertainty in the air. Orders were issued, then cancelled, as Henry Pope recorded on 6 November:

> *Going back to the line today...Raining. Get on road, when lo! 'Halt! About turn!' Wash out! About turn again – carry on D Company – only A [Company] washed out! Marched 6 ¹/₂ miles to shelled billets.*

In just over three months on the Western Front, the battalion had advanced with 30th Division over fifty miles and taken part in two great attacks. It had suffered over 200 casualties. Nearly half of those killed were original men – an indicator of the different pattern of attrition from that of the 1st Battalion (see Appendix 5).

On 10 November, the battalion was back near Avelghem, the Germans having evacuated Mont de l'Enclus on the opposite shore. There were exhilarating rumours, first that British cavalry was sweeping eastwards, then that an armistice was imminent. That evening the battalion held a spontaneous celebration in the village of Heerstert, parading up and down the main street with drums and fifes. The brigade staff considered it premature, and sent a message which dampened everyone's spirits, as Henry Pope recorded:

> *Great rejoicing and firework displays with Verey lights. [Our] band gets a 'bird' for rejoicing too loudly near Brigade headquarters!*

Thus when the official telegram arrived the following morning, there was a sense of anti-climax.

1. *A Brief History of the 30th Division*, London, 1919, p 47

Regimental Christmas card, 1918. In a conscious echo of his 1914 card (page 44) Henry Sayer depicted a victorious Civil Service Rifleman standing on the German eagle as clouds herald the dawn of 1919. Lady Vera Houghton

---

2nd Battalion casualties: Flanders July – November 1918

Wounded	143	
Killed or died	66	
Total*	209	*including men attached from other units

Dead are buried or commemorated at:
Arneke, Bailleul, Cement House, Godewaersvelde, Klein-Veirstraat, La Kreule, Lijssenthoek, Somer Farm, Tyne Cot Memorial, Wulverghem, Wytschaete, Terlincthun

Sources: Brigade and Battalion war diaries, CWGC, SDGW, CSR History

Chapter Eleven

'England, Home and Beauty'

For both battalions of the CSR, the period following the armistice was rather unsatisfactory. Demobilization did not begin until the new year. It was a gradual process, with men released in small groups and the last did not get home until September 1919. The dwindling ranks were occupied with drill, educational courses, football competitions and some duties at a prisoner of war camp. Deaths continued at a depressingly high rate from wounds, gas, and illness – mostly influenza. Twenty-five men died before the end of 1919, nearly half of them originals from 1914 and 1915. The last graves overseas may be seen today in Dunkirk Town Cemetery.

In February 1919 Rowland Feilding wrote presciently to his wife about the likely effects of the war on the warriors. His analysis of their camaraderie helps to explain the extraordinary strength and longevity of their mutual bonds, which is the essence of this story from 1919 onwards:

> After all, there was a good deal to be said in favour of the old trench life...The rations were the same for the 'haves' and the 'have nots', and the shells fell, without favour, upon both. In a life where no money passes the ownership of money counts for nothing. Rich and poor alike stand solely upon their individual merits, without discrimination. You can have no idea, till you have tried it, how much pleasanter life is under such circumstances...There was an atmosphere of selflessness, and a spirit of camaraderie, the like of which has probably not been seen in the world before – at least on so grand a scale. Such is the influence of the shells! The life was a curious blend of discipline and good fellowship; wherein men were easily pleased...In short, there was no humbug in the trenches, and that is why – with all their disadvantages – the better kind of men who have lived in them will look back upon them hereafter with something like affection.[1]

Plans for an Old Comrades Association (OCA), already mooted in 1917, were quickly realized. To this was added the idea of a regimental club, as a memorial to the fallen. Demobilization brought about the disbandment of the 2nd and Reserve Battalions and the temporary reduction of the 1st Battalion to a cadre. In the immediate aftermath of war there was a general disinclination to continue soldiering, but the regiment had a strong London-based nucleus keen to remain active. Like many units, the CSR experienced some difficulty in reconstituting itself.

Government delay in reorganizing the Territorial Force (or Territorial Army (TA) as it became) did not help, nor did anxiety over its possible use in breaking strikes. The Civil Service was still not taking in young men, depriving the regiment of its principal source of recruits. When the Defence Force was created in the face of a threatened miners' strike in 1921, the Treasury ruled that civil servants could not join. This force was based on the organization and premises of the TA, which was temporarily suspended. It only lasted three months but on disbandment most of its members in London joined their respective territorial units. The CSR had no similar source of recruits.

THE LONDON TROOPS MEMORIAL
ERECTED IN FRONT OF THE ROYAL EXCHANGE
15TH(COUNTY OF LONDON)BN THE LONDON REGT.
(CIVIL SERVICE RIFLES)

Replica of Great War memorial to London troops. The original, designed by Sir Aston Webb and sculpted by Alfred Drury, stands outside the Royal Exchange. This bronze replica plaque was presented to the CSR in 1923 and hangs today in the Drill Hall in Putney, of F Company (Royal Green Jackets) the London Regiment, Mortar Platoon.

Nevertheless, the regiment was successfully reconstituted. Sufficient recruits had been forthcoming for a voluntary camp in 1920 and again the following summer, with an impressive attendance of 200. The Prince of Wales agreed to become Honorary Colonel, in succession to his grandfather, and the new commanding officer was Viscount Bury, the third of his family to hold this appointment. A history of the CSR in the Great War was produced by Paul Davenport and A C H Benké, published in 1921. This fine volume ends on an inconclusive and slightly unsettling note, as though the authors have seen writing on the wall.

Amalgamation

The blow fell in November 1921 when national expenditure cuts were announced entailing retrenchment of the army. The Civil Service Rifles was to amalgamate with its erstwhile rival, the Queen's Westminster Rifles. No regiment may be expected to take such news calmly. Within the CSR, so soon after the most momentous period in its history, it evoked shock and disbelief. A rearguard action was mounted but failed to stop the amalgamation. The CSR was reduced to two

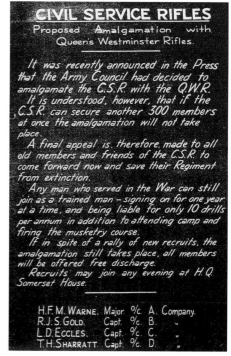

CIVIL SERVICE RIFLES
Proposed Amalgamation with Queen's Westminster Rifles.

It was recently announced in the Press that the Army Council had decided to amalgamate the C.S.R. with the Q.W.R. It is understood, however, that if the C.S.R. can secure another 300 members at once the amalgamation will not take place.

A final appeal is, therefore, made to all old members and friends of the C.S.R. to come forward now and save their Regiment from extinction.

Any man who served in the War can still join as a trained man – signing on for one year at a time, and being liable for only 10 drills per annum in addition to attending camp and firing the musketry course.

If in spite of a rally of new recruits, the amalgamation still takes place, all members will be offered free discharge.

Recruits may join any evening at H.Q. Somerset House.

H.F.M. WARNE. Major °/c A. Company.
R.J.S. GOLD. Capt. °/c B. „
L.D. ECCLES. Capt. °/c C. „
T.H. SHARRATT. Capt. °/c D. „

An unsuccessful attempt to save the regiment from 'extinction' was organized by four wartime officers. When the amalgamation went ahead, many old members resigned.

companies in a combined regiment. The Prince of Wales' feathers had equal prominence with the Westminster portcullis in the new badge. In the regimental title, however, the words 'Civil Service Rifles' came last, which the veterans took as a sign they were junior partners, notwithstanding that they had precedence in the London Regiment. There was a feeling that the CSR, whose members had served loyally in civil as well as military fields, deserved better treatment from its government masters and indeed more support from senior levels in the Service. It must have seemed a far cry from 1914 when the Adjutant could lobby the Prime Minister on the regiment's behalf and achieve an instant reversal of policy. Some members felt strongly enough to resign. A sufficient number, however, accepted the amalgamation and resolved to make the best of it.

Both parties in the new unit were determined not to let the memory of their old regiment be submerged and initially they each retained their old drill halls, badges and buttons. In 1924 the headquarters building at Somerset House was reluctantly surrendered and the CSR companies, B and D, moved to the Westminster headquarters at 58 Buckingham Gate. Eventually the parties were successfully welded together under the tactful management of Lieutenant Colonel E G H Cox. In the inter-war years B and D Companies retained a 'Civil Service' character, led by wartime officers including Second Lieutenant (later Major) J S Oldcorn, Lieutenant (later Major) T H E Clark, Major H F M Warne, Captain L D Eccles and Lieutenant (later Major) J L Hutchison. They were supported by experienced NCOs, some of whom had reverted after holding wartime commissions. When Civil Service recruiting returned to normal, new members came in from various departments. As in the old days, encouragement was given by Exchequer & Audit Department, Inland Revenue, GPO, Post Office Savings Bank and also by the Bank of England. B and D Companies preserved the old CSR reputation, achieving high levels of efficiency and winning a good share of sporting and other competitions. The feeling of a 'family' regiment continued as sons and younger brothers of former members joined.

There were no more jealous guardians of the old regiment than the retired members. Their associations and commemorations were supported from the beginning by those Regular commanding officers from the war with whom strong bonds of mutual respect, even affection, had been forged. The OCA took over from the wartime regimental aid fund the role of looking after cases of hardship. The war memorial project, begun with the opening of the club in 1920, was completed in 1924 with the erection at Somerset House of a handsome column designed by Sir Edwin Lutyens. Names of regimental casualties appeared on departmental rolls of honour which sprang up all over the Civil Service. A small but steady trickle of deaths due to the war continued and a tradition grew of a bereaved relative laying the official

'Joe' Oldcorn, Inland Revenue. Awarded the DCM at Beersheba as CSM of C Coy, 2nd Battalion. He was a leading personality in the post-war regiment and by 1939 had risen to Major. Oldcorn's death in a motor accident during training deprived the regiment of a fine officer who would have achieved higher rank.

Crowds at Somerset House watch the
Prince of Wales unveil the war memorial,
27 January 1924. The dedication was
performed by the 1st Battalion's padré,
Rev E H Beattie. The same order of service
was used when the memorial was
rededicated in July 2002.

The Prince of Wales pulls the cord and two
real flags fall away. Designed by Lutyens,
the stone pier is finished with solid
painted flags – the Union flag and the blue
regimental flag. The names of 1,240 fallen
were inscribed on a scroll placed within
the column.

In 1932 the London, Midland &
Scottish Railway named one of
its 'Royal Scot' class locomotives
'Civil Service Rifleman'. The
nameplate was unveiled by Sir
Josiah Stamp, who had begun his career in the Inland Revenue as a boy clerk in 1896.
Number 6163, painted in Midland red, hauled express trains from London to Liverpool
and Manchester. Inset: close-up of nameplate on the original engine in 1935. It was also
used on the rebuilt engine, 46163, until this was scrapped during the last days of steam in
1965. LMS Railway/National Railway Museum

'Party - Number!' Veterans form up during a tour of the battlefields in 1937.

wreath at the war memorial every November. This honour was performed by, among others, Mrs Parish, Mrs Trembath, Mrs Middleton, Mrs Renny and Mrs W H D Clark. In the 1930s the first of many tours were organized to the battlefields and cemeteries.

Another war

In 1939 scenes in the drill hall were reminiscent of August 1914, though this time there were more journalists, stockbrokers and actors than civil servants. In ten days the regiment was brought up to strength and a 2nd Battalion formed. As the Boer War veterans had done in 1914, so the NCOs from the Great War supervised the training of new recruits, ensuring the regiment's efficiency when it eventually went overseas. The 1st Battalion embarked in May 1942 and served in the Western Desert (El Alamein), Syria, Italy and Greece. The 2nd Battalion took part in fighting from the Normandy beaches in June 1944 until the German surrender. They fought under the KRRC badge as 11th and 12th Battalions (Queen's Westminsters) The King's Royal Rifle Corps. Many from the old CSR served in the second war. Some achieved senior positions at home and overseas, but mostly with other units.

When the regiment was reconstituted in the TA after the war, the 1921 badge was revived. After the ending of National Service in 1960, active recruitment was resumed and once again civil servants were encouraged to join. The name 'Civil Service Rifles' had disappeared from the regimental title in 1938 but the badge bearing the Prince of Wales' feathers was worn until the amalgamations of the 1960s, when the remaining London territorial rifle units became part of the Royal Green Jackets. This last vestige of the CSR badge may be seen today on the memorial to the Queen's Westminsters in Westminster Abbey.

The two crests of the amalgamated regiment of 1921. These formed the centrepiece of the cap badge which was worn until the 1960s.

Late flowering

It appears that after the second war the veterans overcame their residual resentment about the amalgamation. Three small OCAs associated with the combined regiment merged into a harmonious and well-supported QW&CSR Retired Members Association (RMA). The pre-1914 regiment was often described as a club and the same atmosphere is discernible in the veterans' proceedings from the 1950s onwards. As they reached retirement age, more found time to join in regimental activities, often for the first time since the Great War.`

A survey of obituaries reveals that veterans reached senior levels in their chosen fields and especially in the Civil Service. Many civil honours were bestowed, including a knighthood and a baronetcy for that brace of subalterns who had received such a dusty reception from Colonel Hayes in 1914: Kenneth Wills and Kenneth Pickthorn. A few went into Parliament, including Douglas Houghton as Labour member for Sowerby and Kenneth Pickthorn as Conservative member for Cambridge University and later Carlton. Houghton was a cabinet minister in the 1960s and subsequently a life peer, impishly describing himself to the RMA as a 'rifleman in robes'. As eighteen year-olds, the tax clerk Houghton and the future sculptor Henry Moore had travelled together from the North to enlist; now they were Companions of Honour. In 1964 an honour of a different kind was bestowed on Percy Merriman of the *Roosters*, when he was interviewed by Roy Plumley on the BBC radio programme *Desert Island Discs*. Fifty years after the war, Merriman wanted to take to his desert island *Roses of Picardy*, the regimental march *God Bless the Prince of Wales* and *The Last Post*.

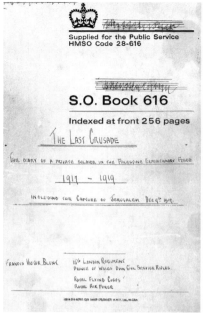

Many civil servants were moved to write memoirs. In 1979 Vic Blunt finished transcribing his war diaries: 'What a period of heroics it was...what a wonderful period to live through'. Kathryn E W Blunt

It is evident from the rich crop of memoirs how enduring were the impressions left by the war. Some never spoke of it to their families, but many were moved to write of it. When Charles Jones took up his pen in 1934, he began:

> Since the war the author has found not only that all his actions, all his standards of values have been influenced by his wartime experiences, but also that these experiences refused to be driven out of his conscious mind. No day passed without some recollection of incident which occurred on active service coming into his thoughts, and all too often into his speech, until his long suffering friends must wonder if his power of assimilating new experiences ceased to function on Armistice Day 1918. Now...he feels the need of a fresh start.

Many returned to the topic in retirement and found satisfaction in recalling the greatest adventure of their lives. Thus wrote Edgar Powell, on ending his memoir in 1970:

> It has carried me back to live again those years which made such an indelible impression on my youthful mind that everything else in my life seems trivial by comparison.

The RMA was blessed with active and dedicated organizers, notably Frank 'Chappie' Chapman of the 2nd Battalion, editor of the flourishing *Newsletter*, and York Rickard who for twenty-three years led the 17th March men and masterminded their well-attended reunions. As a 1st Battalion cook he had looked after 'the boys', a role he continued and cherished long afterwards. In the days before

'Beersheba night', 31 October 1962: some of these men 45 years earlier had charged the Turkish trenches and ejected the occupants with the bayonet. J R Rickard

Annual Remembrance Day services were held at Somerset House until the 1980s. In 1961, the service was led by the Rev George Mitchell, formerly a private in the 2nd Battalion. Veterans 'snapped to attention' on hearing the opening bars of 'God Bless the Prince of Wales'. J R Rickard

York Rickard sporting regimental tie (grey, blue and silver). One of few 17th March men to serve throughout the war. He worked tirelessly for the veterans until his death in 1974. On receiving his MBE in 1973, Rickard was delighted that the Regiment's title appeared in the citation. J R Rickard

computerized burial records were available, Rickard spent his holidays assiduously tracing and recording the graves of former comrades all over France and Belgium.

The many official and unofficial reunions ranged from battalion and company level down to platoons and specialist sections like transport and signals. Everywhere was evidence of strong and lasting bonds forged in adversity. For example, Sir Kenneth Wills came from Australia to attend C Company reunions; D Company for many years published and circulated its own *Bulletin*; and Colonel Benké's sons attended Company functions after their father died in 1951. The strength and nature of the bonds between the former warriors may perhaps be summed up in one humorous anecdote. Four or five veterans were yarning one evening at the drill hall, when one of them suddenly flung his arm around York Rickard's shoulders and exclaimed 'By God Yorkie, if you were a woman I'd *marry* you!'

Inevitably the RMA's membership declined as the survivors entered their eighties and nineties. The 17th March men, however, could be relied upon to turn up so long as they were physically able. In 1969 over 200 were known to be still alive and in March 1970 ninety-nine of them paraded. Every year an 'In Memoriam' notice appeared in the *Daily Telegraph* and loyal greetings were sent to the Queen. Always they would sing *God Bless the Prince of Wales* with feeling before observing a silent toast in memory of lost comrades. They eventually substituted a lunch for their annual dinner, preceded by a pilgrimage to lay a wreath at Somerset House. In 1977, when they erected a diamond anniversary plaque in the Inland Revenue offices, a 17th March man explained:

Diamond Jubilee edition of the retired members' Newsletter.

> With the passing of the years there has been a change of meaning from the gatherings of years ago. This act of remembrance and comradeship has taken the place of the old-time glorious binge, when we let our hair down.[2]

In the 1980s the RMA was given a home by the King's Royal Rifle Corps Association, which still today looks after the interests of the Second World War generation and arranges the CSR plot at the annual Field of Remembrance at Westminster Abbey. The remaining 17th March men fulfilled their vow of 1916 to meet annually so long as any still lived. Seven octogenarians visited Somerset House in March 1981 and signed a special nominal roll held in the Inland Revenue. Their chairman was Harry Old, who spent his twenty-first birthday at La Beuvrière in 1915 and whose war story is told in Chapter 3. After that the record grows rather hazy. Reg Letheren, Ernie Cooke DCM and Reg Wadland met in March 1983 and exchanged the customary greetings with the Royal Family. In 1987 Ernie Cooke, then in his early nineties, made a solitary pilgrimage to Somerset House. He returned,

NOT FORGOTTEN

BREED, ROBERT (Rob), 4634, 1/15 Bn. London Regiment, Civil Service Rifles.—In loving and constant memory of my dear fiancé, killed in action High Wood, Somme, Sept. 15/16, 1916. Name on Thiepval Memorial.—Ruth and 'Aunt Lucy'.

Daily Telegraph, 15.9.66.

We wrote to Pte. Breed's fiancée, Miss R. Plummer, who replied stating that Pte. Breed, then serving in the Hydrographic Dept. of the Admiralty, joined 3/CSR in the Autumn of 1915, and was posted to the 1st Bn. in France in the following spring. His service with us was tragically brief, as he was killed at High Wood on 15th September. Though she had letters of sympathy from his platoon officers, she knew little of the circumstances until her 'In Memoriam' notice brought a reply from ex-Cpl. R. Stent, 9 Pln. 'C' Coy. She would be grateful for further information from any other survivor of the High Wood engagement, if sent c/o the Editor.

Not forgotten, 50 years after High Wood. A poignant notice from the Daily Telegraph, *as reported in the RMA Newsletter, 1966.*

apparently alone, in 1989. After that the nominal roll has no more signatures – only blank pages.

Postscript

In the 1980s the government decided to allow parts of Somerset House to be leased for purposes other than government offices, in particular to house the Courtauld Institute and galleries. When the necessary legislation went through Parliament in 1983, one member took a close interest. This was the 'rifleman in robes', Lord Houghton of Sowerby, then aged eighty-five. He wanted to safeguard the war memorial on its site in the courtyard. Lord Skelmersdale replied for the government:

> This Regiment had a distinguished record of service in the Great War and it is entirely fitting that the memorial should be situated in the courtyard of the first purpose-built Government office building. I can assure the House that there has been no thought of moving it, nor will there be.[3]

But moved it was, during the redevelopment in the late 1990s when the courtyard was prepared for public use and the staging of arts events. The column was restored and the flags carefully repainted before being re-erected on the river terrace of Somerset House in front of the Navy

Ex-Pte Herbert Sparrow with the Lord Lieutenant of Cambridgeshire after receiving the Légion d'Honneur in January 1999. 'Dickie' Sparrow was wounded near Rancourt in September 1918 – one of those 18 year-olds so admired by Colonel Feilding, who described them advancing 'as though they were beating up partridges'. Dickie, despite his wound, lived into his hundredth year. Of the Great War he said 'There has to be a better way of settling differences...war is not the answer'. Betty Baff

Ex-Pte Walter Humphrys, aged 101, receiving the Légion d'Honneur from Lt Col P Champenois in December 1998. Walter fought at Messines and Bourlon Wood and was taken prisoner in March 1918. He said 'I am very proud to be receiving this ... but it was something of a trial too ... I have a photographic memory and I remember things very vividly. It was worse than what people imagine'. Pat Welch

Walter Humphrys with relatives of CSR officers and men at Somerset House, 25 July 2002, after the rededication of the war memorial. The two buglers, who sounded Last Post *and* Reveille, *are from the Band and Bugles of the Light Division.* A J Sollars

Treasurer's doorway. It fell to the Royal Green Jackets to arrange its rededication. This was performed with due reverence in a moving ceremony on 25 July 2002. A wreath was laid by the Chairman of the Inland Revenue Board, whose department had been among the regiment's founding members in 1859 and whose own war memorial, also at Somerset House, bears the names of about ninety staff who died while serving in the CSR. The last known Civil Service Rifleman from the Western Front, Walter Humphrys, was present, along with relatives of officers and men who served in the Great War – that greatest phase in the life of a fine regiment which has now passed into history.

1. R C Feilding, *War Letters to a Wife*, Medici, 1929, p 373
2. QW&CSR *Newsletter*, Vol 8, No.12, October 1976, p 186
3. Official Report [HL] 20 December 1983, Col 677

THE DEAD IN FRANCE GREET THE SPRING

Here, while we sleep in silence
    In unremembered graves,
By fallow field and hedgerow
    Wherein the long grass waves,
We hear a far-off music
    Foot-followed as in dance,
And guess a joyous presence -
    Spring, on the plains of France.

We have not, by our dying,
    Delayed the feet of Spring.
The cries of our last anguish
    Blend with her carolling.
Our hands, set free from slaughter,
    Shall not retard her ways,
Her fickleness and frailty,
    And myriad moods and days.

And tread she ne'er so lightly
    Wher'er we lie at rest,
Her footfall shall arouse us,
    And stir within our breast
Some old forgotten memory
    To raise a slumb'rous head,
Saying, "Spring goes a-roving
    Thro' France - and we are dead!"

Extract from poem by 2/Lt Ernest Denny, of the Second Battalion, Civil Service Rifles, who died of wounds 4 August 1917.

APPENDIX 1: LINE OF DESCENT

1798 'Loyal Volunteers of London' - Somerset House Volunteer Association; Bank of England Volunteers.
Volunteers of 1802 - Bank of England Corps; Custom House Corps; Excise Office Corps.
(all disbanded by 1814)

January/February 1860	21st Middlesex Rifle Volunteer Corps (Audit Office and Post Office)
	27th Middlesex Rifle Volunteer Corps (Inland Revenue)
	31st Middlesex Rifle Volunteer Corps (Whitehall)
	34th Middlesex Rifle Volunteer Corps (Admiralty)
June 1860	21st Middlesex (Civil Service) Rifle Volunteer Corps
1875	21st Middlesex (Civil Service) Rifle Volunteer Corps
	50th Middlesex (Bank of England) Rifle Volunteer Corps (later renumbered 25th)
1880	12th Middlesex (Civil Service) Rifle Volunteer Corps
1898	The Prince of Wales' Own 12th Middlesex (Civil Service) Volunteer Rifle Corps
1908	15th (County of London) Battalion, The London Regiment
	(Prince of Wales' Own Civil Service Rifles)
The Great War	1/15th, 2/15th and 3/15th (Reserve) (County of London) Battalions
	The London Regiment (Prince of Wales' Own Civil Service Rifles)
1921	15th/16th (County of London) Battalion The London Regiment
1923	16th (County of London) Battalion The London Regiment
	(Queen's Westminster & Civil Service Rifles)
1938	The Queen's Westminsters, The King's Royal Rifle Corps
1939	1st and 2nd Battalions The Queen's Westminsters, The King's Royal Rifle Corps
	subsequently 11th and 12th Battalions The King's Royal Rifle Corps
1947	The Queen's Westminsters, The King's Royal Rifle Corps
1961	Queen's Royal Rifles, The King's Royal Rifle Corps
1967	4th (Volunteer) Battalion The Royal Green Jackets
1969	4th (Volunteer) Battalion The Royal Green Jackets London (cadre only)
1975	4th (Volunteer) Battalion The Royal Green Jackets
1999	The London Regiment

APPENDIX 2: BRIGADE ORDERS OF BATTLE

FIRST BATTALION

August 1914 - 2nd London Division

<u>4th London Infantry Brigade</u>
1/13th Battalion London Regiment (Kensington)
1/14th Battalion London Regiment (London Scottish)
1/15th Battalion London Regiment (Civil Service Rifles)
1/16th Battalion London Regiment (Queen's Westminster Rifles)

November 1914 - 2nd (London) Division, renamed May 1915 as 47th (London) Division

<u>4th London Infantry Brigade - later renamed 140th Infantry Brigade</u>
1/6th Battalion London Regiment
1/7th Battalion London Regiment
1/8th Battalion (Post Office Rifles)
1/15th Battalion (Civil Service Rifles)

February 1918 - 47th (London) Division

<u>140th Infantry Brigade</u>
1/15th Battalion London Regiment (Civil Service Rifles)
1/17th Battalion London Regiment (Poplar and Stepney Rifles)
1/21st Battalion London Regiment (First Surrey Rifles)

September 1914 - 2/2nd London (Reserve) Division - renamed January 1916 as 60th London Division

4th (London) Reserve Infantry Brigade - renamed February 1916 179th Infantry Brigade
2/13th Battalion London Regiment (Kensington)
2/14th Battalion London Regiment (London Scottish)
2/15th Battalion London Regiment (Civil Service Rifles)
2/16th Battalion London Regiment (Queen's Westminster Rifles)

July 1918 - 30th Division

90th Infantry Brigade
2/14th Battalion London Regiment (London Scottish)
2/15th Battalion London Regiment (Civil Service Rifles)
2/16th Battalion London Regiment (Queen's Westminster Rifles)

APPENDIX 3: BATTLE HONOURS AND COMMEMORATIONS

South Africa 1900-02 • **Festubert, 1915** • Loos • **Somme, 1916, '18**
Flers-Courcelette • Le Transloy • **Messines, 1917** • **Ypres, 1917, '18**
Cambrai, 1917 • St Quentin • Ancre, 1918 • Albert, 1918 • **Bapaume, 1918**
Amiens • Courtrai • France and Flanders, 1915-18 • Doiran, 1917
Macedonia, 1916-17 • **Gaza** • El Mughar • Nebi Samwil • **Jerusalem**
Jericho • Jordan • Tell 'Asur • Palestine, 1917-18

The honours in **heavy** type were selected to be borne on the Colours and Appointments.

From 1925, annual reunions were held to commemorate the following important anniversaries. All relate to 1st Battalion unless indicated otherwise.

Departure for France	17 March 1915
Festubert	25 May 1915
Loos	25 September 1915
Vimy Ridge	21 May 1916
High Wood	15 September 1915
Butte de Warlencourt	7 October 1916
Karasuli trek (2nd Battalion)	17 March 1917
Messines Ridge	7 June 1917
Beersheba (2nd Battalion)	31 October 1917
Bourlon Wood	30 November 1917
Graincourt	6 December 1917
Jerusalem (2nd Battalion)	8 December 1917
Tel el Ful (2nd Battalion)	27 December 1917
Jebel Ektief (2nd Battalion)	20 February 1918
The Retreat (Metz to Albert)	23 March 1918
Es Salt (2nd Battalion)	30 April 1918
Happy Valley	24 August 1918
Moislains	2 September 1918

Inscribed on base of regimental war memorial, unveiled at Somerset House in January 1924:

(South face) - Festubert 1915, Loos, Somme 1916 1918, Flers Courcelette
(East face) - Transloy, Messines 1917 1918, Ypres 1917 1918, Cambrai 1917
(West face) - Doiran 1917, Lys, Kemmel, Gaza, Nebi Samwil, Jerusalem
(North face) - St Quentin, Albert 1918, Ancre 1918, Bapaume 1918, Selle

APPENDIX 4: HONOURS AND AWARDS

Distinguished Service Order	5
Bar to Distinguished Service Order	2
OBE	3
MBE	1
Military Cross	45
Bar to Military Cross	4
Albert Medal (2nd Class)	1
Distinguished Conduct Medal	31
Bar to Distinguished Conduct Medal	1
Military Medal	185
Bar to Military Medal	6
Meritorious Service Medal	22
Légion d'Honneur	1
Croix de Guerre	6
Croix de Guerre (Belgian)	4
Other foreign decorations	12
Total	**329**

In addition there were 116 'mentions' in despatches and 5 men were 'brought to notice' for gallant and distinguished conduct in the field. The above list may be incomplete. The details are taken from the CSR *History* and have not been checked against other sources, apart from some rationalization of awards of the Distinguished Conduct and Meritorious Service Medals.

Campaign medals: Members of the CSR who served overseas before 11 November 1918 were entitled to the British War Medal and the Victory Medal. Those who saw service on the Western Front before the end of 1915 were, in addition, entitled to the 1914-15 Star.

In 1998 the Légion d'Honneur was awarded to surviving British soldiers who had served on the Western Front, including ex-Privates W Humphrys and H H Sparrow, both of the 1st Battalion.

APPENDIX 5: ATTRITION RATES

Source	Number of wounded
National Archives: WO 95/2706, 2707 (47 Division HQ)	c2,200: 1st Battalion, May 1915-November 1918
National Archives: WO 95/3030, 4928, 4668, 2340 (2nd Battalion war diaries)	563: 2nd Battalion, June 1916-November 1918

Source	Number of deaths (both Battalions)
History of the Prince of Wales Own Civil Service Rifles (1921)	1,227 (including 112 attached to other units)
Soldiers Died in the Great War 1914-19 (1921)	1,306 (excluding 117 formerly in CSR)
Programme for War Memorial ceremony (January 1924)	1,240
Commonwealth War Graves Commission *Debt of Honour* Register	1,254 (excluding 77 for whom CSR was 'secondary unit')

In all 7,000 men served overseas in the CSR (including those subsequently transferred in or out).[1] The casualty figures shown above should be treated with caution. They do not distinguish between those serving when the battalions first went overseas and subsequent reinforcements. The figures for wounded include casualties who recovered and returned to action as well as those who were eventually discharged and/or died. The number of 2nd Battalion wounded may be understated. There was also heavy attrition in both battalions due to sickness. In the 1st Battalion for every 11 wounded there were 9 evacuated due to sick wastage. No figures are available of men dying in later decades as a result of the war. The variations in total deaths quoted above are hard to reconcile. Adjustments can be made for obvious anomalies, but the main difficulty lies in counting casualties who transferred into or out of the CSR. Classification of these 'attached' men is not consistent within each source, let alone across all of them. For example, men who died having moved from the CSR to the Kensingtons or *vice versa* are treated differently in the sources and some are claimed in both regimental rolls of honour. At this distance it is not possible to produce a definitive figure for deaths, except that the total from all causes up to the early 1920s is in the range 1,200 to 1,300, depending on how attached men are counted.

Attrition of original men
Of the 1st Battalion which sailed to France in March 1915 (about 1,080) about 230, or around 21%, died while classed as still serving in the regiment.[2] The 2nd Battalion spent less time on the Western Front and had fewer deaths overall: by 1919 it had lost only around 10% of its originals killed or died (101 of the 973 of June 1916). The different patterns of attrition are shown in the two bar charts, in which dead original men (excluding any known to have died while attached elsewhere) are distinguished from total monthly deaths throughout the war. The monthly figures are taken from the above sources and adjusted for obvious anomalies and duplications; men attached from other units are included but, so far as possible, CSR men killed while serving elsewhere are excluded.

Commissions
Another significant cause of attrition was the exceptionally high number of commissions granted to CSR rankers. These amounted to 967, or nearly 14% of those who served overseas. In fact large numbers of men were creamed off for commissions during training in England, a practice which began in August 1914 and continued until at least the end of 1917. In France, the 1st Battalion ranks were regularly combed for officer material. Around 330 17th March men were commissioned (or 31% of all 17th March rankers). 70% of them left the battalion for this purpose during 1915 and 1916. Some later served as officers in the 1st or 2nd Battalion but the great majority were posted elsewhere. By the time the 1st Battalion arrived on the Somme in September 1916, it had lost more men to officer training than it had lost killed in seventeen months and nearly 200 of them were original men.[3]

Effect of attrition on character of 1st Battalion
The highest proportions of original men were killed during 1915. In a year in which fighting strength declined steadily, 88% of deaths were of 17th March men (90 out of 102). In autumn and winter, evacuations from sickness were high and, in addition, over 100 originals left for officer training. It is thus not surprising that in May 1916 the proportion of originals killed fell to 39% (13 out of 33). Fighting strength was then rebuilt, largely with new men, and in summer 1916 reached over 1,000 for the first time. At High Wood the proportion of originals killed was 31% (51 out of 163). To those original men who survived, it seemed as though an era had ended, 'so many of the flower of the Battalion' having fallen, most of them on one day. The only comparable action in terms of total casualties took place three weeks later. By then the 17th March men were so depleted (including by temporary absences due to wounds and post-battle leave) that the proportion of originals killed at the Butte de Warlencourt was down to 16% (21 out of 127).

In early 1917, some original men returned after hospital treatment. In June, originals constituted 17% of deaths at Messines (10 out of 59). After that the percentage of originals lost in big actions was very low. This is hardly surprising, given the downward trend and the other factors discussed above. Put simply, from the beginning of 1916 there were declining numbers of 17th March men left in the battalion in France to be killed. Those originals who survived until 1918 were mostly among the transport, stores or cooks who tended to be exposed to danger for shorter periods. Given this high attrition rate, one might expect some change after 1916 in the character of the 1st Battalion, in contrast to the 2nd Battalion where the survival rate of originals was higher. This did not happen, as is demonstrated in Chapters 5 and 6, and this brief analysis serves to underline just how remarkable was the survival of the 1st Battalion's original character until the last days of the war.

1. CSR *History*, Appendix VI
2. The overall number of 17th March men who died in the war is probably significantly higher but this analysis deals only with those who died while still in the regiment.
3. The 967 figure is quoted in the CSR *History* (Appendix VI). The main sources consulted for commissions from the ranks are the campaign medal rolls (WO 329/1931,1932, 2868 at the National Archives). CSR rankers commissioned before leaving England and posted to other units are not listed in these rolls.

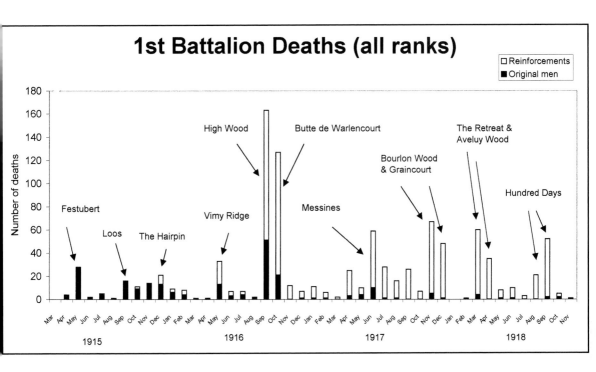

1st Battalion Deaths (all ranks)

□ Reinforcements
■ Original men

Number of deaths (y-axis: 0, 20, 40, 60, 80, 100, 120, 140, 160, 180)

Festubert
Loos
The Hairpin
Vimy Ridge
High Wood
Butte de Warlencourt
Messines
Bourlon Wood & Graincourt
The Retreat & Aveluy Wood
Hundred Days

1915   1916   1917   1918

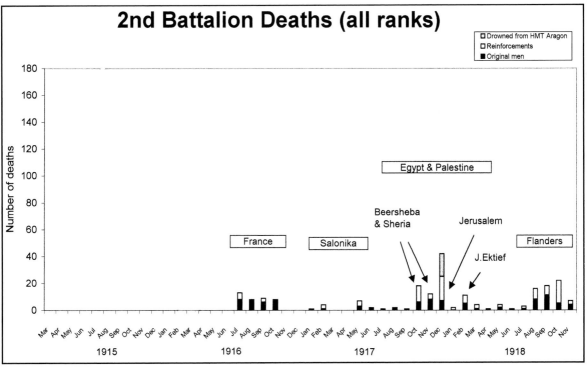

2nd Battalion Deaths (all ranks)

□ Drowned from HMT Aragon
□ Reinforcements
■ Original men

Number of deaths (y-axis: 0, 20, 40, 60, 80, 100, 120, 140, 160, 180)

Egypt & Palestine

Beersheba & Sheria
Jerusalem
France
Salonika
J.Ektief
Flanders

1915   1916   1917   1918

James R Petch

233

APPENDIX 6: GRAVES AND MEMORIALS

The Commonwealth War Graves Commission *Debt of Honour* Register lists 1,254 men for whom Civil Service Rifles was the 'primary' unit. Their graves and memorials are scattered round the world in 221 locations in eight countries:

	Known (57%)	Unknown (43%)	Total (100%)
France	436	421	857
Belgium	116	100	216
Egypt & Israel	74	24	98
Greece	14		14
Germany	4		4
Ireland	1		1
UK	64		64
	709	**545**	**1254**

On the Western Front the largest concentrations of graves and memorials may be visited at:

Thiepval Memorial to the Missing of the Somme: 198 names. All but one are 1st Battalion men killed in four weeks in the autumn of 1916. Most were killed on 15-19 September (121 'missing' in High Wood) and 7 October (70 'missing' at Butte de Warlencourt). Graves of a small number of these missing men, identified only by CSR badge, may be found in local cemeteries, notably Caterpillar Valley and Delville Wood Cemeteries, Longueval; Serre Road Cemetery No.2; Warlencourt British Cemetery; and Cerisy-Gailly French National Cemetery. In fact many bodies from High Wood were identified and reported as buried in marked graves immediately after the battle. Many of these graves were lost in later fighting. Thus only a small proportion of those killed now have known graves. The highest concentration of known graves (19) is at Caterpillar Valley, Longueval. Another 17 are scattered around local cemeteries including some of those mentioned above, also London Cemetery close to High Wood and Flat-Iron Copse Cemetery at Mametz. (Some of the High Wood missing may be in a communal burial of London men in a large shell hole where London Cemetery now stands.[1])

Warlencourt British Cemetery: Graves of 39 known and 6 unknown 1st Battalion men, nearly all killed on 7 October 1916 in the attack on the Butte de Warlencourt, which can be seen from the cemetery.

Loos Memorial, Dud Corner Cemetery, Loos-en-Gohelle: 44 names of 1st Battalion men missing between September and December 1915. These include most of the bomb-carrying party at the Battle of Loos and the men killed at Hairpin Trench.

Arras Memorial, Faubourg d'Amiens Cemetery, Arras: 71 names, nearly all 1st Battalion, from February 1916 to April 1918. Most significant dates are May 1916 (24 missing on Vimy ridge) and March/April 1918 (40 missing in the Retreat). Also two 2nd Battalion men entombed in a dugout in October 1916.

Cambrai Memorial, Louverval: 70 names of 1st Battalion men missing in the defence of and subsequent withdrawal from Bourlon Wood, most of them killed on 30 November and 6 December 1917.

Vis-en-Artois Memorial, Vis-en-Artois British Cemetery: 23 names of 1st Battalion men killed in the advance to victory, August and September 1918.

Maroeuil British Cemetery: largest concentration of 2nd Battalion graves outside the Middle East. 21 graves of men killed while based opposite Vimy ridge between July and October 1916.

Menin Gate Memorial, Ypres: 76 names of 1st Battalion men missing between October 1916 and September 1917. 35 are from one day: 7 June 1917 (Battle of Messines).

Bedford House Cemetery, Ypres: 24 graves of 1st Battalion men who died between February and June 1917, including 15 killed in shelling and enemy trench raids in April and two from Battle of Messines in June.

Tyne Cot Memorial, Zonnebeke: 24 names and one burial. Except for six 2nd Battalion men missing in August-October 1918, all were 'missing' in fighting at Passchendaele while attached to other units, notably 6th Londons and KRRC.

Lijssenthoek Military Cemetery, Poperinghe: 22 graves of 1st Battalion men who died of wounds at a nearby dressing station between October 1916 and December 1917.

Only the sites commemorating 19 or more CSR men are listed here. CSR men are buried in 140 more locations on the Western Front, as well as in several other countries. Information on the location of cemeteries and memorials is available from Commonwealth War Graves Commission, 2 Marlow Road, Maidenhead, Berkshire, SL6 7DX or www.cwgc.org

1. Terry Norman, *The Hell They Called High Wood,* 1984, p 235

ACKNOWLEDGEMENTS

I count myself enormously fortunate in having been able to research and write this book. I could not possibly have done it without the help of a great many people. My foremost debt is to members of the Civil Service Rifles who left a wealth of written material, vital to understanding the regiment's character. Most had died before my interest was awakened and it was thus a unique privilege to know and listen to Walter Humphrys in the last two years of his life. I am profoundly grateful to the many families I tracked down. Repeatedly, I was touched by their kindness, ready cooperation and willingness to entrust me with treasured memorabilia, not all of which could be included in the book. I am grateful to copyright holders for permission to reproduce photographs and quote from published and unpublished works. Every effort has been made to trace them all and I regret that in a few cases it proved impossible. For extensive quotes from memoirs my special thanks are due to Mr W J A Wills AM and Mr F B Jones; also to Mrs Margaret Tims for the extract from Ernest Denny's poem. I acknowledge my debt to the authors of the CSR *History* of 1921, particularly A C H Benké, some of whose sketch maps have been redrawn.

My research task would have been immeasurably harder without the generous help I received from the Royal Green Jackets Museum. I should like to record my warm appreciation of assistance from Major Ron Cassidy MBE, who put himself out on my many visits to Winchester and patiently answered numerous questions by email. Mr Richard Frost MBE, Honorary Secretary of the King's Royal Rifle Corps Association, was unfailingly helpful in the search for regimental memorabilia. Many of the photographs are reproduced by courtesy of the Royal Green Jackets Museum and the King's Royal Rifle Corps Association.

I encountered many experts and enthusiasts of the Great War who generously shared their expertise and material. Particular help came from members of the Western Front Association, the Centre for First World War Studies (University of Birmingham), the Great War Forum (http://www.1914-1918.org/forum) and the Territorial Force Study Group. Arthur Potton, Editor of *Firestep*, gave shrewd advice and asked tough questions. A number of experts read and commented on individual draft chapters including Charles Messenger; Monty Rossiter; Alan Wakefield; and Ian Passingham who in addition helped me to identify features on the aerial photograph of the White Château and allowed me to use his 1997 interview with Walter Humphrys. Others who read and suggested improvements to various chapters include Henry & Mary Pickthorn; Denys Stephenson; Kathryn Blunt; and Ione Bates who also contributed valuable insights from her research on 17th March officers. The final text is, of course, my responsibility including any imperfections and errors.

For permission to quote from particular documents and to reproduce photographs I am grateful to the Trustees of the Imperial War Museum; the Brotherton Library, University of Leeds; the Local Studies Library Croydon; the National Archives; the Director, the National Army Museum, London; the Trustees of the Liddell Hart Centre for Military Archives; the National Railway Museum; The Naval & Military Press; and Wakefield MDC Museums & Arts. I am indebted to the Commonwealth War Graves Commission for permission to use material from the *Debt of Honour* Register and to the French regional office for advice on 'unknown' burials. The images and quotations on pages 116 and 146 are reproduced by kind permission of the Henry Moore Foundation. I am grateful to the Earl Haig for permission to quote from his father's diary. I also acknowledge courteous help from librarians and staff at the Bank of England, Churchill College Cambridge, HM Customs & Excise, Defra, DTI, Eton College, FCO, HMSO, Home Office, Inland Revenue, London Symphony Orchestra, MOD, Modern Records Centre (University of Warwick), National Audit Office, National Savings & Investments, Office of National Statistics, Ordnance Survey, Prudential Assurance, Royal Mail Heritage, RUSI Library, Somerset House Trust and HM Treasury. I am indebted to Charles Fair for advice and material on 47th Division attrition rates; to Hedley Malloch for making a special journey to take photographs in Noeux-les-Mines; and to the editor of *Options* (at the Civil Service Retirement Fellowship) and secretaries of family history societies for publishing appeals for information.

The following people have helped in diverse ways and I am grateful to them all: Ian Alexander, Denise Aylmer-Aylmore, Betty Baff, Peter Barton, Patrick Baty, Tim Benké, Cynthia Bonham-Carter,

Neil Bright, Lord Bruntisfield, Col Terry Cave, Lt Col Peter Chamberlin, Major Tom Craze, Janis Croom, Arthur Dark, Eleanor Edwards, James Farquhar, Anthony & Jenny Fereday, Jennifer & Mark Gaze, Judith Gibbons, Janet Gill & Margaret Shaw, Roger & Doug Goodman, Caroline Gordon-Duff, Edward Hancock, Bernard Harris, Nigel Harris, Norman Harris, A W Higgins, Lady Houghton, Michael Hull, Joe & Adrienne Ibbett, Evelyn Kench, Deborah Lake, David Langford, Barry Langridge, Jean Lindley, Bruce Lothian, Lt Col Ian McCausland, Helen McPhail, Donald Martin, Mike Milne, Bill Mitchinson, Alan Newson, Eric Old, Andrew Page, Sheila Parish, Pat Phillips, Trevor Pidgeon, Frank Price, Joan Price, Martin Pym, Adrian Ray, Bev Renny, J R Rickard, Molly Snart, Edna, Denys & Paul Stephenson, Ian Townsend, Allan & Andrée Trembath, Liz Vyvyan, Michael Warrender, Pat & John Welch, Ray Westlake, Barbara Westmuckett and Peter Wiseman. I received generous help from specialist medal collectors, in particular Doug Honychurch on awards of DCM and MSM and Ian Cook on Capt Rathbone's rare group. I am grateful to Gabriel Sayyed for his painstaking work on redrawing the maps; to Martin Middlebrook and Ross Davies for access to veterans' questionnaires; to Andy Sollars for his excellent photographs at Somerset House in 2002; to Malcolm & Angela Carpenter of Prédefin for help in France; and to Peter Simkins who, with Lt Col Mike Martin of Holts Tours, first encouraged me to channel my enthusiasm into more serious study.

My special thanks go to Henry Wilson at Pen & Sword Books for taking me on and to Roni and Paul Wilkinson in Barnsley for all their work on the manuscript and photographs. This study grew out of the DTI war memorial project and I shall always be grateful to the many work colleagues who encouraged and helped me in so many ways, particularly Lyndon Edwards for research and advice on Civil Service history; Gavin Bennett; Jan Dixon; Michael Forsyth; Paul Hamilton; Peter Lambert; Maureen Verrall; and also Ann Morrison to whom credit is due for the inspired if ambitious suggestion of turning my research into a book. Only brief reference is possible here to friends and neglected family whose support, practical help and wise counsel have sustained me over several years. I hope I may be forgiven for mentioning but a small sample of a distinguished circle: Caroline & Philip Catlow, Jim Petch, Polly & Michael Richardson, Janina Slater, the 'PAWs' group; and my husband David Petch who endured the intrusion of the Great War into his domestic life with the fortitude of a rifleman and to whom is owed more than I can say.

The author would be pleased to receive information about any CSR officers and men. She may be contacted via the publishers.

SOURCES

Unpublished personal recollections, letters, diaries

Key: F = family papers and recollections; IWM = Imperial War Museum Department of Documents; KCL = Liddell Hart Centre for Military Archives, King's College London; L = Liddle Collection, Brotherton Library, University of Leeds; MD = Martin Middlebrook/Ross Davies; RGJ = Royal Green Jackets Museum.

Amsden C S (L), Angel R L (IWM), Armfield A R (IWM), Ballands J H (IWM), Bassett C (RGJ), Bazley G (IWM in Pounds G S), Blackaby N (F), Blunt F V (F; IWM), Brookling H W (IWM; L), Carr W R (IWM), Cornwell P D (IWM), Dark V (F), Edwards H C (IWM; L), Edwards L M (L), Edwards W N (L; F), Fautley C (IWM), Fereday A H (F; Malaspina University College http:www.mala.bc.ca/history/letters), Fisher W L (IWM), French H J A (L), Galloway J M (IWM), Gardiner J T (L), Garner W J (F), Goldby H (L), Hennessey C R (IWM), Honychurch C R (F), Houghton ALND (F; L), Hull C B (F), Humphrys W (F; I Passingham; author interviews), Ibbett C (F), Jones C F (F; KCL), Jones T I (IWM), March J E (IWM), Martin F A (F), Moore H S (Henry Moore Foundation; L), Moore L G (IWM), Mummery F J (IWM; MD), Mundy P D (IWM), Old H (F; L), Parish F W (F), Pearce H L (F; IWM), Pearce J (L), Pearson L (IWM in Pearson H), Pickard L W (MD), Pope H T (IWM), Powell E C (IWM), Price W J (F; L), Quinton C J (F), Radice F R (L), Reader B A (F; IWM), Richards E C (IWM), Rickard R Y (F), Roberts A (IWM), Robins A L (L; MD), Smith T A (F), Sparrow H H (F), Stileman Rev (L), Thompson R J (IWM; RGJ), Tibbs W J (F), Titmuss C D (L), Tombleson B (L; MD), Warrender H V (Churchill College Cambridge CHAR28/127; F), Wills K A (F; L; RGJ), Young K H (IWM).

Medal rolls, service records, war diaries and departmental records were consulted at the National Archives.

Main published sources

Merrick, Edward, *A History of the Civil Service Rifle Volunteers 1798-1891*, Sheppard and St John, 1891
Davenport P & Benké ACH (eds), *The History of the Prince of Wales' Own Civil Service Rifles*, Wyman & Sons, 1921 (referred to in the text as 'the CSR *History*')
Civil Service Rifles Gazette; *QW&CSR RMA Newsletter*; *Red Tape*; *British Imperial Calendar & Civil Service List*, 1914; *Civil Service Year Book*, 1913
Dalbiac, P H, *History of the 60th Division*, George Allen & Unwin, 1927
Maude, Alan H, *The History of the 47th (London) Division 1914-1919*, Amalgamated Press, 1922
Soldiers Died in the Great War 1914-19, 1921 republished by Naval & Military Press, 1998 (referred to in text as 'SDGW'),
-- *A Brief History of the 30th Division*, London, 1919
Brett, T P, *Memories of a CSM*, privately published, 1950s
Denny, Ernest, *Triumphant Laughter, Poems 1914-1917*, Brentham Press, 1978
Feilding, Rowland, *War Letters to a Wife*, Medici Society, 1929
French, Anthony, *Gone for a Soldier*, Roundwood Press, 1972
Houghton of Sowerby, Rt Hon Lord: *A memorial tribute to his life and work*, Lady Houghton CBE, 1998
Loxdale, Edward, *Souvenir of a Soldier*, 1916
Portch, W T, *Journal 1915*, privately published
Young, Desmond, *Try Anything Twice*, Hamish Hamilton, 1963

Numerous military, regimental and departmental histories, biographies and rolls of honour were consulted. The following is a selection only of those which were particularly illuminating.

Beckett Ian F W & Simpson Keith, *A Nation in Arms*, Tom Donovan Publishing, 1990
Berthoud, Roger, *The Life of Henry Moore*, Faber & Faber, 1987
Bruce, Anthony, *The Last Crusade*, John Murray, 2002
Cunningham, Hugh, *The Volunteer Force*, Croom Helm, 1975
Lloyd, Mark, *The London Scottish in the Great War*, Leo Cooper, 2001
Messenger, Charles, *Terriers in the Trenches*, Picton Publishing, 1982
Mitchinson, K W, *Gentlemen and Officers*, Imperial War Museum, 1995
Norman, Terry, *The Hell They Called High Wood*, William Kimber, 1984
Passingham, Ian, *Pillars of Fire, the Battle of Messines Ridge 1917*, Sutton Publishing, 1998
Pellew, Jill, *From Clerks to Bureaucrats, the Home Office 1848-1914*, Heinemann, 1982
Pidgeon, Trevor, *The Tanks at Flers*, Fairmile Books, 1995
Reader, K M, *The Civil Service Commission, 1855-1975*
Sheffield, G D, *Leadership in the Trenches: officer-man relations in the British Army in the era of the First World War*, Macmillan, 2000
Simkins, Peter, *Kitchener's Army, the Raising of the New Armies 1914-16*, Manchester University Press, 1988
Wigham, Eric, *From Humble Petition to Militant Action, a History of the CPSA 1903-1978*, CPSA, 1980

INDEX